AF739741

# AI Safety in Healthcare Systems

This book provides an in-depth exploration of artificial intelligence (AI) safety in healthcare. It bridges the gap between technical innovation and patient protection. It examines emerging methodologies for risk management, transparency, and robust AI system design used specifically in medical applications.

Readers will gain insights into the ethical considerations that surround AI deployment, techniques for improving the explainability and accountability of AI models, and the implementation of safety protocols to detect and prevent AI failures. The book also discusses the evolving regulatory view that shapes AI adoption and how privacy-preserving technologies can enable safer data sharing across institutions. In highlighting both current challenges and future directions, the book makes a meaningful contribution to the safe, responsible, and trustworthy integration of AI in healthcare systems.

This is an illuminating read for researchers, practitioners, policymakers, and healthcare providers interested in acquiring the knowledge needed to harness AI's potential while safeguarding human health and well-being.

# AI Safety in Healthcare Systems

## Resilience, Transparency, and Accountability

Edited by
Azadeh Zamanifar, Amirfarhad Farhadi, and Amir Taherkordi

CRC Press
Taylor & Francis Group
Boca Raton London New York

CRC Press is an imprint of the
Taylor & Francis Group, an **informa** business
A CHAPMAN & HALL BOOK

First edition published 2027
by CRC Press
2385 NW Executive Center Drive, Suite 320, Boca Raton FL 33431

and by CRC Press
4 Park Square, Milton Park, Abingdon, Oxon, OX14 4RN

CRC Press is an imprint of Taylor & Francis Group, LLC

© 2027 selection and editorial matter, Azadeh Zamanifar, Amirfarhad Farhadi, and Amir Taherkordi

Reasonable efforts have been made to publish reliable data and information, but the author and publisher cannot assume responsibility for the validity of all materials or the consequences of their use. The authors and publishers have attempted to trace the copyright holders of all material reproduced in this publication and apologize to copyright holders if permission to publish in this form has not been obtained. If any copyright material has not been acknowledged please write and let us know so we may rectify in any future reprint.

Except as permitted under U.S. Copyright Law, no part of this book may be reprinted, reproduced, transmitted, or utilized in any form by any electronic, mechanical, or other means, now known or hereafter invented, including photocopying, microfilming, and recording, or in any information storage or retrieval system, without written permission from the publishers.

For permission to photocopy or use material electronically from this work, access www.copyright.com or contact the Copyright Clearance Center, Inc. (CCC), 222 Rosewood Drive, Danvers, MA 01923, 978-750-8400. For works that are not available on CCC please contact mpkbookspermissions@tandf.co.uk

For Product Safety Concerns and Information please contact our EU representative GPSR@taylorandfrancis.com. Taylor & Francis Verlag GmbH, Kaufingerstraße 24, 80331 München, Germany.

**Trademark notice:** Product or corporate names may be trademarks or registered trademarks and are used only for identification and explanation without intent to infringe.

ISBN: 9781041249610 (hbk)
ISBN: 9781041247630 (pbk)
ISBN: 9781003743422 (ebk)

DOI: 10.1201/9781003743422

Typeset in Times
by KnowledgeWorks Global Ltd.

# Contents

# Preface

This is a comprehensive book that explores how explainable artificial intelligence (XAI), particularly large language models (LLMs), is transforming healthcare. The book covers foundational concepts of XAI, emphasizing the need for transparency, accountability, and interpretability in AI-driven medical systems, which are crucial for clinician and patient trust. It examines the principles and methodologies in explainable AI. It details how LLMs can make complex machine learning outputs understandable through explanations, model design, and human-centered descriptions.

Part of the book is dedicated to real-world applications, such as disease diagnosis, treatment planning, and patient management. It demonstrates how XAI improves clinical decision-making and patient outcomes. It discusses the integration of explainable LLMs into electronic health records (EHRs) and clinical workflows. It shows how these technologies facilitate data analysis, improve documentation, and support care. The book also addresses the challenges and limitations of deploying explainable LLMs in healthcare. It includes issues of privacy, data complexity, and adapting models to specific domains. Evaluation techniques for explainability are discussed, with attention to metrics, benchmarks, and human-centered assessment methods that ensure AI explanations are both accurate and clinically relevant. Ethical considerations, such as fairness, accountability, and privacy, are discussed. We highlight the importance of balancing transparency with patient confidentiality. The book provides case studies and empirical evidence illustrating the benefits and challenges of implementing XAI in real clinical settings.

Future directions are discussed. It includes adaptive explanations according to different user needs, integration with genomic medicine, and improving human–AI collaboration for shared decision-making. The book is aimed at healthcare professionals, AI researchers, policymakers, and anyone interested in the intersection of AI and medicine. Its final goal is to empower healthcare stakeholders to use AI safely and effectively. It ensures that AI-driven decisions are transparent, trustworthy, and aligned with clinical best practices. By bridging technical depth with practical relevance, this book is a vital resource for understanding and advancing XAI in modern healthcare.

# Editor Biographies

**Azadeh Zamanifar** is currently the head of the computer engineering department at Islamic Azad University, Science and Research Branch, Tehran, Iran. She received her B.Sc. degree in Computer Engineering (Hardware) from Tehran University in 2002. She went on to complete her M.Sc. degree in Computer Engineering (Software) at the Iran University of Science and Technology in 2008, before obtaining her Ph.D. in Software Engineering from Shahid Beheshti University, Tehran, Iran. Currently, Dr. Zamanifar serves as a head of the Software and AI Department at Islamic Azad University, Science and Research Branch. Her research interests include healthcare systems, machine learning, and distributed systems.

**Amirfarhad Farhadi** holds a Ph.D. in artificial intelligence and is currently a post-doctoral fellow at Iran University of Science and Technology. He also serves as an adjunct professor in the Department of Computer Engineering at the Science and Research Branch of Islamic Azad University. His research expertise spans artificial intelligence (AI), machine learning, deep learning, transfer learning, reinforcement learning, natural language processing (NLP), and healthcare systems. Dr. Farhadi serves as a reviewer for esteemed journals, including IEEE *Transactions on Pattern Analysis and Machine Intelligence* (TPAMI) and IEEE *Transactions on Neural Networks and Learning Systems*, among others. In addition to his academic contributions, he holds patents in robotics and actively participates in the AI industry, focusing on innovative applications and technological advancements.

**Amir Taherkordi** (Member, IEEE) is a full professor at the Department of Informatics, University of Oslo (UiO). He received his Ph.D. degree from the Informatics Department, UiO, in 2011. After completing his Ph.D. studies, Dr. Taherkordi joined Sonitor Technologies as a senior embedded software engineer. From 2013 to 2018, he was a researcher in the Networks and Distributed Systems (ND) group at the Department of Informatics, UiO. He has so far published several articles in high-ranked conferences and journals, and he has experience with several national (Norwegian Research Council) and international (European research funding agencies) research projects. He is an associate editor of IEEE *Transactions on Mobile Computing* and IEEE *Transactions on Network Science and Engineering.* Dr. Taherkordi's research interests are broadly on resource efficiency, scalability, adaptability, dependability, mobility, and data intensiveness of distributed systems designed for emerging computing technologies, such as Internet of Things (IoT), fog/edge/cloud computing, and cyber-physical systems (CPS).

# List of Contributors

**Ehsan Bahrami**
Department of Computer Engineering
University of Science and Culture
Tehran, Iran

**Amirfarhad Farhadi**
School of Computer Engineering
Iran University of Science and Technology
Tehran, Iran

**Moein Hedayati**
Department of Computer Engineering
SR.C., Islamic Azad University
Tehran, Iran

**Homayoun Safarpour Motealegh Mahalegi**
University of Limerick
Limerick, Ireland

**Farshid Babapour Mofrad**
Department of Medical Radiation Engineering
SR.C., Islamic Azad University
Tehran, Iran

**Omid Mohebi**
Department of Computer Engineering
University of Science and Culture
Tehran, Iran

**Nasser Mozayeni**
Department of Computer Engineering
Iran University of Science and Technology
Tehran, Iran

**Roya Noori**
Department of Computer Engineering
SR.C, Islamic Azad University
Tehran, Iran

**Tarannom Sadegh**
Department of Computer Engineering
Iran University of Science and Technology
Tehran, Iran

**Azadeh Tabatabaei**
Department of Computer Engineering
University of Science and Culture
Tehran, Iran

**Alireza Taheri**
Department of Computer Engineering
Science and Research Branch, Islamic Azad University
Tehran, Iran

**Amir Taherkordi**
Department of Informatics
University of Oslo
Oslo, Norway

**Parisa Tavana**
Minimally Invasive Surgery Research Center
Iran University of Medical Sciences
Tehran, Iran

**Neda Yousefi**
Department of Computer Engineering
SR.C, Islamic Azad University
Tehran, Iran

**Midya Yousefzamani**
Department of Medical Radiation Engineering
SR.C., Islamic Azad University
Tehran, Iran

**Azadeh Zamanifar**
Department of Computer Engineering
SR.C, Islamic Azad University
Tehran, Iran

**Mohammad Zareinejad**
Department of Computer Engineering
South Tehran Branch, Islamic Azad University
Tehran, Iran

# 1 Introduction to AI Safety in Healthcare Systems

*Azadeh Tabatabaei and Ehsan Bahrami*

## 1.1 INTRODUCTION

Imagine an artificial intelligence (AI) model with 98% accuracy in detecting brain tumors based on training data, then deployed in a busy hospital. Months later, clinicians discover the system is dangerously overconfident, missing rare but critical conditions. This isn't just a hypothetical. Such real-world gaps between lab performance and clinical reality have pushed **AI safety** past academic debate, making it a practical, ethical necessity in healthcare [1].

AI is transforming health systems at an unprecedented pace [2]. This technology promises greater accuracy and personalized treatment and helps with complex decision-making in areas like advanced diagnostic imaging and predictive risk models. Still, its rapid adoption quickly raises important questions about these systems' reliability, transparency, and ethics [3]. Today, **ensuring safe, predictable, and human-aligned behavior** for AI in healthcare is as critical as achieving high performance [4].

Healthcare is unique among safety-critical fields. Unlike financial systems or consumer apps, where mistakes might cause economic loss or inconvenience, clinical decisions directly and irreversibly affect a patient's survival, long-term well-being, and quality of life. Given these high stakes, building safe, trustworthy AI systems for medicine isn't just important; it's essential. This focus on AI safety stems from the profound clinical impact of errors, the deeply personal nature of health data, the practical challenges of implementation, and the evolving regulatory landscape needed to foster public confidence.

Medical decisions often involve life-or-death situations. Diagnostic errors, incorrect treatment recommendations, or misleading predictive scores can directly harm patients and expose clinicians to liability. While older machine learning systems operated within narrow limits, today's foundation models and generative AI offer impressive generalization abilities but also introduce new, complex failure modes. These include generating plausible but wrong information (hallucination), overconfidence in their predictions, and a worrying sensitivity to small changes in data [5]. Such vulnerabilities highlight that robustness and reliability must be engineered as core, non-negotiable components of AI systems in clinical settings, not merely afterthoughts [4].

The imperative for safety is further amplified by the sensitive nature of healthcare data itself, which represents some of the most personal information about an individual. Any misuse, leakage, or improper inference poses severe ethical and legal risks [6]. Advanced models, particularly those that learn rich latent representations of data, risk

DOI: 10.1201/9781003743422-1

inadvertently memorizing or revealing identifiable patient features [7]. Consequently, a comprehensive safety framework must rigorously incorporate privacy-preserving design principles, aligning technical development with established and emerging ethical guidelines for AI in healthcare [8].

Furthermore, the promise of AI must be realized within the complex, dynamic, and often resource-constrained environment of real-world healthcare delivery. Hospitals require fast, robust decision-support tools that function consistently despite corrupted inputs, sensor noise, missing data, or previously unseen clinical conditions. A technical cornerstone of safety, therefore, is ensuring model stability and performance under real-world distributional shifts and against potential adversarial perturbations—a known challenge in fields like medical imaging [9]. Managing these operational risks necessitates structured approaches, such as those outlined in frameworks like the NIST AI Risk Management Framework.

This drive for technical reliability intersects directly with a tightening regulatory landscape. Authorities in the EU, US, and Asia are increasingly classifying medical AI models as high-risk devices, establishing evolving frameworks for their approval and monitoring [10]. Achieving and maintaining compliance demands a demonstrable commitment to transparency, auditability, explainability, and robust performance evaluation across diverse populations [11, 12]. In this context, AI safety functions as the essential bridge between sophisticated technical design and the legal, ethical, and social accountability required to earn and sustain public trust in these transformative technologies [13].

Moving beyond a narrow focus on accuracy, the contemporary scientific discipline of AI safety encompasses a broader set of engineering practices aimed at ensuring systems behave as intended [4, 5]. For healthcare, this expanded view includes: ensuring **robustness** against noise and adversarial attacks; maintaining **alignment** with clinically valid and ethical goals; guaranteeing **reliability** across diverse patient subgroups and clinical contexts; providing well-calibrated **uncertainty quantification**; enabling **interpretability and explainability** to support clinician understanding; and designing **fail-safe mechanisms** for graceful degradation and effective human oversight [14].

Ultimately, healthcare does not merely present a set of challenges for AI safety; it serves as a vital proving ground for the entire field. The domain benefits from a deeply ingrained culture of systematic risk management—using methods like root-cause analysis and failure mode and effects analysis—providing a natural scaffold for integrating AI-specific safety protocols [15]. Moreover, healthcare uniquely concentrates high-stakes imperatives: stringent regulation, profound ethical responsibility, and intense operational pressure for reliability. This convergence creates a forcing function where safety cannot remain abstract but must be engineered into robust, auditable systems. The lessons learned and frameworks validated within healthcare are thus poised to establish foundational benchmarks for trustworthy AI across all safety-critical industries.

## 1.2 A SYSTEM-LEVEL VIEW OF AI IN HEALTHCARE

Before delving into safety challenges, it is essential to clarify the position of AI models within the complex modern healthcare ecosystem. Viewing AI as an isolated "black box" that merely ingests data and produces an output is an incomplete and potentially misleading perspective. Instead, a system-level view recognizes AI as one component within a broader socio-technical ecosystem, whose success is

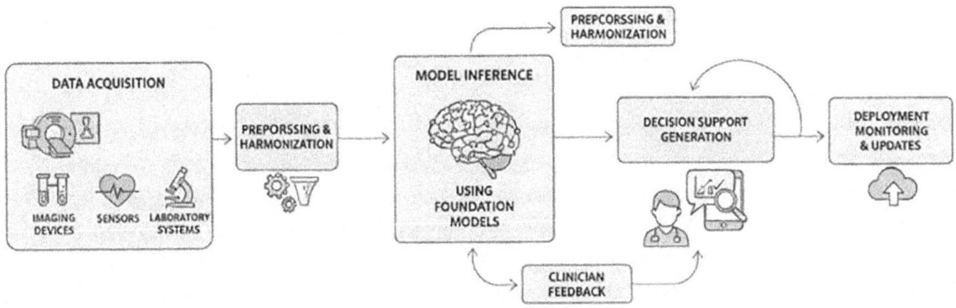


**FIGURE 1.1** A high-level pipeline for AI-enabled healthcare systems.

critically dependent on its interaction with all other elements [16]. Figure 1.1 illustrates a typical end-to-end pipeline.

This ecosystem encompasses intertwined technical, human, and organizational layers. The technical layer involves the crucial challenge of interoperability—seamlessly integrating AI with existing health information infrastructure such as Electronic Health Records (EHRs), picture archiving and communication systems (PACSs), and data exchange protocols like HL7 FHIR [17]. An advanced diagnostic model fails to deliver value if its outputs cannot be presented in an understandable and integrated format within the clinical workflow.

The human layer focuses on the interaction between AI and its end-users, including physicians, nurses, technicians, and patients. Factors such as user interface (UI) and user experience (UX) design, the provision of interpretable explanations (explainability), and the management of expectations determine whether a model's output is correctly interpreted and incorporated into decision-making [1]. Phenomena like automation bias and alert fatigue are classic examples of failures at this human–system interface.

A strong system architecture accounts for AI's entire operational lifecycle. This means continuous performance monitoring in real-world settings to catch data and concept drift. It also involves having processes ready for updating, retraining, and redeploying models. Such an approach needs clear governance and risk management frameworks. These frameworks outline roles, responsibilities, and incident response protocols [18].

Therefore, the success of AI in healthcare should not be measured solely by isolated metrics like accuracy, sensitivity, or specificity. The ultimate metric is its tangible impact on improving patient outcomes, enhancing clinical efficiency, and elevating the overall quality of care within the complex socio-technical environment of modern medicine [19].

## 1.3 KEY DIMENSIONS OF AI SAFETY IN HEALTHCARE

The safety of AI systems in healthcare cannot be reduced to a single metric but must be evaluated across multiple, interdependent dimensions. Each dimension addresses a unique aspect of potential failure or harm, and together they form a comprehensive framework for assessing and ensuring safety. These key dimensions are summarized in Table 1.1.

**TABLE 1.1**
**Key Dimensions of AI Safety in Healthcare**

| Dimension | Description |
|---|---|
| **Robustness** | Stability of model outputs under input noise, data corruption, distribution shifts, or adversarial perturbations [5, 20]. |
| **Reliability** | Consistent performance and behavior across diverse patient populations, clinical settings, and over time [16]. |
| **Privacy and Security** | Protection of sensitive health data against unauthorized access, leakage, or inference attacks [21]. |
| **Fairness and Bias Mitigation** | Equitable performance across demographic groups and prevention of discriminatory outcomes [22]. |
| **Explainability** | Ability to provide interpretable reasons for AI decisions to support clinical understanding and trust [23]. |
| **Human-AI Collaboration** | Effective integration into clinical workflows with appropriate trust calibration and clear role definition [24, 25]. |
| **Clinical Validity and Impact** | Demonstrated real-world improvement in patient outcomes and care processes, beyond technical accuracy [17, 26]. |
| **Regulatory and Ethical Compliance** | Adherence to medical device regulations (e.g., EU AI Act, FDA guidelines) and ethical principles [12]. |
| **Operational Resilience** | Robust lifecycle management, continuous monitoring, and graceful degradation under real-world operational pressures [18]. |

### 1.3.1 Interdependence and Systemic Integration

The dimensions in the table aren't independent; they form a closely linked system. A weakness in one can quickly lead to problems in others. For instance, a technical flaw in a generative model—say, if it hallucinates—can directly undermine clinical validation and erode clinician trust, damaging effective human-AI collaboration. Similarly, ignoring data bias can result in unfair outcomes that go against regulatory and ethical standards [16]. Therefore, a system-level view (see the previous section) is essential, where safety is treated as an emergent property of the entire socio-technical ecosystem, requiring continuous monitoring and adaptive management across all dimensions simultaneously.

### 1.3.2 From Principles to Practice

Translating these safety dimensions into actionable practice involves creating structured processes and checkpoints throughout the AI lifecycle—from design and development to deployment and decommissioning. Tools such as the NIST AI Risk Management Framework [18] and reporting standards like MI-CLAIM [26] provide concrete starting points. Ultimately, the goal is to build healthcare AI systems that are not only intellectually sophisticated but also operationally resilient, ethically aligned, and worthy of the profound trust placed in them by patients and clinicians alike.

## 1.4 HISTORICAL EVOLUTION OF AI SAFETY AND ITS RELEVANCE TO HEALTHCARE

The idea of "AI safety" has evolved quite a bit over the last six decades. While early discussions about safety in AI were speculative and philosophical, contemporary AI safety is a serious, interdisciplinary science. It brings together engineering principles, clinical risk management, ethics, and regulatory frameworks [4, 18]. This evolution has been especially important for healthcare systems, where the consequences of erroneous decision-making are immediate and potentially life-threatening [1]. In this section, we explore the historical development of AI safety, with an emphasis on how its conceptual and technical frameworks have shaped modern healthcare applications.

### 1.4.1 Early AI Systems and the Roots of Safety Thinking (1950s–1980s)

The origins of AI safety can be traced to early work on automated reasoning and expert systems. The pioneering ideas of McCarthy, Minsky, Newell, and Simon established foundational questions about machine intelligence, knowledge representation, and automated decision-making [27, 28]. Although safety was not explicitly identified as a research domain, early researchers recognized the risks of brittle logic-based systems that failed in unpredictable ways when exposed to incomplete or ambiguous information [29].

By the 1980s, rule-based expert systems such as MYCIN had demonstrated the promise of AI-assisted diagnosis but also revealed critical limitations—including poor generalization, sensitivity to missing rules, and the difficulty of encoding medical knowledge manually [30]. The failures of expert systems planted the seeds for later discussions about robustness, uncertainty, and the need for continuous monitoring in clinical AI tools [15].

### 1.4.2 The Statistical Learning Era and Empirical Safety (1990s–2010)

The rise of statistical machine learning in the 1990s introduced new opportunities and new risks. Unlike symbolic systems, statistical models derived patterns from data, enabling improved generalization. However, these systems were significantly more opaque and vulnerable to dataset bias, data leakage, and overfitting [31].

In healthcare, machine learning models were increasingly used for disease classification, risk stratification, and prognosis prediction. Yet studies began to show that models trained on limited datasets often failed to generalize across clinical populations [22]. This discrepancy highlighted the need for safety-centered practices such as the following:

- External validation [26]
- Recalibration [32]
- Dataset shift analysis [16]
- Fairness assessment [22]
- Subgroup performance evaluation [17]

During this period, regulators, including the U.S. Food and Drug Administration (FDA) and the European Medicines Agency (EMA), began developing frameworks for software as a medical device (SaMD). This marked the first time officials recognized that AI systems, much like drug treatments, required systematic safety evaluations.

### 1.4.3 Deep Learning and the Rise of Safety Concerns (2010–2020)

The advent of deep learning introduced unprecedented leaps in performance, enabling AI to achieve near-human or superhuman accuracy in tasks such as medical image classification, radiology triage, dermatology lesion detection, and pathology slide interpretation [33–35]. However, deep neural networks also introduced new safety risks:

- **Adversarial vulnerabilities:** Small perturbations causing severe misclassification [20, 36].
- **Distributional shift failures:** Sensitivity to scanner differences, demographic changes, and imaging protocols [16].
- **Lack of explainability:** Opaque internal representations complicating clinical validation [23].
- **Overconfidence:** High-probability predictions even when wrong [5, 32].

These challenges motivated a new subfield: *machine learning safety*. Studies demonstrated that even clinically deployed AI systems could be manipulated by adversarial attacks on medical images [20]. This revelation was a major turning point: healthcare AI safety could no longer be treated as an abstract research concern—it had become a concrete operational risk [37].

### 1.4.4 Foundation Models and the New Era of AI Safety (2020–Present)

[37–39]The emergence of large foundation models, including large language models (LLMs), vision-language transformers, diffusion-based medical image generators, and multimodal clinical models, has revolutionized healthcare AI. These models demonstrate strong transfer learning, generate clinically plausible text and images, and provide flexible reasoning across complex clinical contexts [38–40].

### 1.4.5 Why Healthcare Magnifies AI Safety Challenges

Healthcare systems amplify the risks of AI for several reasons:

1. **Heterogeneity of clinical data:** Medical images vary across scanners, contrasts, hospitals, and populations [16].
2. **High stakes of error:** A single incorrect prediction may lead to delayed diagnosis, harmful treatment, or even mortality [1].

3. **Implicit trust in clinical technology:** Clinicians often assume FDA-approved or CE-marked systems are safe [25].
4. **Systemic interconnectedness:** Clinical AI interacts with EHRs, PACS systems, laboratory data, and decision support tools, increasing the chance of cascading failures [17].

Thus, AI safety in healthcare must be approached not as a model-level problem but as a system-level discipline [18, 41].

## 1.5 A HISTORICAL VIEW OF FAILURES AND COMPARATIVE ANALYSIS

Figure 1.2 gives us a timeline of important moments for AI safety in healthcare. It shows how safety concerns grew as AI's abilities advanced. Each new AI generation brought its own set of risks, which then pushed us to improve safety, both in theory and in practice.

### 1.5.1 Failures of Early Clinical Expert Systems

Early expert systems suffered from brittleness, a lack of generalization, and the inability to adapt to new medical knowledge. Their failures motivated the integration of probabilistic reasoning, Bayesian approaches, and uncertainty quantification in later models [42].

### 1.5.2 Machine Learning Failures in Real Clinical Settings

Statistical and early deep learning systems often failed when deployed outside the training environment. Examples include:

- Models trained on one hospital failing on data from another.
- Triage algorithms producing racially biased risk scores.
- Imaging models misclassifying due to scanner artifacts.

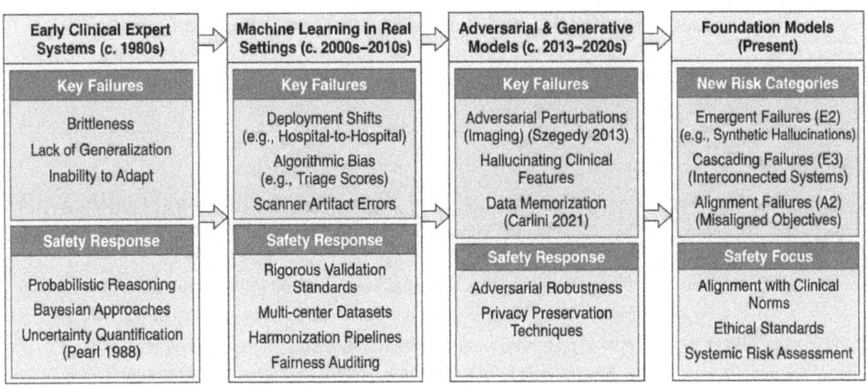


**FIGURE 1.2** A Conceptual Timeline Summarizing Major Milestones in AI Safety and the Co-evolution of Risks in Healthcare.

These failures led to rigorous validation standards, including multicenter datasets, harmonization pipelines, and fairness auditing.

### 1.5.3 Adversarial and Generative Model Failures

The discovery of adversarial perturbations in deep models [36] raised major concerns for safety-critical imaging tasks. Later, diffusion and GAN-based generative models were shown to hallucinate clinical features or memorize patient data [43]. These behaviors highlighted the tension between expressiveness and safety in large generative models.

### 1.5.4 A Comparative Analysis of Safety Risk Categories

The foundation models also introduce new categories of risk not present in traditional deep learning. These include:

**Emergent failures ($E_2$):** Unexpected behaviors arising from scale, model complexity, or training diversity. For example, hallucinating nonexistent tumors in synthetic MRI scans or generating fabricated clinical rationales in medical LLMs [44].

**Cascading failures ($E_3$):** Errors that propagate across interconnected hospital systems. For instance, a misinterpreted EHR note generated by an LLM may influence downstream radiology workflow triage or medication recommendation modules [17].

**Alignment failures ($A_2$):** Cases where the model optimizes for objectives misaligned with clinical norms, patient well-being, or institutional ethical standards [4].

Table 1.2 summarizes key differences and examples in healthcare contexts.

This taxonomy gives us a practical grasp of modern AI risks in clinical settings, especially with generative and foundation models becoming more common.

**TABLE 1.2**

**Comparison of Emergent, Cascading, and Alignment Failures in Healthcare AI**

| Risk Type | Description and Healthcare Examples |
|---|---|
| $E_2$: Emergent Failures | Unexpected behaviors arising at scale. Example: hallucination of nonexistent lesions in CT scans. |
| $E_3$: Cascading Failures | Errors propagating through interconnected systems. Example: incorrect LLM-generated clinical summary influencing radiology triage. |
| $A_2$: Alignment Failures | Misaligned optimization objectives. Example: maximizing report brevity at the cost of clinical completeness. |

## 1.6 TECHNICAL SAFETY CHALLENGES IN GENERATIVE AND FOUNDATION MODELS

Bringing foundation models and generative AI into healthcare transforms how clinical decisions get supported. Models such as LLMs, vision-language models (VLMs), and diffusion-based image generators bring powerful new abilities. But they also create safety challenges different from those in traditional machine learning systems. Their emergent behaviors, complex internal representations, and dynamic reasoning can lead to failures that are tough to predict, interpret, or control in high-stakes clinical settings [40, 45].

We'll explore these challenges across three related areas, as shown in Figure 1.3. These include intrinsic model limitations, system-level integration risks, and vulnerabilities specific to different modalities. Each area affects clinical workflows and raises unique safety concerns. Tackling these will require thorough safety frameworks.

### 1.6.1 Intrinsic Limitations of Foundation Models

#### 1.6.1.1 Emergent Behaviors and Unpredictability

Emergent behaviors—capabilities or failure modes that arise only at sufficient scale or complexity—represent a fundamental challenge [46]. These include unexpected generalization (e.g., models inferring patient demographics from unintended correlations), hallucination in medical LLMs [47, 48], and synthetic feature creation in diffusion models [49]. Such behaviors, categorized as $E_2$ risks, cannot be reliably predicted from small-scale testing and may manifest only in production clinical environments.

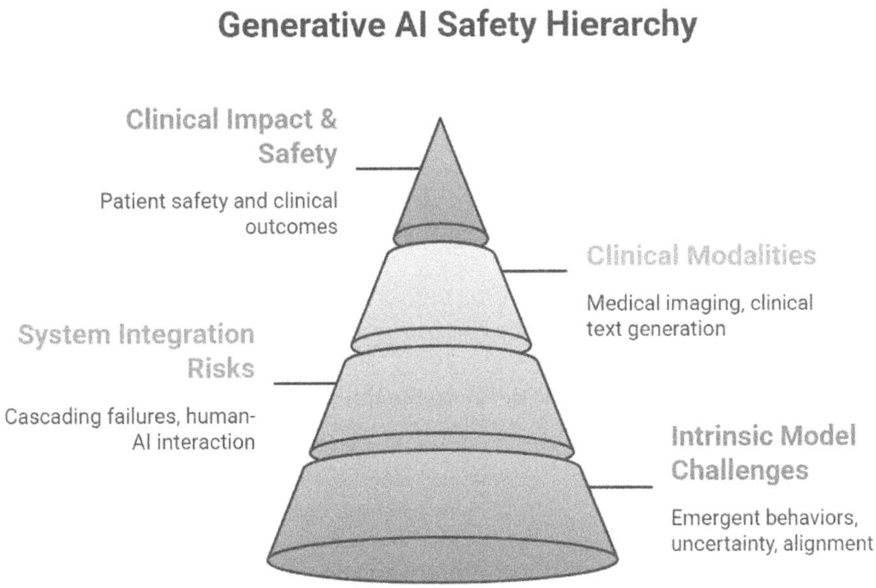


**FIGURE 1.3** A Hierarchical Safety Challenges of Generative AI in Healthcare.

#### 1.6.1.2 Uncertainty Quantification Failures

Foundation models often exhibit poor uncertainty calibration, producing overconfident predictions even when incorrect [32, 50]. This is particularly dangerous in radiology and pathology, where diagnostic ambiguity is common. Two critical forms of uncertainty must be addressed:

- **Aleatoric uncertainty:** Inherent data noise (sensor artifacts, motion blur, incomplete information).
- **Epistemic uncertainty:** Model limitations for out-of-distribution samples, rare diseases, or underrepresented populations [16].

#### 1.6.1.3 Robustness to Clinical Distributional Shifts

Medical imaging models face unique robustness challenges due to scanner heterogeneity, protocol variations, and population diversity. Major risks include domain shifts across hospitals, variations in imaging protocols, scanner-specific reconstruction algorithms, and vulnerability to adversarial perturbations [20]. Table 1.3 shows common robustness risk in medical imaging and their clinical examples.

#### 1.6.1.4 Alignment with Clinical Objectives

Alignment failures ($A_2$) happen when a model's optimization goals don't match clinical objectives, ethical standards, or patient well-being. A few issues contribute to this, such as complex clinical aims, varying safety rules between institutions, missing ground truth data, and improving accuracy in ways that could hurt minority groups [22].

### 1.6.2 System-Level Integration Risks

#### 1.6.2.1 Cascading Failures in Clinical Ecosystems

Modern healthcare systems comprise interconnected components—EHRs, PACS, laboratory systems, and decision support tools—where failures can propagate catastrophically ($E_3$ risks) [15]. Examples include erroneous LLM-generated reports influencing downstream treatment decisions, flawed risk scores disrupting triage prioritization, and synthetic training data degrading diagnostic model performance. These cascades are particularly dangerous given healthcare's time-sensitive, high-stakes nature [17].

**TABLE 1.3**
**Common Robustness Risks in Medical Imaging AI Systems**

| Robustness Risk | Clinical Example |
|---|---|
| **Domain Shift** | MRI model trained on 1.5T data failing on 3T scans |
| **Protocol Variation** | CT model misclassifying low-dose protocol images |
| **Scanner Differences** | Siemens vs. GE reconstruction pipeline variability |
| **Artifact Sensitivity** | Motion artifacts causing false positives |
| **Adversarial Perturbations** | Subtle pixel changes leading to misdiagnosis |

#### 1.6.2.2 Human-AI Interaction Failures

Even technically sound models can fail due to human factors: automation bias, confirmation bias, misunderstanding of uncertainty estimates, poor interface design, and alert fatigue [24]. Effective safety requires a user-centered design that supports appropriate trust calibration and transparent decision support.

### 1.6.3 Modality-Specific Vulnerabilities

#### 1.6.3.1 Clinical Text Generation Risks

Using LLMs in clinical documentation and healthcare communication brings unique vulnerabilities. These systems can hallucinate, inventing incorrect clinical facts or even fake citations. LLMs might also "context drift," meaning they gradually lose touch with clinical rules or the time-based details in patient histories. Adding to this, their answers often sound overly confident and authoritative, even when they're wrong. On top of all this, there's a significant risk of privacy leaks, as these models could accidentally reveal or recreate patient-identifiable information [43].

#### 1.6.3.2 Medical Image Synthesis Challenges

Generative models, when applied in medical imaging for tasks like data augmentation, modality translation, or image reconstruction, bring specific risks. One major concern involves "hallucinated lesions." Here, synthetic images might show fabricated pathological features, or they could completely miss important clinical abnormalities [49]. These models can also reinforce or amplify preexisting dataset biases, particularly when trained on demographically skewed data. Furthermore, similar to text-based systems, image-based generative models may memorize sensitive visual patterns and reproduce patient-specific content, thereby posing substantial privacy threats.

### 1.6.4 Toward Comprehensive Safety Evaluation

Traditional performance metrics such as Area Under the Receiver Operating Characteristic (AUROC) curve and accuracy, while useful, are insufficient for establishing the safety of foundation models in healthcare. A comprehensive evaluation regime must instead incorporate a broader set of criteria, including assessments of distributional robustness under adversarial or out-of-distribution stressors, as well as systematic examination of uncertainty calibration and mechanisms for detecting hallucinations. Ensuring fairness across demographic groups is essential, particularly in high-stakes clinical contexts, and red-teaming methodologies have become an increasingly vital component of generative model assessment [51]. Such practices rely on deliberately challenging the system with adversarial perturbations, ambiguous scenarios, and edge-case inputs to uncover latent failure modes. Ultimately, safety evaluation must extend beyond isolated model behavior to encompass system-level integration and continuous post-deployment monitoring, thereby ensuring that clinical AI systems operate reliably within dynamic healthcare environments [52].

### 1.6.5 Case Studies: From Theory to Clinical Reality

#### 1.6.5.1 Adversarial Attacks on Chest X-ray AI

Finlayson et al. demonstrated that imperceptible pixel perturbations could cause dramatic misclassification in radiology AI, potentially altering clinical triage [20].

#### 1.6.5.2 Hallucinated MRI Lesions from Diffusion Models

Diffusion models may generate nonexistent lesions or obscure subtle tumor boundaries, compromising diagnostic integrity when synthetic images inform clinical decisions [49].

#### 1.6.5.3 LLM Fabrication in Radiology Reports

Medical LLMs sometimes produce exam findings that sound real but aren't. This poses a danger, especially when clinicians are busy and might miss the mistakes.

Such instances demonstrate how safety issues, once just theoretical, become real-world problems. So, strong safeguards are vital throughout an AI's entire life: during development, validation, deployment, and monitoring.

## 1.7 GOVERNANCE, REGULATION, AND SYSTEM-LEVEL SAFETY

Keeping healthcare AI safe requires a multilayered governance system. This system should integrate regulatory guidance, ethical principles, risk management, and technical safeguards. As foundation models increasingly shape diagnostic, predictive, and generative workflows, traditional device regulations simply aren't enough. Instead, governance needs an adaptive approach, one that covers the entire lifecycle and aligns with international standards [53].

### 1.7.1 International Governance Landscape

Healthcare AI governance is shaped by global organizations and national regulatory bodies. The WHO framework emphasizes ethical principles such as transparency, human oversight, and accountability to ensure equitable deployment [41]. The OECD provides high-level recommendations for trustworthy AI, defining robustness, safety, and accountability as core requirements [8]. The EU AI Act categorizes most clinical AI systems as high-risk and mandates strict documentation, monitoring, and traceability mechanisms [54]. Similarly, the U.S. FDA introduces Good Machine Learning Practice (GMLP), focusing on data quality, reproducibility, and lifecycle governance [12]. NIST's AI Risk Management Framework provides systematic guidelines for identifying, assessing, and mitigating risks associated with AI systems, including drift and sociotechnical vulnerabilities [18].

While these frameworks vary in scope, they converge on shared commitments: transparency, continuous monitoring, human oversight, and robust documentation. These principles are particularly critical for foundation models whose behavior may evolve with updates or new deployment contexts.

### 1.7.2 Lifecycle Governance of Healthcare AI

Lifecycle governance addresses safety throughout a system's development and deployment. Data curation demands close attention to provenance, demographic balance, annotation quality, and privacy. Then, during model development, methods for robustness evaluation, uncertainty quantification, fairness assessment, and interpretability become central [55]. Pre-deployment evaluation typically includes multi-site external validation to assess generalizability in real-world environments.

Post-deployment monitoring is indispensable. Drift detection, surveillance metrics, incident reporting, and recalibration cycles ensure the AI system remains aligned with its clinical purpose [2]. This lifecycle view acknowledges that clinical environments evolve dynamically, requiring ongoing governance rather than static certification.

### 1.7.3 System-Level Architectures for Safety

A robust safety architecture for any system combines careful input validation, strong model design, secure output generation, and continuous human oversight.

#### 1.7.3.1 Input Safety

Clinical data requires thorough integrity checks, like noise removal, anomaly detection, and harmonization, to prevent models from behaving unpredictably.

#### 1.7.3.2 Model Safety

Safeguards within models include adversarial robustness, resilience against distribution shifts, fairness monitoring, and alignment constraints. For foundation models, specific protections are essential to curb hallucinations or clinically implausible outputs.

#### 1.7.3.3 Output Safety

Filtering outputs, setting uncertainty thresholds, and detecting hallucinations help keep unreliable model recommendations from reaching clinicians.

#### 1.7.3.4 Human Oversight and Monitoring

Clinician-in-the-loop systems ensure interpretability, accountability, and override options. Monitoring dashboards and audit logs support ongoing safety evaluation.

### 1.7.4 Unique Safety Challenges of Foundation Models

Foundation models introduce novel risks not seen in traditional machine learning. Their broad pretraining across heterogeneous datasets can produce medically plausible but incorrect statements—hallucinations—that complicate validation [55]. Privacy leakage remains a major concern, particularly with imaging models capable of memorizing high-resolution features. Techniques such as differential privacy and federated learning help mitigate but cannot completely remove this risk.

Additionally, their performance is highly sensitive to data drift. Changes in imaging protocols, device types, or population health patterns can silently degrade accuracy. Hence, continuous monitoring and periodic auditing are required to ensure safe operation [2].

### 1.7.5 Post-Market Surveillance and Continuous Monitoring

Modern regulations emphasize post-market surveillance as a core requirement for high-risk AI systems [12, 54]. Continuous monitoring mechanisms include shift detection, fairness tracking, calibration analysis, and incident reporting pipelines. Hospitals must also maintain procedural oversight, such as audit logs, documentation of decision rationales, and transparent reporting of adverse system behaviors.

### 1.7.6 Reporting, Transparency, and Explainability

Transparency and interpretability are central to clinician trust. Documentation tools—such as Model Cards and Dataset Datasheets—provide standardized descriptions of model development processes, limitations, and known risks [8]. Explainability is particularly critical in medical imaging, where tools like Grad-CAM and integrated gradients help clinicians understand model reasoning [55].

### 1.7.7 Integrated Governance Framework for Foundation Models in Healthcare

As shown in Figure 1.4, an integrated governance framework **synthesizes** ethical principles, regulatory requirements, technical controls, clinical workflow integration, and organizational oversight.

#### 1.7.7.1 Ethical and Regulatory Foundations

Governance begins with adherence to ethical guidelines from WHO and OECD, supported by legal requirements from bodies such as the EU and the FDA [12, 41, 54].

#### 1.7.7.2 Technical Lifecycle Controls

Technical Lifecycle Controls ensure responsible data management, thorough robustness testing, and careful bias auditing. These controls also involve evaluating how well systems generalize, keeping generative consistency, and stopping privacy leaks.

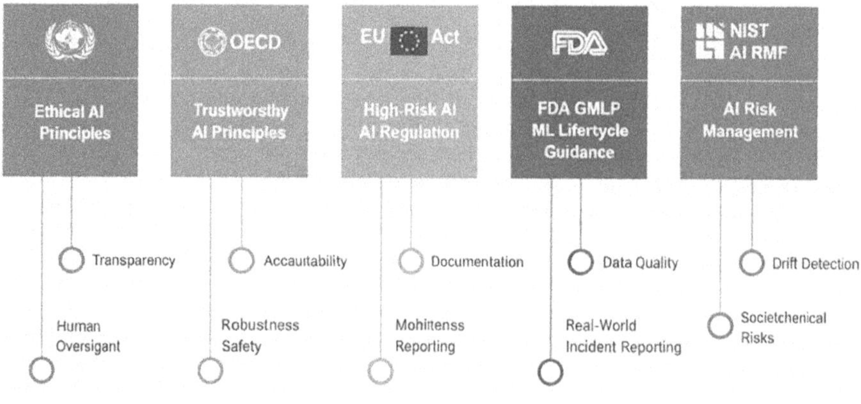


**FIGURE 1.4** Comparison of major AI governance frameworks relevant to healthcare.

#### 1.7.7.3 Deployment and Workflow Integration

Deploying these systems safely requires integrating them with PACS and EHR systems. It also means training clinicians, establishing access control, and having solid incident-reporting mechanisms in place.

#### 1.7.7.4 Continuous Monitoring and Adaptation

Once deployed, ongoing monitoring and adaptation become essential. This involves watching for system drift, regularly reevaluating performance, handling controlled updates, retraining workflows, and keeping rollback procedures ready [18].

#### 1.7.7.5 Organizational Governance and Oversight

Hospitals establish AI oversight committees, multidisciplinary review teams, and compliance officers.

These groups ensure safety, transparency, and accountability. Together, this governance approach offers a clear, adaptable way to safely introduce foundation models into healthcare.

## 1.8 CONCLUSION

AI safety in healthcare is a fundamental prerequisite for the trustworthy and effective deployment of transformative technologies. While foundation and generative models offer unprecedented capabilities, they introduce novel and complex risks—such as emergent behaviors, cascading failures, and alignment challenges—that transform safety from a technical feature into a systemic, multidimensional property. Ensuring safety requires the integration of robust technical frameworks, rigorous regulatory governance, and responsible integration into clinical workflows. Ultimately, success in this endeavor depends not only on engineering advances but also on interdisciplinary collaboration and a collective ethical commitment to the principle of *primum non nocere*—first, do no harm.

## REFERENCES


1. E. J. Topol, "High-Performance Medicine: The Convergence of Human and Artificial Intelligence," *Nature Medicine*, vol. 25, no. 1, pp. 44–56, 2019, doi: 10.1038/s41591-018-0300-7.
2. A. Esteva *et al.*, "A Guide to Deep Learning in Healthcare," *Nature Medicine*, vol. 25, no. 1, pp. 24–29, 2019.
3. P. M. Doraiswamy, C. Blease, and K. Bodner, "Artificial Intelligence and the Future of Psychiatry: Insights from a Global Physician Survey," *Artificial Intelligence in Medicine*, vol. 102, p. 101753, 2020, doi: 10.1016/j.artmed.2019.101753.
4. D. Amodei, C. Olah, J. Steinhardt, P. Christiano, J. Schulman, and D. Mané, "Concrete Problems in AI Safety," *arXiv preprint arXiv:1606.06565*, 2016. [Online]. Available: https://doi.org/10.48550/arXiv.1606.06565
5. D. Hendrycks, N. Carlini, J. Schulman, and J. Steinhardt, "Unsolved Problems in ML Safety," *arXiv preprint* arXiv:2109.13916, 2021. [Online]. Available: https://arxiv.org/abs/2109.13916
6. "Ethics and governance of artificial intelligence for health." Accessed: Dec. 04, 2025. [Online]. Available: https://www.who.int/publications/i/item/9789240029200

7. T. Stadler, B. Oprisanu, and C. Troncoso, "Synthetic Data – Anonymisation Grounding Day," in *Proceedings on Privacy Enhancing Technologies (PoPETs)*, Sciendo, July 2022, pp. 252–271. doi: 10.56553/popets-2022-0088.
8. Organisation for Economic Co-operation and Development, *OECD Principles on Artificial Intelligence*, Paris, France, OECD Publishing, 2019. [Online]. Available: https://www.oecd.org/ai/oecd-principles-on-artificial-intelligence-b2d6eae5-en.htm
9. "Artificial Intelligence (AI) Advisory Services | VeraSafe." Accessed: Dec. 04, 2025. [Online]. Available: https://verasafe.com/advisory-and-audit/ai-advisory-services/
10. S. Gerke, T. Minssen, and G. Cohen, "Ethical and Legal Challenges of Artificial Intelligence-Driven Healthcare," *Artificial Intelligence in Healthcare*, pp. 295–336, 2020, doi: 10.1016/B978-0-12-818438-7.00012-5.
11. European Parliament and the Council of the European Union, "Regulation (EU) 2024/... of the European Parliament and of the Council on laying down harmonised rules on artificial intelligence (Artificial Intelligence Act)." 2024. [Online]. Available: https://eur-lex.europa.eu/legal-content/EN/TXT/?uri=CELEX:32024R1689
12. U.S. Food and Drug Administration (FDA), Health Canada, and the United Kingdom's Medicines and Healthcare products Regulatory Agency (MHRA), "Good Machine Learning Practice for Medical Device Development: Guiding Principles," U.S. Food and Drug Administration, Oct. 2021. [Online]. Available: https://www.fda.gov/medical-devices/software-medical-device-samd/good-machine-learning-practice-medical-device-development-guiding-principles
13. D. B. Larson, H. B. Harvey, M. O'Connell, and C. J. Harvey, "Regulating Artificial Intelligence in Health Care: Principles, Applications, and Perspectives," *Journal of the American College of Radiology*, vol. 20, no. 1, pp. 154–162, 2023, doi: 10.1016/j.jacr.2022.09.015.
14. "Ethical implications for LLMs | 8 | Applications of Large Language Mod." Accessed: Dec. 06, 2025. [Online]. Available: https://www.taylorfrancis.com/chapters/edit/10.1201/9781003665083-8/ethical-implications-llms-mohammad-saleh-azadeh-tabatabaei?utm_source=researchgate.net&medium=article
15. E. Coiera, *Guide to Health Informatics*, 3rd ed. Boca Raton, FL: CRC Press, 2015. [Online]. Available: https://www.routledge.com/Guide-to-Health-Informatics/Coiera/p/book/9781444170498
16. M. Ghassemi, T. Naumann, P. Schulam, A. L. Beam, I. Y. Chen, and R. Ranganath, "A Review of Challenges and Opportunities in Machine Learning for Health," *AMIA Summits on Translational Science Proceedings*, vol. 2021, pp. 191–200, 2021.
17. C. J. Kelly, A. Karthikesalingam, M. Suleyman, G. Corrado, and D. King, "Key Challenges for Delivering Clinical Impact with Artificial Intelligence," *BMC Medicine*, vol. 18, no. 1, p. 195, 2020, doi: 10.1186/s12916-020-01661-3.
18. National Institute of Standards and Technology (NIST), "Artificial Intelligence Risk Management Framework (AI RMF 1.0)," U.S. Department of Commerce, Standard, Jan. 2023. doi: 10.6028/NIST.AI.600-1.
19. R. L. Wears, E. Hollnagel, and J. Braithwaite, "Socio-Technical Systems Analysis in Health Care: A Research Agenda," *IIE Transactions on Healthcare Systems Engineering*, vol. 1, no. 3, pp. 145–160, 2011, doi: 10.1080/19488300.2011.619158.
20. S. G. Finlayson, H. W. Chung, I. S. Kohane, and A. L. Beam, "Adversarial Attacks on Medical Machine Learning," *Science*, vol. 363, no. 6433, pp. 1287–1289, 2019.
21. G. A. Kaissis, M. R. Makowski, D. Rückert, and R. F. Braren, "Secure, Privacy-Preserving and Federated Machine Learning in Medical Imaging," *Nature Machine Intelligence*, vol. 2, no. 6, pp. 305–311, 2020.
22. Z. Obermeyer, B. Powers, C. Vogeli, and S. Mullainathan, "Dissecting Racial Bias in an Algorithm Used to Manage the Health of Populations," *Science*, vol. 366, no. 6464, pp. 447–453, 2019, doi: 10.1126/science.aax2342.

23. J. Amann, A. Blasimme, E. Vayena, D. Frey, and V. I. Madai, "Explainability for Artificial Intelligence in Healthcare: A Multidisciplinary Perspective," *BMC Medical Informatics and Decision Making*, vol. 20, no. 1, p. 310, 2020.
24. R. T. Sutton, D. Pincock, D. C. Baumgart, D. C. Sadowski, R. N. Fedorak, and K. I. Kroeker, "An Introduction to Clinical Decision Support Systems," *Journal of Healthcare Engineering*, vol. 2020, pp. 1–9, 2020, doi: 10.1038/s41746-020-0221-y.
25. A. Bussone, S. Stumpf, and D. O'Sullivan, "The Role of Trust in Automation Reliance," *International Journal of Human-Computer Studies*, vol. 80, pp. 1–13, 2015.
26. B. Norgeot *et al.*, "Minimum Information about Clinical Artificial Intelligence Modeling: The MI-CLAIM Checklist," *Nature Medicine*, vol. 26, no. 9, pp. 1320–1324, 2020.
27. J. McCarthy, M. L. Minsky, N. Rochester, and C. E. Shannon, "A Proposal for the Dartmouth Summer Research Project on Artificial Intelligence," 1955.
28. J. McCarthy, "Programs with Common Sense," *Proceedings of the Teddington Conference on the Mechanization of Thought Processes*, England, pp. 75–91, 1960.
29. S. Russell, *Artificial Intelligence and the Problem of Control.* New York: Penguin Books, 2021.
30. E. H. Shortliffe, *Computer-Based Medical Consultations: MYCIN.* New York, NY: Elsevier, 1976.
31. R. Caruana, Y. Lou, J. Gehrke, P. Koch, M. Sturm, and N. Elhadad, "Intelligible Models for Healthcare: Predicting Pneumonia Risk and Hospital 30-day Readmission," *Proceedings of the 21th ACM SIGKDD International Conference on Knowledge Discovery and Data Mining*, pp. 1721–1730, 2015.
32. C. Guo, G. Pleiss, Y. Sun, and K. Q. Weinberger, "On Calibration of Modern Neural Networks," *Proceedings of the 34th International Conference on Machine Learning*, vol. 70, pp. 1321–1330, 2017.
33. A. Esteva *et al.*, "Dermatologist-Level Classification of Skin Cancer with Deep Neural Networks," *Nature*, vol. 542, no. 7639, pp. 115–118, 2017, doi: 10.1038/nature21056.
34. P. Rajpurkar *et al.*, "CheXNet: Radiologist-Level Pneumonia Detection on Chest X-Rays with Deep Learning," *arXiv preprint arXiv:1711.05225*, 2017.
35. G. Litjens *et al.*, "A Survey on Deep Learning in Medical Image Analysis," *Medical Image Analysis*, vol. 42, pp. 60–88, 2017, doi: 10.1016/j.media.2017.07.005.
36. C. Szegedy *et al.*, "Intriguing Properties of Neural Networks," *arXiv preprint arXiv:1312.6199*, 2013.
37. A. L. Beam, J. M. Drazen, I. S. Kohane, T. Leong, A. K. Manrai, and E. J. Rubin, "Clinical Artificial Intelligence: A Practical Review for Clinicians," *New England Journal of Medicine*, vol. 388, no. 15, pp. 1426–1436, 2023, doi: 10.1056/NEJMra2302038.
38. K. Singhal *et al.*, "Large Language Models Encode Clinical Knowledge," *Nature*, vol. 620, no. 7972, pp. 172–180, 2023, doi: 10.1038/s41586-023-06291-2.
39. A. Pal *et al.*, "Med-PaLM 2: Towards Expert-Level Medical Question Answering with Large Language Models," *arXiv preprint arXiv:2305.09617*, 2023.
40. R. Bommasani *et al.*, "On the Opportunities and Risks of Foundation Models," *arXiv preprint*, vol. arXiv:2108.07258, 2021. [Online]. Available: https://arxiv.org/abs/2108.07258
41. World Health Organization, "Ethics and Governance of Artificial Intelligence for Health," World Health Organization, Geneva, Switzerland, 2021. [Online]. Available: https://www.who.int/publications/i/item/9789240029200
42. J. Pearl, *Probabilistic Reasoning in Intelligent Systems: Networks of Plausible Inference.* San Francisco, CA: Morgan Kaufmann, 1988.
43. N. Carlini *et al.*, "Extracting Training Data from Large Language Models," *Proceedings of the USENIX Security Symposium*, 2021.

44. Z. Ji *et al.*, "Survey of Hallucination in Natural Language Generation," *ACM Computing Surveys*, vol. 55, no. 12, pp. 1–38, 2023.
45. A. Tabatabaei and A. ZadZiabari, "Generative AI in Medical Imaging," in *Application of Generative AI in Healthcare Systems*, Cham, Springer, 2025, pp. 1–33. doi: 10.1007/978-3-031-82963-5_1.
46. J. Wei *et al.*, "Emergent Abilities of Large Language Models," *Transactions on Machine Learning Research*, 2022. [Online]. Available: https://openreview.net/forum?id=yzkSU5zdwD
47. A. Gilson *et al.*, "How Well Do Large Language Models Support Clinical Information Retrieval?," *JAMA Network Open*, vol. 6, no. 11, p. e2344027, 2023, doi: 10.1001/jamanetworkopen.2023.44027.
48. S. Raza, D. Reji, Y. Ding, and H. Li, "Hallucination in Large Language Models: A Survey," *arXiv preprint 10.48550/arXiv.2311.05232*, 2023.
49. G. Somepalli, V. Singla, M. Goldblum, J. Geiping, and T. Goldstein, "Understanding Diffusion Models: A Unified Perspective," *arXiv preprint arXiv:2303.02165*, 2023.
50. Y. Ovadia *et al.*, "Can You Trust Your Model's Uncertainty? Evaluating Predictive Uncertainty under Dataset Shift," *Advances in Neural Information Processing Systems*, vol. 32, 2019.
51. D. Ganguli *et al.*, "Red Teaming Language Models to Reduce Harms: Methods, Scaling Behaviors, and Lessons Learned," *arXiv preprint arXiv:2209.07858*, 2022.
52. M. Saleh and A. Tabatabaei, "Building Trustworthy Multimodal AI: A Review of Fairness, Transparency, and Ethics in Vision-Language Tasks," *International Journal of Web Research*, vol. 8, no. 2, pp. 11–24, 2025, doi: 10.22133/ijwr.2025.503147.1264.
53. A. ZadZiabari, and A. Tabatabaei, "Ethics and Regulations in Generative AI," in *Application of Generative AI in Healthcare Systems*, A. Zamanifar and M. Faezipour, Eds., Cham: Springer Nature Switzerland, 2025, pp. 197–211. doi: 10.1007/978-3-031-82963-5_8.
54. European Commission, "Artificial Intelligence Act." 2024. [Online]. Available: https://eur-lex.europa.eu/legal-content/EN/TXT/?uri=CELEX:32024R1689
55. F. Doshi-Velez and B. Kim, "Towards A Rigorous Science of Interpretable Machine Learning," *arXiv preprint arXiv:1702.08608*, 2017.

# 2 Ethical and Legal Considerations in AI Safety

*Azadeh Tabatabaei, Omid Mohebi, and Tarannom Sadegh*

## 2.1 INTRODUCTION

The integration of artificial intelligence (AI) into clinical practice marks a paradigm shift with the potential to redefine diagnosis, treatment, and patient management [1, 2]. However, this transformation introduces profound ethical questions, novel legal liabilities, and complex governance challenges that extend far beyond technical performance metrics [3–5]. The "safety" of an AI system in this high-stakes domain is not merely a function of its accuracy but an emergent property of its alignment with human values, its compliance with legal standards, and its accountable integration into socio-technical healthcare ecosystems [6–8].

Conventional approaches to medical device safety are ill-equipped to address the dynamic, opaque, and adaptive nature of modern AI, particularly foundation and generative models [9–11]. These technologies can perpetuate historical biases [1, 12], obscure decision-making rationale [9, 10], and operate within diffuse accountability structures [5, 13], thereby risking patient harm, eroding autonomy, and undermining equitable care [4, 14]. Consequently, a siloed focus on engineering or regulation is insufficient. A proactive, multidisciplinary framework is necessary to anticipate and mitigate risks across the entire AI lifecycle [7, 8, 14].

This chapter provides a comprehensive synthesis of this essential framework, structured around three interdependent pillars: ethics, law, and governance. First, it grounds the discussion in the established principles of biomedical ethics—autonomy, beneficence, non-maleficence, and justice—and demonstrates their practical application and limitations through contemporary AI healthcare scenarios [4, 14–16]. It then explores complementary ethical theories to navigate complex moral trade-offs in the design and deployment of technology [6, 17].

The second pillar confronts the practical challenge of operationalizing ethical principles, focusing on algorithmic fairness. It details formal fairness metrics [7], critically examines their limitations in clinical contexts [1, 7], and outlines technical strategies for bias mitigation across the data pipeline [1, 18]. The discussion then transitions to the concrete legal and regulatory landscape, analyzing evolving international guidelines [8, 14] and region-specific regulations [5, 19, 20] that govern high-risk AI systems.

The third pillar addresses implementation through governance and accountability. It dissects the complex issue of liability distribution among developers,

DOI: 10.1201/9781003743422-2

clinicians, and institutions [5, 13, 21] and proposes organizational structures—such as oversight boards and clear stewardship roles—necessary for responsible risk management [1, 8, 12]. Finally, the chapter examines technical privacy-preserving techniques (e.g., differential privacy and federated learning) [18, 22, 23] and concludes with imperative human-factors principles for interface and workflow design, aimed at preserving critical clinical judgment and mitigating automation bias [1, 24, 25].

By weaving these strands together, this chapter argues that the path to safe and trustworthy healthcare AI is fundamentally integrative [26]. It requires a deliberate and continuous effort to align technical capabilities with enduring ethical commitments [6, 14, 15, 27, 28], to navigate evolving legal obligations [5, 20, 29], and to institute transparent and accountable governance [1, 8, 12]. The following sections elaborate on this framework, providing the conceptual tools and practical guidance needed to ensure that AI fulfills its promise as a beneficial and equitable force in medicine.

## 2.2 ETHICAL FOUNDATIONS FOR HEALTHCARE AI

The integTechnological advancements, specifically artificial intelligence (AI) and robotics, will require an ethical framework to be developed for use in the practice of medicine and biomedicine. An ethical framework should be built on the same principles of morality and professional responsibility (i.e., concepts) that characterize the field of biomedical ethics. Therefore, the subsections will address both (1) classical ethical theories (i.e., Judeo-Christian) and (2) more current philosophical methods for evaluating technology (i.e., utilitarianism and deontological). By constructing these backgrounds, we can assess how to evaluate AI's presence in medicine.

### 2.2.1 Classic Biomedical Ethics and AI

The four classical principles of biomedical ethics, autonomy, beneficence, nonmaleficence, and justice, serve as foundational ethical frameworks for medicine [15]. Their application is crucial when evaluating AI systems, particularly because AI introduces novel complexities related to data, algorithms, and accountability into clinical practice [14].

#### 2.2.1.1 Beneficence (Maximizing Benefit)

Beneficence involves the moral obligation to promote the well-being of others, maximize expected benefits, and minimize risks of harm [14, 16]. It requires ensuring that AI technologies promote the prosperity of individuals and society as a whole [6].

#### 2.2.1.2 Non-Maleficence (Preventing Harm)

Non-maleficence, or "Do no harm" (primum non nocere), requires that AI technologies should not cause mental or physical harm [14] and minimize the risks of misuse or abuse [15]. Harm can arise from algorithmic bias, errors, or over-reliance on the technology [4].

#### 2.2.1.3 Autonomy (Respect for Persons)

Patients' rights include autonomy. Patients must have the ability to make their own decisions regarding their care. AI in medicine will necessitate human beings remaining in total control of decision-making concerning medical care, with sufficient information to provide a basis for an informed decision. An essential component of this will be the need for an individual to give their consent with full knowledge of the capabilities and limitations of AI, along with the uncertainties associated with using AI [3, 14].

#### 2.2.1.4 Justice (Fairness and Equity)

Finally, the principle of justice must be addressed to complete the ethical framework. Justice requires ensuring that all persons are treated fairly and that AI is designed to reduce inequity and bias [14]. Algorithmic bias, often stemming from unrepresentative or historically biased training data, can perpetuate existing healthcare disparities [12]. Justice concerns include ensuring equitable access to AI-driven personalized healthcare solutions [3].

A consolidated mapping of AI scenarios to the four principles of biomedical ethics is provided in Table 2.1.

**TABLE 2.1**
**AI Scenarios and Their Ethical Relevance**

| Corresponding Classic Biomedical Ethic | AI Scenario | Relevance to Beneficence |
|---|---|---|
| Beneficence | Predictive Risk Scores/Personalized Medicine | AI excels at tailoring treatment plans based on extensive patient data, aiming for unparalleled precision and efficacy in treatments [3, 30]. AI should be used to support healthy living by coaching, preventing, and treating diseases. |
| | Drug Discovery and Operational Efficiency | AI accelerates drug discovery by predicting molecule interactions [3] and optimizes resource allocation in healthcare settings (e.g., predicting patient inflow) [1]. This maximizes system-wide good and reduces costs. |
| | Autonomous Diagnostic Systems | These systems analyze medical data to make diagnostic decisions, improving the speed and accuracy of diagnoses, thereby maximizing positive health outcomes [3, 31, 32], [33, p. 201820]. |
| Non-maleficence | Diagnostic Imaging Analysis (Radiology/ Pathology) | If an AI algorithm, trained on biased or incomplete data, provides an incorrect diagnosis or treatment recommendation, it can lead to patient harm [3]. If AI-based decision-making tools increase the risk of diagnostic error (false positives or false negatives), their use is unethical [4]. |
| | Clinical Decision Support Software (CDSS) | The over-reliance (automation bias) of a healthcare professional (HCP) on AI-driven recommendations can lead to errors of omission or commission, causing harm by displacing critical human judgment [2, 7, 13]. |

*(Continued)*

**TABLE 2.1** *(Continued)*
**AI Scenarios and Their Ethical Relevance**

| Corresponding Classic Biomedical Ethic | AI Scenario | Relevance to Beneficence |
|---|---|---|
| | Autonomous Systems/Robotic Surgery | Responsibility for errors or adverse outcomes becomes complex when AI is increasingly autonomous, making it challenging to assign liability and ensure patients are protected from harm resulting from algorithmic failure [1, 3]. |
| Autonomy | AI-Driven Diagnostics and Treatment Plans | Patients must be fully aware of how AI is used in their care, including its function, accuracy, and limitations, to ensure their choices are informed and voluntary [3, 14]. |
| | Black-Box Algorithms (Deep Learning) | The complexity and lack of transparency (opacity or black-box nature) of AI systems hinder patients' ability to understand the rationale behind recommendations, making truly informed consent challenging [9]. |
| | AI in End-of-Life Care | When AI recommends life-sustaining treatments or end-of-life care plans, ensuring the system respects patient values, preferences, and the right to refuse intervention is essential [3, 14]. |
| Justice | Triage and Resource Allocation Algorithms | Algorithms, if trained on biased data reflecting past inequities, may systematically disadvantage marginalized populations, leading to unequal access to care [34, 35]. |
| | Predictive Risk Scores (e.g., for intervention referral) | If a model uses biased metrics (like historical healthcare spending instead of actual health needs, as seen in the Optum case [3]), it can underestimate the needs of certain groups, contributing to health inequities [1, 34, 35]. |
| | Inclusive Access | AI benefits should be accessible to all, particularly those from underserved or marginalized communities, and limited access due to socioeconomic factors can worsen disparities [3, 14]. |

### 2.2.2 Ethical Frameworks for Decision-Making

While the classical principles of biomedical ethics provide a foundational moral compass, decision-making in complex clinical and technological scenarios often benefits from applying broader ethical theories. Three key frameworks, utilitarianism, deontology, and care ethics, offer distinct perspectives on evaluating the moral permissibility of integrating AI and robotics into healthcare. Understanding these frameworks is essential for navigating the trade-offs and ensuring responsible innovation.

#### 2.2.2.1 Utilitarianism

Utilitarianism evaluates ethical permissibility by assessing whether actions maximize overall utility or happiness, aiming to produce the greatest good for the greatest number [17]. As a consequentialist framework, it focuses primarily on outcomes [36], grounding moral judgment in the balance of expected benefits and harms. Its core principle aligns beneficence with non-maleficence by requiring that anticipated risks be weighed against anticipated gains [7, 13]. The overarching goal is to determine whether a decision promotes the well-being of affected individuals and communities [7].

#### 2.2.2.2 Deontology (Duty-Based Ethics)

Deontological ethics assesses actions according to duties and moral rules, emphasizing their inherent rightness or wrongness independent of consequences [17]. This framework prioritizes adherence to universal obligations, including respect for autonomy [13, 17], the avoidance of harm, and the fair and just treatment of all persons [7, 14]. Its central aim is to ensure that actions conform to principles that safeguard individual dignity and protect fundamental rights [7, 17].

#### 2.2.2.3 Care Ethics (Relational Ethics)

Care ethics highlights the relational dimensions of moral life, focusing on empathy, trust, and responsiveness to context-specific needs [17]. In AI, this perspective emphasizes designing and deploying systems that foster stakeholder welfare and preserve meaningful human connections, relationships, and mutual understanding [4, 7]. Its core principle insists that AI should serve human interests rather than technological goals alone [6]. The objective is to maintain the fiduciary relationship in healthcare and support compassionate, human-centered interactions, particularly in high-stakes settings [1, 4].

## 2.3 FAIRNESS METRICS AND LIMITATIONS, AND BIAS MITIGATION STRATEGIES

This section outlines how bias can manifest in algorithmic systems, how fairness is formally measured, where these metrics fall short in clinical environments, and the strategies used to mitigate discriminatory outcomes.

### 2.3.1 Common Fairness Metrics

Fairness aims to ensure that the outcomes and decisions produced by AI systems do not discriminate against specific groups or individuals based on protected characteristics like race, gender, or age [6, 8]. Fairness constraints can be introduced during the model training process to ensure that predictions do not disproportionately favor one group over another [3].

Fairness metrics offer formal mechanisms for assessing whether algorithmic outcomes vary across demographic groups. Statistical parity evaluates whether optimistic predictions are proportionally distributed across protected groups, aiming to prevent disparate impact [7]. Equal opportunity and equalized odds refine this by examining error-rate parity, ensuring that true-positive and false-positive rates remain comparable across groups [7]. Together, these formulations express the core goal of fairness: to ensure that models do not systematically advantage or disadvantage any population subgroup in terms of access to beneficial outcomes or exposure to error.

### 2.3.2 Limitations of Fairness Metrics in Clinical Settings

Although mathematically precise, fairness metrics often diverge from ethical and clinical conceptions of equity. Many definitions are mutually incompatible, and selecting among them requires normative judgment shaped by the clinical use case [7, 33]. Proxy variables introduce additional complexity: historical inequities embedded in healthcare spending or access can be inadvertently encoded into model predictions, as demonstrated by systems trained on cost rather than clinical need [1, 6]. Further, demographic attributes needed for fairness auditing are frequently unavailable or unreliable, hindering meaningful subgroup evaluation. Even when protected attributes are removed, hidden proxies can perpetuate structural bias [7]. In healthcare, where diverse populations and heterogeneous data are the norm, these limitations underscore the need for careful interpretive use of fairness metrics rather than blind adherence.

### 2.3.3 Bias Mitigation Strategies

Bias mitigation spans the full AI development lifecycle and aims to reduce representational and statistical distortions that lead to inequitable outcomes. As illustrated in Figure 2.1, interventions operate at three stages: pre-processing, in-training, and post-processing, each contributing distinct mechanisms for promoting fairness [7].

#### 2.3.3.1 Data Augmentation/Resampling (Pre-processing Stage)

Techniques such as data augmentation and resampling modify the training distribution to correct demographic imbalance and reduce representation bias [1, 3, 6, 7, 13, 18]. Ensuring inclusive and demographically representative datasets is essential for improving model generalizability and avoiding systematic underperformance on minority populations [3], while maintaining data quality and integrity helps address biases originating from flawed or uneven collection processes [6, 7]. Adversarial augmentation further enhances robustness by introducing controlled perturbations or adversarial examples during training [18].

#### 2.3.3.2 Fairness-aware Loss/Adversarial De-biasing (In-training)

Fairness-aware loss functions and adversarial de-biasing embed fairness constraints directly into the optimization process, penalizing biased predictions and suppressing the model's ability to encode sensitive attributes [7, 18]. These methods ensure that accuracy is not achieved through discriminatory shortcuts and support fairness-aware algorithmic design choices [3]. Optimizing models against fairness metrics, such as equal opportunity, helps align performance across demographic subgroups [7].

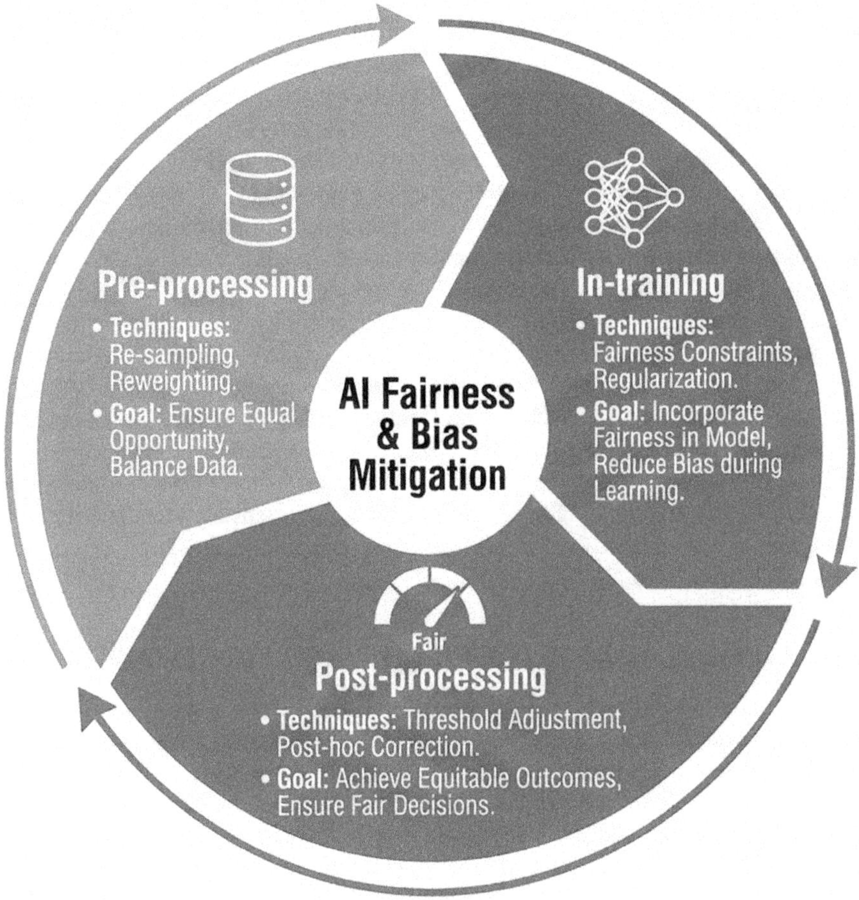


**FIGURE 2.1** Demonstrate mitigation strategies in different stages.

#### 2.3.3.3 Threshold Adjustments (Post-processing)

To increase equality after a model has been trained, threshold adjustments alter the outputs to create a new set of boundaries for classifying data. This is achieved by adjusting thresholds such that they reduce the difference between groups for key error rates (true positives vs. false positives), which allows for equal treatment and prevents the uneven impact of misclassification on certain groups [7].

### 2.3.4 Evaluation Protocol

Rigorous testing and validation are crucial for ensuring safety, reliability, and ethical compliance before and after AI systems are implemented [8, 13]. The evaluation pillar proposes a comprehensive approach covering technical ability, societal implications, and risk assessment [6].

Regular algorithmic audits are necessary to identify how AI systems perform across demographic groups and to detect disparities that may systematically disadvantage specific populations [3]. Accuracy measurements should therefore be disaggregated by race, ethnicity, gender, age, and other relevant characteristics to ensure equitable performance [14]. Beyond internal audits, external validation is essential for establishing generalizability, as models trained in one institution may not function reliably in different clinical or geographic contexts [14, 37, 38]. Rigorous testing must occur in the intended clinical environment, with prospective evaluations, such as randomized trials that are recommended over retrospective dataset comparisons [14]. Accuracy measures must also demonstrate external validity beyond initial training conditions [8]. Because many AI systems evolve over time, continuous monitoring is required to maintain fairness and safety, incorporating feedback loops to detect emerging biases and assess whether outputs remain appropriate in real-world use [3, 14, 39]. Such monitoring supports proactive risk management, aligning with regulatory expectations that emphasize tracking system performance and identifying unanticipated risks post-market, such as the FDA's framework for adaptive AI [8, 39]. Ongoing oversight and auditability ensure accountability and transparency throughout the AI lifecycle by documenting incidents, errors, and emergent behaviors [6, 8].

## 2.4 CONSENT, DATA SUBJECT RIGHTS AND CONTESTABILITY

In this section, the ethical and legal framework that dictates the way patient information is collected, used, and protected in an AI-enabled healthcare environment will be discussed. The first part of this section will discuss the differences in the level of consent required when collecting patient information from a clinical setting versus a research setting. The second part will discuss the need to protect vulnerable and/or at-risk populations. Finally, the third part will provide an overview of the fundamental rights of the patient over their information, as well as their ability to dispute automated decisions. The last section discuss secondary uses for model training.

### 2.4.1 Informed Consent in Clinical AI vs. Research AI

The challenge of informed consent in AI-driven healthcare encompasses both ethical and legal dimensions, requiring updated frameworks to address the complexities introduced by these technologies [3].

#### 2.4.1.1 Decision Support (Clinical AI)

When AI functions as decision support, it is intended to augment rather than replace clinician judgment, offering evidence-based recommendations derived from large datasets such as imaging or clinical records [14, 37]. Although the clinician remains the ultimate decision-maker, AI outputs can significantly influence medical choices [3, 13]. The opacity of many machine-learning systems creates challenges for interpretability, which is frequently described as "black boxes" [5, 6, 16], potentially hindering adoption and constraining patient autonomy by limiting shared decision-making [6]. Meaningful consent, therefore, requires transparency about the AI's role, rationale, and limitations so that clinicians and patients can make informed choices [3]. In this standard model, AI functions as a tool to augment or support the judgment of a human clinician.

#### 2.4.1.2 Direct Clinical Use/Autonomous Decisioning

Where AI systems operate with minimal human oversight, the challenge of informed consent is amplified, as patients must understand not only what data are collected but also the extent of the system's autonomy in their care [14]. If AI decision-making undermines human autonomy, it violates a core ethical principle, underscoring the need to preserve human authority in clinical judgment. A lack of meaningful human oversight in fully or partially autonomous systems may also challenge existing legal frameworks when machines take on functions traditionally reserved for clinicians [3]. Ensuring valid consent, therefore, requires clear communication about how responsibility is distributed within the human-AI collaboration and reaffirming that humans retain ultimate control over medical decisions [14].

#### 2.4.1.3 Secondary Uses for Model Training (Research AI)

This refers to the crucial process of using collected health data to develop, train, and continuously refine AI models, which often requires large datasets. AI models, especially those for personalized medicine, require access to vast amounts of sensitive data, including genetic information and clinical histories. This data is used to find hidden patterns and develop predictive models [3, 13, 14, 37].

The relationship between clinical practice and research is changing with the advent of digital technology. Data collected during treatment can now be used to develop algorithms to improve patient care (a secondary use). Patients may have provided consent to use this data for one particular purpose, but the use of this data in a different capacity (e.g., for research and/or to develop commercial products) may require a patient's additional consent or will be outside of the scope of the initial consent. Often, the traditional model of providing "notice and consent" is insufficient, as in many cases the data subject has no control over either current or future use of his/her data. Furthermore, the continual evolution of algorithms to improve treatment methods through the use of patient data conflicts with a hospital's obligation to protect the privacy of patients [6, 14].

#### 2.4.1.4 Special Populations and Consent Language

To keep AI-supported care ethical and legal, we must offer specific protections to vulnerable groups and understand when stronger consent is necessary.

#### 2.4.1.5 Best Practices for Vulnerable Populations (Minors, Cognitively Impaired)

When dealing with patients who are vulnerable (such as minors, the elderly, or those with cognitive impairments), the ethical and legal frameworks emphasize stricter controls, greater transparency, and often rely on surrogate decision-makers [14].

To address this issue, special provisions must be made to protect the rights and welfare of vulnerable persons, including mechanisms for redress if bias or discrimination arises. This will be done through targeted protection. Regulations may need to be tailored according to risk, ensuring that those who are especially vulnerable, including people with mental illness, children, and the elderly, are protected from misinformation and poor advice from health applications that might exploit them [14]. When designing AI systems and providing explanations for their outputs, experts should prioritize the needs of the most disadvantaged stakeholders first. This means fine-tuning explanatory strategies to accommodate their requirements and providing precise, non-technical details about the algorithmic rationale [7].

Moreover, obtaining consent is considered critical and obligatory for both competent and incompetent users of intelligent assistive technology, ensuring their respect and privacy are maintained when exposed to monitoring technologies [40]. For senior citizens, strategies include applying advance directives to understand their expressed wishes and respect their autonomy throughout the progression of their disease. It is also necessary to fully comprehend vulnerable groups' decisions about intelligent assistive technology before their cognitive impairment worsens [40].

Behavioral observation may be used as a method to detect behaviors that indicate a patient is withdrawing previously obtained consent, mainly due to discomfort or disease progression [40]. Moreover, in minors' cases, parents are considered the personal representatives for their minor children under the Health Insurance Portability and Accountability Act (HIPAA), granting them the ability to exercise individual rights like accessing the medical record on the minor's behalf [41].

#### 2.4.1.6 When "Notice-Only" Is Insufficient and Active Consent Must Be Obtained!

The distinction between "notice-only" or implied consent and required active or explicit authorization often hinges on the purpose of the data usage, particularly in the US legal context (HIPAA) versus European regulations (GDPR) [29, 41].

In the United States, obtaining "consent" (written permission) for certain routine healthcare activities is generally optional for covered entities under the HIPAA Privacy Rule [41]. Covered entities are permitted to use and disclose Protected Health Information (PHI) for their own treatment, payment, and healthcare operations (TPO) activities. For these specific purposes, obtaining consent is optional. Providers are required to give patients a Notice of Privacy Practices, which outlines how their information can be used, particularly for TPO. Covered entities may rely on informal permission for certain limited disclosures, such as information used for a facility directory or information directly relevant to a family member's involvement in the individual's care or payment [41].

Active or explicit consent (Authorization under HIPAA) is required when the use of data moves outside the scope of routine care or when handling sensitive data, especially in the context of AI and secondary data use or anything beyond TPO. A covered entity must obtain the individual's written authorization for any use or disclosure of PHI that is not for treatment, payment, or healthcare operations or otherwise permitted or required by the Privacy Rule. Examples include disclosing information to a life insurer for coverage purposes or to a pharmaceutical company for marketing [41].

### 2.4.2 Data Subject Rights

AI applications touch on how much control and freedom people have, making it vital to enforce their data rights. The GDPR protects data subjects through specific rights. For instance, patients can access, correct, and delete their data. Article 17 gives individuals the right to ask for their personal data to be removed. This right gets legally tricky with AI, though, because erasing data might affect an algorithmic model's credibility and accuracy. Article 20 also lets individuals transfer their personal data. Article 22 prohibits automated decisions that lead to legal consequences or significantly impact the data subject, affecting things like their work performance, economic situation, or health. There are exceptions, of course, like decisions based on explicit consent or those legally authorized with built-in safeguards. Closely tied to Article 22 is the right to get clear information about the logic behind automated decisions (found in Article 15 and Recital 71). However, the "black box" problem, where complex machine learning models are opaque, makes upholding this right difficult [29].

HIPAA also grants patients significant rights over their PHI. Patients have the right to access and request amendments to their health information (aligned with the ethical principle of autonomy and individual control). Patients must be fully informed about the types of data being collected, how it will be used, and the potential risks to their privacy. This is a critical ethical safeguard for AI-driven care. Patients are entitled to information regarding how their health records have been shared, which reinforces transparency and individual control [41].

### 2.4.3 Contestability

Contestability is primarily enabled through two core mechanisms: transparency/explainability (understanding why the decision was made) and human oversight/final judgment (the ability to override the decision) [3, 7, 8, 14].

#### 2.4.3.1 Patient Rights and Recourse

Contestability requires that patients and advocates have mechanisms to understand and challenge automated decisions. Explanations should clarify the rationale behind the system's recommendation to support informed critical assessment [7]. Under the GDPR, individuals hold the right to contest decisions based solely on automated processing and to obtain human intervention, including access to "meaningful information about the logic involved" [1, 29, 42]. Patients also retain the right to refuse AI-assisted treatment; they may seek second opinions or alternative care, and essential services cannot be withheld on the basis of declining AI use [3, 14, 43]. Counterfactual explanations provide actionable avenues for recourse by identifying how specific factors could change to produce a different outcome [7]. Under HIPAA, individuals may request amendments to inaccurate or incomplete health records used in clinical decision-making, allowing corrections when flawed data influence AI-generated recommendations [41].

#### 2.4.3.2 Clinician's Right to Contest and Override

Clinicians remain the central point of accountability—serving as the "human warranty"—and bear responsibility for evaluating and, when appropriate, overriding AI recommendations [7, 14]. AI systems must support, not replace, clinical judgment, and clinicians must be able to intervene whenever automated outputs are medically or ethically inappropriate [6, 13, 14]. Operational safeguards are needed to mitigate automation bias, which may lead clinicians to over-rely on AI or accept outputs uncritically [7]. Training should reinforce that AI-generated insights contribute to, rather than substitute for, professional deliberation [7, 14]. When disagreements arise—particularly with opaque models—dialogue and multidisciplinary review are essential to mediate conflicting interpretations and maintain accountability [44].

## 2.5 REGULATORY AND POLICY LANDSCAPE

To interpret how AI for healthcare is shaped by the global framework, as well as the regulatory and policy landscape governing the use and development of AI for healthcare via national laws and regulations, as well as health data protection legislation, an understanding of this regulatory and policy environment is necessary. The next sections will provide details regarding the various international approaches and agreements in the field, regional and country-specific regulations, and the key elements of the legal framework for health data handling.

### 2.5.1 Global and Supranational Frameworks

Global and supranational frameworks provide harmonized principles, shared standards, and cross-border governance mechanisms that guide countries, institutions, and developers toward responsible AI practices. These frameworks are designed to address the inherently international nature of AI technologies, where data, models, and risks often transcend jurisdictional boundaries, and to promote consistency in ethical norms, risk management, human rights protections, and accountability structures. By establishing common reference points such as ethical principles (e.g., WHO) [14] and operational risk-management guidelines (e.g., NIST) [8], these frameworks help align diverse stakeholders and encourage the trustworthy, inclusive, and sustainable use of AI for health across different regions and socioeconomic contexts.

#### 2.5.1.1 WHO Guidance: Ethics and Governance of AI for Health

The WHO's Ethics and Governance of Artificial Intelligence for Health, developed through expert consensus, offers foundational principles intended to guide governments, developers, and healthcare institutions toward ethically grounded AI deployment [14]. Its six principles emphasize protecting autonomy; promoting well-being, safety, and the public interest; ensuring transparency and intelligibility; fostering responsibility and accountability; supporting inclusiveness and equity; and promoting responsiveness and sustainability through continuous assessment and environmental attention [14].

The WHO guidance is explicitly grounded in international human rights law, outlining the following key expectations [3, 14]:

- AI for health must align with ethical norms and human rights standards.
- Human rights, including those in the Universal Declaration of Human Rights, provide the baseline for dignity and protection.
- Human rights principles relevant to AI include equality, non-discrimination, privacy, freedom, participation, solidarity, and accountability.
- Governments must restrict or prohibit AI uses that violate or endanger human rights.
- AI can advance the human right to health if designed accountably but also poses risks such as dehumanization, erosion of autonomy, and privacy violations.
- Private sector actors must respect human rights and avoid contributing to rights abuses, independent of state obligations.

#### 2.5.1.2 NIST AI Risk Management Framework (AI RMF 1.0)

The NIST AI RMF 1.0 is a voluntary, rights-preserving framework designed to help organizations manage the risks posed by socio-technical AI systems, particularly those shaped by shifting data and human behavior [8]. Emphasizing human centricity, social responsibility, and sustainability, the framework is structured around four high-level functions that organize risk-management activities across the AI lifecycle [8]. Table 2.2 explains these four functions in detail.

**TABLE 2.2**
**AI RMF Four core Functions**

| Function | Core Focus | How It Supports Lifecycle Risk Management |
|---|---|---|
| GOVERN | Fosters a culture of risk management. | The overall purpose of the governance function is to align the technical aspects of AI system design and development to organizational values and principles and strategic priorities [8]. |
| MAP | Establishes the context to frame risks related to an AI system. | It helps AI actors understand the intended purposes, constraints, potential settings, context-specific laws, and norms. The MAP function requires characterizing the likelihood and magnitude of both positive and negative impacts (harms) on individuals, communities, and society. It informs the initial go/no-go decision about designing, developing, or deploying an AI system. |
| MEASURE | Employs tools and methodologies to analyze, assess, benchmark, and monitor AI risk. | It involves rigorous Test, Evaluation, Verification, and Validation (TEVV) processes. Systems must be tested before deployment and regularly while in operation. MEASURE ensures that systems are evaluated for all trustworthy characteristics (validity, reliability, safety, security, fairness, privacy, and explainability) and that methods for tracking existing and emergent risks are in place. |

*(Continued)*

**TABLE 2.2** *(Continued)*
**AI RMF Four core Functions**

| Function | Core Focus | How It Supports Lifecycle Risk Management |
|---|---|---|
| MANAGE | Prioritizes, responds to, and manages risks based on assessments from the MAP and MEASURE functions. | This function includes making a determination on whether development or deployment should proceed. It establishes strategies to maximize benefits and minimize negative impacts. It ensures that post-deployment monitoring plans are implemented, including mechanisms for collecting user feedback, processing appeals, incident response, recovery, and continuous improvement. |

## 2.5.2 Region and Country Examples

Different regions and countries have developed regulatory approaches tailored to their legal systems, healthcare infrastructure, and risk tolerance for AI technologies. The EU AI Act and the FDA AI/ML SaMD Action Plan illustrate how high-risk AI systems in healthcare are classified, regulated, and monitored.

### 2.5.2.1 Europe: The EU AI Act

The EU AI Act introduces a harmonized, common regulatory and legal framework for AI, classifying them into four tiers with corresponding regulatory obligations (Figure 2.2): systems posing an Unacceptable Risk to fundamental rights, such as government social scoring, are strictly prohibited; systems deemed Limited Risk (e.g., general-purpose chatbots or deepfakes) must comply with minimal transparency requirements

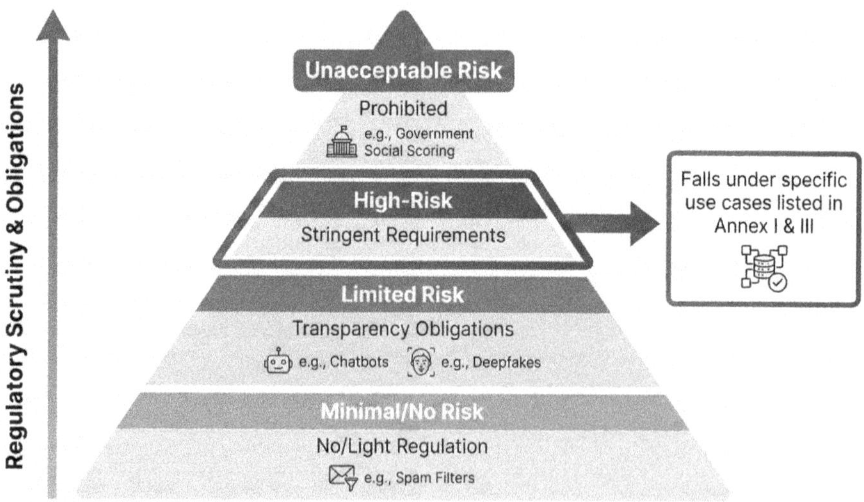


**FIGURE 2.2** The EU's regulatory framework for AI, which classifies AI systems into four hierarchical risk categories based on the potential harm they pose.

to inform the user of the AI interaction; Minimal/No Risk systems (like spam filters) are largely unregulated; and finally, High-Risk systems; the majority of the AI Act's stringent requirements are directed toward systems deemed "High-Risk" [19]. An AI system is classified as high-risk if it meets one of two criteria:

1. It is intended to be used as a safety component or a product covered by existing EU harmonization legislation listed in Annex I (e.g., medical devices and machinery). It is required to undergo a third-party conformity assessment under those laws.
2. It falls under specific use cases listed in Annex III.

AI used in medical care is predominantly captured under the high-risk categorization due to its relationship with existing regulations like the Medical Device Regulation (MDR) 2017/745 [3, 5].

- Software is considered a medical device if it is intended for the diagnosis, cure, mitigation, prevention, or prognosis of a disease. The MDR expands the range of devices covered compared to older directives, specifically by including terms like "prediction" and "prognosis" of disease in the medical device definition [39].
- AI-based tools and decision-making software used for diagnosis or therapeutic.
- Purposes are frequently classified as Class IIa devices under Rule 11 of the MDR [5].
- If the system may result in death or an irreversible deterioration of a person's state of health (or a surgical intervention), it is classified as a Class IIb or Class III (highest risk) device [4, 5].

### 2.5.2.2 United States: FDA AI/ML SaMD Action Plan

The US Food and Drug Administration (FDA) regulates medical devices and technologies, including AI systems, through existing pathways like premarket clearance (510(k)) or premarket approval. Recognizing that the traditional regulation paradigm was not designed for adaptive AI/ML technologies, the FDA has taken steps to create a fit-for-purpose framework [20].

The FDA published the "Artificial Intelligence and Machine Learning Software as a Medical Device Action Plan" (AI/ML SaMD Action Plan) in January 2021. This plan is part of the FDA's coordinated approach to AI across its centers [20]. The core goal is to ensure that AI applications meet the same standards of safety and effectiveness as traditional medical devices. The FDA approach emphasizes managing AI/ML-driven devices throughout their entire Total Product Lifecycle (TPLC), rather than relying on a single, fixed premarket approval [5, 20]. In other words, the FDA focuses on regulating the entire life cycle, monitoring, managing, and identifying risks that arise from the dynamic nature of AI, such as concept drift, instability, and covariate shift. This necessitates continuous monitoring and robust validation mechanisms [3].

The FDA acknowledges the transformative potential residing in AI's ability to learn and adapt from real-world use, positioning its regulatory framework to manage the risks inherent in continuous learning systems rather than attempting to freeze their capability at the time of initial approval. The framework is designed to allow AI devices to continuously improve their performance in real-time when used in a clinical setting [5, 20, 39].

### 2.5.3 Data Protection Laws That Affect Healthcare AI

The deployment of AI in healthcare relies heavily on the use and processing of massive amounts of sensitive health data. Consequently, the field is critically regulated by robust, region-specific data protection laws designed to safeguard patient privacy, ensure data security, and mandate ethical handling of personal information. This section will elaborate on two of the most significant frameworks governing healthcare AI: the General Data Protection Regulation (GDPR) in the European Union (EU) and the HIPAA in the United States.

#### 2.5.3.1 GDPR Highlights: Automated Decision-Making and Profiling

The GDPR establishes strict requirements for processing personal and sensitive health data, particularly when AI systems engage in automated decision-making or profiling [29]. Article 22 prohibits decisions based solely on automated processing when they produce legal or similarly significant effects, subject to narrow exceptions such as contractual necessity, legal authorization with safeguards, or explicit consent for those exceptions that generally do not apply to decisions involving genetic, biometric, or other health data. Profiling is defined as automated processing intended to evaluate personal aspects of an individual, while automated decision-making refers to decisions made without human involvement. Data subjects, therefore, retain the right not to be subject to such decisions and to receive meaningful information about the logic involved.

#### 2.5.3.2 HIPAA Basics for US Clinical Data Flows, PHI, and Business Associate Responsibilities

The HIPAA of 1996 is the key federal law in the United States that safeguards individuals' health data privacy. It establishes national standards for protecting identifiable health information, defining PHI, and regulating how it may be used or disclosed [41]. Covered entities, like healthcare providers, plans, and clearinghouses, require patient authorization for most uses of PHI, with exceptions for TPO [6, 41]. The Privacy Rule's "minimum necessary" standard mandates limiting PHI use to what is strictly required, and business associates handling PHI must be contractually bound to safeguard it [5, 41]. Patients retain rights to access and amend their records and receive an accounting of disclosures [5, 6]. HIPAA leaves gaps for health-related data falling outside its scope, prompting calls for additional state and federal protections, including proposals such as the Algorithmic Accountability Act requiring impact assessments for high-risk AI systems [5, 13, 37].

## 2.6 LIABILITY, ACCOUNTABILITY, AND GOVERNANCE

Data protection laws in healthcare govern both automated decision-making and routine data flows, as seen in frameworks like the GDPR in Europe and HIPAA in the United States.

### 2.6.1 Liability Regimes and Allocation of Responsibility

AI deployment involves numerous actors, including developers, algorithm trainers, data collectors, manufacturers, hospitals, and clinicians [21]. This complexity creates the "many hands problem" or traceability challenge, making it difficult, both legally and morally, to assign responsibility [14, 30, 45]. Frameworks must clearly define the roles and responsibilities of both AI developers and healthcare providers to ensure patient protection.

#### 2.6.1.1 Allocation of Responsibility: Developer vs. User

Liability is typically shared between the creators of an AI system and the clinicians or institutions that apply it in practice. A central question concerns whether AI should be treated as a product subject to strict liability, a regime traditionally applied to defective goods regardless of negligence [1, 20, 35, 42]. While software has historically been classified as a service, legal consensus increasingly supports treating AI as a product, making developers accountable when flawed design or inadequate data produce harmful outcomes [42]. Strict liability may also apply when a safer alternative design could have prevented foreseeable injury [21].

The model becomes more complex when machine-learning systems evolve after deployment, raising questions about developer responsibility for post-market changes [14, 39]. Developers may invoke the "learned intermediary" doctrine, which shifts responsibility to clinicians if adequate warnings are provided [14].

Clinicians remain responsible for patient care under malpractice law [3, 30]. When AI functions as a support tool, clinicians retain final decision-making authority and may be liable if excessive reliance on AI leads to negligent recommendations [1, 13]. They must independently evaluate AI outputs rather than defer unquestioningly to opaque systems [3, 14]. As AI becomes standard practice, clinicians may also be expected to use AI tools when they improve diagnostic or treatment accuracy [4].

Hospitals and health systems can similarly be liable if they fail to exercise due care in selecting, implementing, or maintaining AI technologies through corporate negligence or vicarious liability [1, 14].

#### 2.6.1.2 Legal Scholarship and Liability Debates

Scholars disagree on whether existing tort law is sufficient for AI-related harms. Some argue that traditional doctrines, including product liability, already provide adequate tools for addressing causation and defect claims, a position called the "Law of the Horse" [21]. Others propose harm-based models that classify AI-related injuries and tailor compensation accordingly [21]. Because assigning fault is often difficult with autonomous systems, no-fault compensation schemes have been proposed, modeled on vaccine injury programs and funded through mechanisms such as AI product surtaxes [21, 46, 47]. "Collective" or "faultless responsibility" are other approaches that allocate responsibility across all actors in the AI supply chain to counteract responsibility diffusion and promote shared accountability [14].

## 2.6.2 Organizational Governance Structures

Effective governance is the backbone for the responsible and safe deployment of AI in healthcare. Establishing clear organizational structures, roles, and accountability mechanisms is paramount to managing the inherent risks associated with AI systems and ensuring they align with clinical safety, ethical principles, and patient-centric values. This governance must span the entire AI lifecycle, from design and development to continuous monitoring.

### 2.6.2.1 Governance Board/Accountability Structures

AI governance begins with cultivating a risk-aware organizational culture supported by clear decision-making structures and accountability lines [8]. Senior leadership, management, and Boards of Directors hold responsibility for overseeing AI-related risks and ensuring that system design and deployment align with institutional values and strategic priorities [8]. Policymakers and healthcare organizations are encouraged to establish collaborative bodies, such as Ethical Governance Councils, that bring together AI specialists, clinicians, ethicists, and patient advocates to uphold ethical principles throughout development and implementation [3, 6, 13]. The GOVERN function provides a framework for anticipating, identifying, and managing risks, including potential impacts on users and society [8].

### 2.6.2.2 Chief AI Officer/Clinical AI Steward Roles

Clear assignment of roles is essential for mapping, measuring, and managing AI risks. Governance structures must document the responsibilities of individuals involved in human-AI team configurations and system oversight [8, 30]. AI should augment rather than replace clinical judgment, making human oversight a central principle of patient care [4, 14]. Healthcare professionals require adequate training to understand AI systems and exercise appropriate supervision, consistent with AMA guidance on clinician well-being and competency [1, 48, 49]. The concept of "human warranty" reinforces the need for human evaluation at critical points in AI development and deployment [14].

### 2.6.2.3 Data Governance Committee

Data governance is critical for ensuring privacy, data quality, and ethical use. The WHO's hub-and-spoke model, supported by a Data Governance Committee, exemplifies the importance of maintaining data integrity and establishing shared principles for data collection, sharing, and oversight [14]. Robust policies must include anonymization, encryption, and access controls, regularly updated to address emerging security threats [26]. Governance must also ensure compliance with data protection laws such as HIPAA and GDPR, which impose strict obligations for managing sensitive health information [3, 30] while safeguarding privacy, confidentiality, and informed consent [14, 30].

### 2.6.2.4 Integration into Existing Clinical Governance

AI must be integrated into established clinical safety and quality assurance frameworks. Systems must satisfy regulatory requirements for safety, accuracy, and efficacy, consistent with FDA expectations and AMA recommendations for risk governance [1, 8, 20]. Accountability structures should clearly define the respective roles of manufacturers and clinical users when AI contributes to patient harm. Continuous monitoring, periodic evaluation, and feedback mechanisms are essential for maintaining performance, especially as AI systems evolve through continuous learning [3, 6, 8, 14, 35]. Ethics by Design further embeds ethical considerations across the lifecycle, requiring collaboration among AI specialists, clinicians, policymakers, and patients [1, 4].

## 2.7 PRIVACY AND DATA PROTECTION

The sensitivity of patient health data requires that AI pipelines adhere to stringent legal requirements and utilize advanced technical safeguards. Compliance is fundamentally driven by two core objectives: establishing a lawful basis for every processing activity and deploying privacy-preserving technologies (PPTs) to minimize risk.

### 2.7.1 Legal Requirements Relevant to AI Pipelines

Data protection frameworks like the GDPR and HIPAA impose specific, non-negotiable rules on how sensitive health data can be collected, used, and stored by AI systems.

#### 2.7.1.1 Lawful Bases for Processing (GDPR) and Permitted Uses (HIPAA)

AI systems rely on large volumes of sensitive patient data, which must be collected and used only under strict legal justification [3, 39]. The GDPR requires that personal data, especially sensitive health data, be processed lawfully, transparently, and for specific purposes. Lawful processing (Article 6) means that data processing must be justified by a legal basis. And according to Article 9, health data is categorized as highly sensitive. Processing is generally prohibited unless specific exceptions apply, such as when the individual gives explicit consent or if the use is necessary for health-related operations or scientific research [5, 29]. Consent is central to maintaining privacy. It must be specific (aligned with the original purpose for collection), granular (separate from granting access to a service), and freely given (meaning no significant imbalance exists between the individual and the controlling entity). Legal scholars and authorities note that, particularly in contexts like employment, consent may not be considered freely given, necessitating a reliance on other legal bases, such as necessity for Occupational Safety and Health (OSH) purposes. Processing must remain consistent with the original purpose for data collection. The use of data in AI applications raises a constant challenge regarding the repurposing of data without explicit consent [29].

HIPAA sets forth requirements for protecting patient information, known as PHI [41].

- Authorization vs. Exception: Covered entities are generally prohibited from using or disclosing PHI without the individual's authorization.
- Permitted Uses: PHI disclosure and use are allowed without authorization for purposes of TPO.

- Research: Research use of PHI is allowed under specific conditions, which typically require safeguards like Institutional Review Board (IRB) approval.
- De-identification: If all identifying details are stripped from the data, it is no longer considered PHI, and HIPAA restrictions do not apply.

#### 2.7.1.2 Minimization

Both GDPR and HIPAA require limiting data processing to what is strictly necessary. GDPR's data minimization principle (Article 5-1c) mandates that only relevant data be collected for the intended purpose and embeds minimization within Privacy by Design (PbD) practices [29]. HIPAA similarly requires using or disclosing only the minimum necessary PHI for each task, ensuring that AI systems access no more data than required [41].

#### 2.7.1.3 Retention Policies

GDPR's storage limitation principle (Article 5-1e) requires that personal data be retained only as long as necessary for processing, permitting extended storage for archival, statistical, or research purposes when justified [29]. HIPAA mandates retention of privacy-related documentation for six years from creation or the last effective date, ensuring traceability and compliance [41].

### 2.7.2 Technical Privacy-Preserving Techniques

As AI systems, particularly in healthcare, necessitate vast amounts of highly sensitive data, technical privacy-preserving techniques are crucial for ethical and legal compliance [3, 14, 17]. These technologies offer methods to leverage data for AI development while minimizing the risk of privacy breaches and unauthorized access [18, 30].

#### 2.7.2.1 Differential Privacy

Differential privacy is identified as a technology recommended for adoption to address data privacy and security issues. It is one of the methods used to protect data privacy and prevent leaks [18]. Alongside k-anonymity and coarse-graining through clustering, differential privacy is categorized as a technique that can be selected through consultation to safeguard privacy and assure confidentiality [14].

#### 2.7.2.2 Federated Learning

Federated data systems have grown significantly and are considered a promising approach for preserving privacy and security while enabling access to sensitive data, including genomic data, that must remain within a country or institution. The mechanism involves advancing novel methods to train machine-learning models while preserving personal data confidentiality. This is achieved because the data does not leave the participating organization that holds it [39].

In other words, in federated learning, one person can start training a deep-learning model, and another person can finish it. Hospitals, for instance, can train their models locally using patient data and then share the half-trained model with a centralized location to finalize the training. Moreover, its privacy benefit is that the second company or central entity would never see the raw patient data, only the resulting model or partial model [39].

Federated machine learning is mentioned explicitly in the context of secure and privacy-preserving approaches in medical imaging [22]. It also relates to the future of digital health [23]. Proponents of this approach note that it allows each entity to govern the use of its data and enhances privacy and security. However, the approach does not resolve the concern that informed consent might not have been sought for secondary uses of the data [14].

## 2.8 INTERFACE AND WORKFLOW DESIGN TO MITIGATE AUTOMATION BIAS

To effectively create an interface and workflow for clinicians, you must provide transparency and actively encourage the clinician (e.g., human-in-the-loop) to utilize their knowledge and provide explicit acknowledgement, particularly when it comes to recommendations requiring high levels of risk.

### 2.8.1 Presentation of Confidence and Uncertainty

To combat complacency and unwarranted deference to AI results (the "technological halo effect"), the system must explicitly communicate the probabilistic nature and limitations of its predictions. Explanations should include explicit representations of confidence intervals and error bars. These certainty estimates should make the confidence range of specific predictions as quantitatively explicit as possible [7]. Interfaces should present dynamic system confidence information to help users appropriately calibrate their trust and reliance on the decision aid [24]. The design should convey that algorithmic outcomes are probabilistic and not infallible and clarify the limitations and potential uncertainties in the statistical results to ensure they do not mislead implementers [7].

### 2.8.2 Presentation of Provenance (Rationale and Evidence)

Transparency regarding how a recommendation was reached fosters trust and enables clinicians to validate or challenge the AI's findings using their professional judgment [3, 6]. Transparency regarding how a recommendation was reached fosters trust and enables clinicians to validate or challenge the AI's findings using their professional judgment. For opaque "black box" algorithms, the technical machinery (input, output variables, and parameters) must be translated into the everyday language of human practices and clinical concepts. This translation should make explicit the rational criteria for the determination [3]. Clinicians require access to information about the data on which the system was trained, how the AI model was built, and the variables underlying the model [14]. Mandating transparency includes requiring clear documentation of the training data and the algorithmic decision-making processes. This is crucial for detecting and mitigating potential biases embedded within the data (e.g., historical bias or sampling bias) [3, 6].

The explanation should explicitly state what components are acting as premises (evidence/data), what components are the conclusions, and the inferential rationale connecting them.

### 2.8.3 Presentation of Alternative Suggestions

Providing alternatives or counterfactuals ensures the human user views the AI recommendation not as a singular truth, but as one option among several, promoting comparative judgment. The interface should include a counterfactual explanatory tool [25]. This tool allows implementers and affected individuals to gain a better contrastive understanding of the logic of the outcome and its alternative possibilities. In some scenarios, AI technology should present a set of options from which a physician must select, rather than a single, authoritative decision [14].

### 2.8.4 Requirement for Explicit Clinician Acknowledgment for High-Risk Recommendations

In high-risk scenarios, the workflow must be structured to prevent automation bias by forcing the clinician to take intentional responsibility for the ultimate decision [7, 14] (Figure 2.3). AI systems must be designed to allow the clinician to override

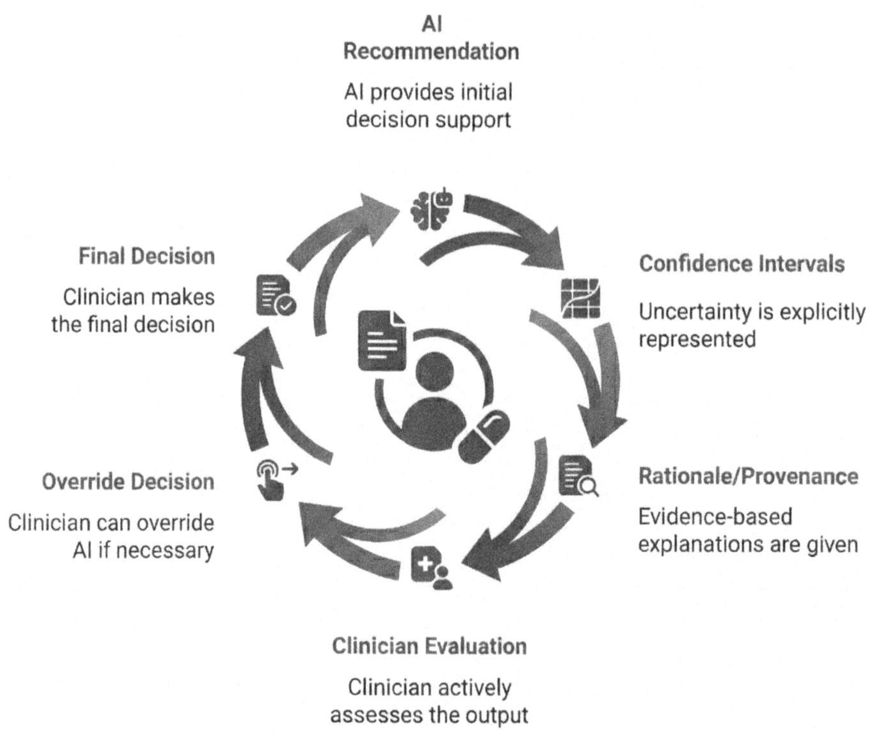


**FIGURE 2.3** Demonstrate interface workflow in high-risk scenarios.

decisions made by the AI. The workflow should incorporate safeguards to allow human judgment to complement AI-generated insights. Operationalizing strong regimes of accountability at the site of user deployment is necessary to steer human decision agents toward using critical judgment. For high-stakes predictive systems (like risk assessments), the interface should include a standard Implementation Disclaimer that explicitly communicates the limitations of the advice and reaffirms the clinician's final role. This disclaimer should state that the results are intended only to assist evidence-based judgment and are not meant to replace reasoned deliberations or constitute the sole evidentiary basis. If a clinician accepts the AI's recommendation, they must be able to rationally evaluate and critically assess the logic and rationale behind the output, demonstrating that their final determination is anchored in solid reasoning and evidence-based judgment [7]. This requirement ensures they can account for the output if they choose to use the data [13].

## 2.9 CONCLUSION

To summarize this chapter, we have established that AI's safe use in healthcare does not exist independently of technical features; it is instead based upon an integrative framework comprised of ethics, laws, and governance. Biomedical ethics provides the ethical underpinning, while both algorithmic fairness and the mitigation of bias provide measures of success as we translate biomedical ethics into quantifiable results. There is also an evolving set of international and regional regulations that create the necessary legal framework and create levels of accountability. When putting this together, it is important to recognize the need for effective governance and the existence of a clear liability framework when operationalizing the guidelines and managing risk throughout the AI lifecycle. The successful and reliable use of AI in healthcare settings will depend on how well we integrate AI into practice while ensuring adequate human oversight, promoting the use of professional judgment, and ensuring that we use AI technology in accordance with our primary duty of care to patients. A comprehensive view of AI throughout its lifecycle will provide the basis for the technical and operational safety approaches that will be explored throughout the remainder of this book.

## REFERENCES

1. M. Bekbolatova, J. Mayer, C. W. Ong, and M. Toma, "Transformative Potential of AI in Healthcare: Definitions, Applications, and Navigating the Ethical Landscape and Public Perspectives," Healthcare, vol. 12, no. 2, p. 125, 2024, doi: 10.3390/healthcare12020125.
2. E. J. Topol, "High-Performance Medicine: the Convergence of Human and Artificial Intelligence," Nat. Med., vol. 25, no. 1, pp. 44–56, 2019, doi: 10.1038/s41591-018-0300-7.
3. T. Pham, "Ethical and Legal Considerations in Healthcare AI: Innovation and Policy for Safe and Fair Use." Accessed: Oct. 20, 2025. [Online]. Available: https://royalsocietypublishing.org/doi/epdf/10.1098/rsos.241873
4. A. Čartolovni, A. Tomičić, and E. Lazić Mosler, "Ethical, Legal, and Social Considerations of AI-Based Medical Decision-Support Tools: A Scoping Review," Int. J. Med. Inf., vol. 161, p. 104738, May 2022, doi: 10.1016/j.ijmedinf.2022.104738.

5. S. Gerke, T. Minssen, and G. Cohen, “Ethical and Legal Challenges of Artificial Intelligence-Driven Healthcare,” in Artificial Intelligence in Healthcare, Elsevier, 2020, pp. 295–336. doi: 10.1016/B978-0-12-818438-7.00012-5.
6. S. Nasir, R. A. Khan, and S. Bai, “Ethical Framework for Harnessing the Power of AI in Healthcare and Beyond,” IEEE Access, vol. 12, pp. 31014–31035, 2024, doi: 10.1109/ACCESS.2024.3369912.
7. D. Leslie, “Understanding Artificial Intelligence Ethics and Safety: A Guide for the Responsible Design and Implementation of AI Systems in the Public Sector,” Zenodo, 2019, doi: 10.5281/ZENODO.3240529.
8. E. Tabassi, “Artificial Intelligence Risk Management Framework (AI RMF 1.0),” National Institute of Standards and Technology (U.S.), Gaithersburg, MD, NIST AI 100-1, Jan. 2023. doi: 10.6028/NIST.AI.100-1.
9. D. S. Watson et al., “Clinical Applications of Machine Learning Algorithms: Beyond the Black Box,” BMJ, vol. 364, p. l886, 2019, doi: 10.1136/bmj.l886.
10. M. Carabantes, “Black-box Artificial Intelligence: An Epistemological and Critical Analysis,” AI Soc., vol. 35, no. 2, pp. 309–317, 2020, doi: 10.1007/s00146-019-00888-w.
11. A. Tabatabaei and A. ZadZiabari, “Generative AI in Medical Imaging,” in Application of Generative AI in Healthcare Systems, Cham: Springer, 2025, pp. 1–33. doi: 10.1007/978-3-031-82963-5_1.
12. S. Reddy, S. Allan, S. Coghlan, and P. Cooper, “A Governance Model for the Application of AI in Health Care,” J. Am. Med. Inform. Assoc., vol. 27, no. 3, pp. 491–497, 2020, doi: 10.1093/jamia/ocz192.
13. N. Naik et al., “Legal and Ethical Consideration in Artificial Intelligence in Healthcare: Who Takes Responsibility?,” Front. Surg., vol. 9, 2022, doi: 10.3389/fsurg.2022.862322.
14. Ethics and Governance of Artificial Intelligence for Health: WHO Guidance, 1st ed. Geneva: World Health Organization, 2021.
15. T. L. Beauchamp and J. F. Childress, Principles of Biomedical Ethics, 8th ed. Oxford University Press, 2019. [Online]. Available: https://global.oup.com/ushe/product/principles-of-biomedical-ethics-9780190640873?cc=fr&lang=en&
16. S. Prakash, J. N. Balaji, A. Joshi, and K. M. Surapaneni, “Ethical Conundrums in the Application of Artificial Intelligence (AI) in Healthcare—A Scoping Review of Reviews,” J. Pers. Med., vol. 12, no. 11, p. 1914, 2022, doi: 10.3390/jpm12111914.
17. M. Alabi, and T. Holmes, “AI Safety and Ethics: Developing Robust Frameworks for Ethical AI Development and Deployment,” Aug. 2024. Accessed: Oct. 23, 2025. [Online]. Available: https://www.researchgate.net/publication/383283895_AI_Safety_and_Ethics_Developing_Robust_Frameworks_for_Ethical_AI_Development_and_Deployment
18. X. Chen, T. Hui, Y. Li, and H. Yang, “Discussion on Artificial Intelligence Safety and Ethical Issues,” ITM Web Conf., vol. 70, p. 04031, 2025, doi: 10.1051/itmconf/20257004031.
19. “High-level Summary of the AI Act | EU Artificial Intelligence Act.” Accessed: Oct. 23, 2025. [Online]. Available: https://artificialintelligenceact.eu/high-level-summary/
20. C. for D. and R. Health, “Artificial Intelligence in Software as a Medical Device,” FDA, July 2025, Accessed: Oct. 23, 2025. [Online]. Available: https://www.fda.gov/medical-devices/software-medical-device-samd/artificial-intelligence-software-medical-device
21. I. Giuffrida, “Liability for AI Decision-Making: Some Legal and Ethical Considerations,” Fordham Law Rev., vol. 88, no. 2, p. 439, 2019.
22. G. A. Kaissis, M. R. Makowski, D. Rückert, and R. F. Braren, “Secure, Privacy-Preserving and Federated Machine Learning in Medical Imaging,” Nat. Mach. Intell., vol. 2, no. 6, pp. 305–311, 2020, doi: 10.1038/s42256-020-0186-1.
23. N. Rieke et al., “The Future of Digital Health with Federated Learning,” Npj Digit. Med., vol. 3, no. 1, p. 119, 2020, doi: 10.1038/s41746-020-00323-1.

24. J. M. McGuirl and N. B. Sarter, "Supporting Trust Calibration and the Effective Use of Decision Aids by Presenting Dynamic System Confidence Information," Hum. Factors, vol. 48, no. 4, pp. 656–665, 2006, doi: 10.1518/001872006779166334.
25. S. Wachter, B. Mittelstadt, and C. Russell, "Counterfactual Explanations without Opening the Black Box: Automated Decisions and the GDPR," Mar. 21, 2018, arXiv: arXiv:1711.00399. [Online]. Available: https://doi.org/10.48550/arXiv.1711.00399.
26. M. Saleh and A. Tabatabaei, "Building Trustworthy Multimodal AI: A Review of Fairness, Transparency, and Ethics in Vision-Language Tasks," Int. J. Web Res., vol. 8, no. 2, pp. 11–24, 2025, doi: 10.22133/ijwr.2025.503147.1264.
27. "Ethical Implications for LLMs | 8 | Applications of Large Language Mod." Accessed: Dec. 06, 2025. [Online]. Available: https://www.taylorfrancis.com/chapters/edit/10.1201/9781003665083-8/ethical-implications-llms-mohammad-saleh-azadeh-tabatabaei?utm_source=researchgate.net&medium=article
28. A. ZadZiabari and A. Tabatabaei, "Ethics and Regulations in Generative AI," in Application of Generative AI in Healthcare Systems, A. Zamanifar and M. Faezipour, Eds., Cham: Springer Nature Switzerland, 2025, pp. 197–211. doi: 10.1007/978-3-031-82963-5_8.
29. "General Data Protection Regulation (GDPR) – Legal Text," General Data Protection Regulation (GDPR). Accessed: Oct. 20, 2025. [Online]. Available: https://gdpr-info.eu/
30. F. Nizamullah, M. Fahad, N. Abbasi, M. U. Qayyum, and S. Zeb, "Ethical and Legal Challenges in AI-Driven Healthcare: Patient Privacy, Data Security, Legal Framework, and Compliance," Int. J. Innov. Res. Sci. Eng. Technol., vol. 13, pp. 15216–15223, 2024.
31. A. Arieno, A. Chan, S. V. Destounis, A. Arieno, A. Chan, and S. V. Destounis, "A Review of the Role of Augmented Intelligence in Breast Imaging: From Automated Breast Density Assessment to Risk Stratification," Am. J. Roentgenol., 2018, doi: 10.2214/AJR.18.20391.
32. J. De Fauw et al., "Clinically Applicable Deep Learning for Diagnosis and Referral in Retinal Disease," Nat. Med., vol. 24, no. 9, pp. 1342–1350, 2018, doi: 10.1038/s41591-018-0107-6.
33. G. Kunapuli et al., "A Decision-Support Tool for Renal Mass Classification," J. Digit. Imaging, vol. 31, no. 6, pp. 929–939, 2018, doi: 10.1007/s10278-018-0100-0.
34. T. A. D'Antonoli, "Ethical Considerations for Artificial Intelligence: An Overview of the Current Radiology Landscape," Diagn. Interv. Radiol., doi: 10.5152/dir.2020.19279.
35. M. E. Fenech and O. Buston, "AI in Cardiac Imaging: A UK-Based Perspective on Addressing the Ethical, Social, and Political Challenges," Front. Cardiovasc. Med., vol. 7, 2020, doi: 10.3389/fcvm.2020.00054.
36. S. Weerts, D. Naous, M. E. Bouchikhi, and C. Clavien, "AI Systems for Occupational Safety and Health: From Ethical Concerns to Limited Legal Solutions," in Electronic Government, in Lecture Notes in Computer Science, M. Janssen, C. Csáki, I. Lindgren, E. Loukis, U. Melin, G. Viale Pereira, M. P. Rodríguez Bolívar, and E. Tambouris, Eds., vol. 13391., Cham: Springer International Publishing, 2022, pp. 499–514. doi: 10.1007/978-3-031-15086-9_32.
37. G. Karimian, E. Petelos, and S. M. A. A. Evers, "The Ethical Issues of the Application of Artificial Intelligence in Healthcare: A Systematic Scoping Review," AI Ethics, vol. 2, no. 4, pp. 539–551, 2022, doi: 10.1007/s43681-021-00131-7.
38. C. R. Swetlitz Ike, "IBM's Watson Supercomputer Recommended 'Unsafe and Incorrect' Cancer Treatments, Internal Documents Show," STAT. Accessed: Oct. 25, 2025. [Online]. Available: https://www.statnews.com/2018/07/25/ibm-watson-recommended-unsafe-incorrect-treatments/
39. E. Fosch-Villaronga, D. Chokoshvili, V. B. Vallevik, M. Ienca, and R. L. Pierce, "Implementing AI in Healthcare: An Ethical and Legal Analysis Based on Case

Studies," in Data Protection and Privacy, vol. 13, Bloomsbury Publishing Plc., 2021, pp. 187–216. Accessed: Oct. 23, 2025. [Online]. Available: https://www.scopus.com/pages/publications/85147942942

40. T. Wangmo, M. Lipps, R. W. Kressig, and M. Ienca, "Ethical Concerns with the Use of Intelligent Assistive Technology: Findings from a Qualitative Study with Professional Stakeholders," BMC Med. Ethics, vol. 20, no. 1, p. 98, 2019, doi: 10.1186/s12910-019-0437-z.
41. "HIPAA Home | HHS.gov." Accessed: Oct. 20, 2025. [Online]. Available: https://www.hhs.gov/hipaa/index.html
42. A. Boch, E. Hohma, and R. Trauth, "Towards an Accountability Framework for AI: Ethical and Legal Considerations," 2022, doi: 10.13140/RG.2.2.10231.50086.
43. T. Ploug and S. Holm, "The Right to Refuse Diagnostics and Treatment Planning by Artificial Intelligence," Med. Health Care Philos., vol. 23, no. 1, pp. 107–114, 2020, doi: 10.1007/s11019-019-09912-8.
44. M. Beil, I. Proft, D. van Heerden, S. Sviri, and P. V. van Heerden, "Ethical Considerations about Artificial Intelligence for Prognostication in Intensive Care," Intensive Care Med. Exp., vol. 7, no. 1, pp. 1–13, 2019, doi: 10.1186/s40635-019-0286-6.
45. E. Racine, W. Boehlen, and M. Sample, "Healthcare Uses of Artificial Intelligence: Challenges and Opportunities for Growth," Healthc. Manage. Forum, 2019, doi: 10.1177/0840470419843831.
46. "Background on: No-Fault Auto Insurance | III." Accessed: Oct. 26, 2025. [Online]. Available: https://www.iii.org/article/background-on-no-fault-auto-insurance
47. K. R. Feinberg, What Is Life Worth? : The Unprecedented Effort to Compensate the Victims of 9/11. New York : Public Affairs, 2005. Accessed: Oct. 26, 2025. [Online]. Available: http://archive.org/details/whatislifeworthu00fein
48. A. Bataineh, A. Mushtaha, I. Abu-AlSondos, S. Aldulaimi, E. Al-Ekir, and M. Abdeldayem, Ethical & Legal Concerns of Artificial Intelligence in the Healthcare Sector. 2024. doi: 10.1109/ICETSIS61505.2024.10459438.
49. N. Ky and K. Iw, "Big Data and Machine Learning Algorithms for Health-Care Delivery," Lancet Oncol., vol. 20, no. 5, 2019, doi: 10.1016/S1470-2045(19)30149-4.

# 3 Data Privacy and Security in AI-Enabled Healthcare

*Neda Yousefi, Azadeh Zamanifar, Amirfarhad Farhadi, and Amir Taherkordi*

## 3.1 INTRODUCTION

The 21st century has seen the merging of the three fields, including healthcare, data science, and artificial intelligence (AI), in a way that has never been possible before, and as a result, patient care will be revolutionized. The array of AI innovations includes, for example, the use of AI in diagnostic tools that can detect malignancies in medical images with accuracy beyond that of a human [1, 2] and the deployment of predictive models that can forecast disease outbreaks [3]. What AI is capable of doing to enhance clinical outcomes [4, 5] is only the tip of the iceberg. AI can also be used to optimize hospital operations [6] and to accelerate biomedical research [7]. This leap in technology is made possible by the massive and still rapidly growing amount of digital health data that goes beyond electronic health records (EHRs) [8] and includes genomic sequences [9] as well as real-time data streams from wearable devices and Internet of Things (IoT) sensors [10–12]. Without this data, which is the core of contemporary AI algorithms, AI would not be able to perform tasks such as learning, inferring, and predicting, which it does to assist human abilities.

### 3.1.1 The Dawn of AI in Healthcare: A Double-Edged Sword

The use of AI in the clinical workflow is a fundamental change in how things work. Machine learning (ML), a subset of AI, is able to detect complicated patterns in large datasets that humans are often unable to observe. Various scholars have pointed out that deep learning (DL) has achieved outstanding results in domains like radiology, pathology, and ophthalmology, where the model trained on a large number of images can be used for making diagnoses quickly and accurately by clinicians [13, 14]. Beyond diagnostics, AI is also being used to personalize treatment plans by analyzing a diverse set of patient-specific data, such as genomics, proteomics, metabolomics, medical history, lifestyle, and environmental factors, to design customized therapeutic strategies and to dynamically adjust treatment dosing [15–18]. In addition, AI is improving patient selection for clinical trials by thoroughly investigating electronic medical records (EMRs) and omics data to find people who would benefit the most from the use of investigational drugs [19, 20]. This integration advances personalized medicine to the next level; thus, the treatment becomes more effective, drug development gets faster [21, 22], and hospital logistics are getting optimized through the prediction of patient admission rates and resource management [23, 24].

DOI: 10.1201/9781003743422-3

However, this data-intensive revolution is a double-edged sword. The very data that empowers these life-saving innovations is also exceptionally sensitive. Sensitive Health Information (SHI), also known as Protected Health Information (PHI) under U.S. law, contains the most intimate details of an individual's life [25]. Its exposure can lead to devastating consequences, including financial fraud, identity theft, employment or insurance discrimination, and profound personal stigma [26]. Consequently, the healthcare sector has emerged as a primary target for cyberattacks, with large hospital systems and insurers experiencing repeated, high-impact intrusions in recent years. Stolen electronic health records (EHRs) command a substantially higher value on underground markets than single financial identifiers because longitudinal medical files contain rich, often irreversible information (demographic data, diagnoses, medications, and biometric identifiers) that can be exploited for identity theft, insurance and benefits fraud, extortion, and other forms of organized cybercrime. Furthermore, the large-scale aggregation of multimodal patient data required to develop and train robust AI models concentrates sensitive information into centralized repositories; this markedly increases the potential impact of a single security breach, with the compromise of one AI training corpus exposing data from thousands to millions of individuals in a single event [27–29].

### 3.1.2 The Imperative of Data Privacy and Security

In a situation where AI is combined with healthcare at a high level, the question of data privacy and security is not only a matter of technology or regulation but goes deep to become the very foundation upon which the whole system of AI is built, ethically, safely, and in line with sustainable development. One of the most important things to do in healthcare is to earn and keep patients' trust, and this trust is mainly based on the fact that proper guarantees are given that personal health information will be kept confidential; however, data breaches or even perceived vulnerabilities can lead to a swift trust collapse, which in turn will limit the sharing of data, a process that is vital both for the personalization of care and for building AI models that can be widely applied [30, 31].

The problem is reflected in different ways. It consists of implementing strong external cybersecurity measures to defend against sophisticated attackers and, at the same time, becoming highly ethical when dealing with data from inside the organization. Privacy describes the right of people to have control over the collection, use, and sharing of their personal information, whereas security refers to a set of protective measures of a technical, administrative, or physical nature, which prevent unauthorized access, disclosure, alteration, or destruction. In AI scenarios, these requirements are interconnected: on the one hand, models can unintentionally store data from their training, and, therefore, privacy attacks like membership inference or reconstruction can take place; on the other hand, biased algorithms may cause certain groups to become more affected by privacy issues than others, thus facing discrimination [30–32].

Furthermore, AI also plays a role in making the issue of opacity more difficult, as it is often the case that "black box" architectures are less interpretable and harder to audit; thus, transparency and accountability, being at the core of the problem, are less referred to. Being in line with very strict frameworks like the U.S. Health Insurance Portability and Accountability Act (HIPAA) and the EU General Data Protection Regulation (GDPR) calls for new governance paradigms, privacy-enhancing technologies (PETs) (e.g., federated learning and differential privacy), and interdisciplinary ethical protocols balancing technological progress and patient rights [33].

### 3.1.3 Chapter Objectives and Structure

This chapter seeks to analyze and debate the issues of data privacy and security when implementing AI-powered healthcare systems deeply and extensively. The goal here is to go beyond just a superficial understanding of the problem and address its technical, regulatory, and ethical dimensions. This would allow for a candid evaluation of both the risks and the most advanced solutions available. This chapter, by exploring these interconnected themes, attempts to provide the knowledge necessary to foster innovation responsibly, building a future where AI can achieve its full potential in healthcare without compromising the fundamental rights to privacy and security.

## 3.2 THE HEALTHCARE DATA ECOSYSTEM: FUEL FOR AI, TARGET FOR ADVERSARIES

The performance of any AI system depends largely on the quality, quantity, and diversity of the data it is trained with. In the case of healthcare, the data ecosystem is naturally complicated and diverse. It is also a highly sensitive ecosystem composed of several data sources. These sources range from structured clinical records to high-dimensional imaging, from genomic sequencing to real-time patient-generated streams. Building a good security and privacy system requires deep knowledge of these components, their complete life cycle, and the variety of threats that target them at each stage [34–38].

### 3.2.1 The Spectrum of Sensitive Health Information (SHI)

AI models in healthcare are possible through a diverse taxonomy of data modalities. The data types represent different categories that vary in their structural properties, contextual nuances, and risk profiles for privacy. These categories, derived from recognized taxonomies of the health information system, are further explained in the text below and are shown in Figure 3.1.

- **Electronic Health Records (EHRs) and Electronic Medical Records (EMRs):** Being the basis for patients' longitudinal documentation, EHRs/EMRs collect information on demographics, the International Classification of Diseases (ICD, 10/11) diagnoses, medication histories, treatment protocols, immunization records, allergies, laboratory results, and unstructured clinical narratives. Since their hybrid structured, unstructured format makes them very useful for training predictive models that forecast disease trajectories, treatment responses, and adverse outcomes; however, the problem of interoperability gaps aggravates that of breaches [34, 39].

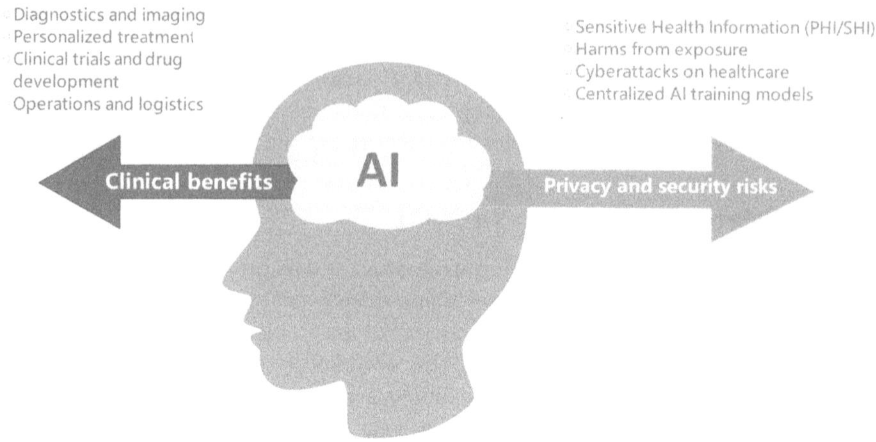


**FIGURE 3.1** AI is a double-edged sword.

- **Medical Imaging Data:** These are basically the images of magnetic resonance imaging (MRI), computed tomography (CT), radiography, ultrasound, and pathology slides standardized in Digital Imaging and Communications in Medicine (DICOM) format. The images are represented by high-dimensional pixel/voxel arrays, which are used for feeding convolutional neural networks (CNNs) for performing tasks such as lesion detection, organ segmentation, and radiomic phenotyping. Even though the images go through the process of de-identification, there is still some possibility of risk from "burnt-in" metadata (e.g., patient names in overlays), unique anatomical signatures, or linkage with ancillary clinical data [40].
- **Genomic and Omics Data:** One instrument here depicts sequencing of deoxyribonucleic acid (DNA), transcriptomics, proteomics, and metabolomics. It is a tool that plays a major role in precision medicine by pointing out the genetic predispositions, pharmacogenomics, and hereditary risks. Its feature of being almost uniquely identifiable, which further extends to biological kinships via polygenic inheritance, necessitates the use of very strict safeguards, as even in such cases where the datasets are aggregated, the kinship inference attacks can still be carried out [41].
- **Patient-Generated Health Data (PGHD):** PGHD is highly detailed, real-time behavioral and physiological data, which is rapidly becoming the main source of information for the monitoring of chronic diseases and preventive care. It is obtained from devices consumable by the general public, such as wearables, mobile applications, and Internet of Medical Things (IoMT) devices (e.g., continuous glucose monitors, ambulatory ECGs) [42]. However, the existence of such data on platforms intended for general consumers introduces significant risks that are brought about by insecure APIs, unpatched firmware, and secondary data marketplaces [43, 44].
- **Clinical Trial and Research Data:** These are highly organized repositories originating from prospective trials that capture participant phenotypes,

intervention responses, and endpoints. They serve as a source of fuel for AI-driven meta-analyses and drug repurposing. Protecting them is very important in order to preserve the scientific nature of the research and the confidentiality of the participants amid the changes brought about by the open data mandates.

- **Administrative, Claims, and Registry Data:** These are additional streams that comprise billing codes (e.g., CPT/HCPCS), insurance claims, and disease registries. They provide the epidemiological scale, but at the same time, they are probably the source of quasi-identifiers (e.g., ZIP codes and time stamps) that are ready for linkage attacks.

The organization of these "multimodal" groups allows AI models to build a more holistic and accurate picture of a patient's health. However, this also tremendously increases the attack surface: the cross-modal fusion increases the chances of reidentification (e.g., through Bayesian linkage of imaging quasi-identifiers with EHR demographics), while the expansion of the life cycle, from edge devices to cloud analytics, increases the number of possible points of attack.

### 3.2.2 The Data Life Cycle in AI-Enabled Healthcare

Appropriate health data protection requires considering its entire life cycle, from the creation of the data to final disposal. Each of the stages shown in Figure 3.2 presents different kinds of vulnerabilities that could be targeted in distinct ways [37, 45].

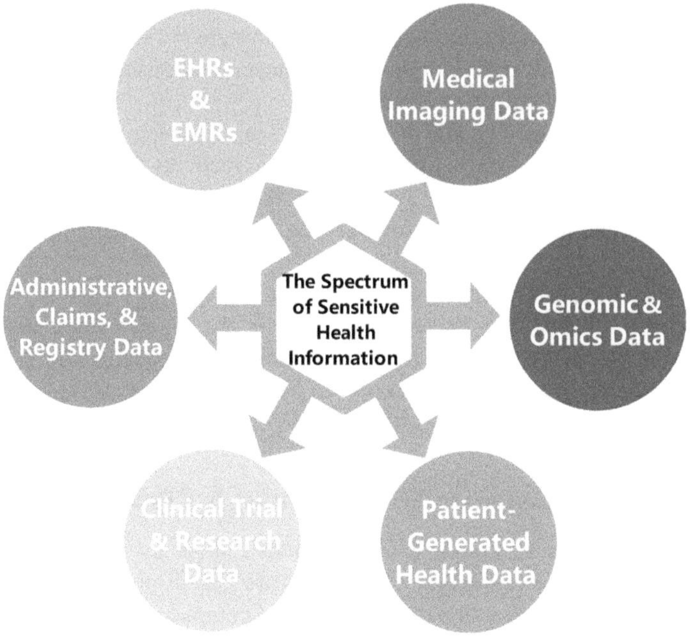


**FIGURE 3.2** The spectrum of sensitive health information.

- **Data Generation/Collection:** Data freshly generated in clinical points of care, laboratories, or even via user-friendly devices is prone to result in insecure input interfaces, unencrypted IoT transmissions, and insufficient consent mechanisms for secondary AI training; thus, unauthorized data capture and provenance breaches get facilitated [37, 45].
- **Data Transmission:** Besides local transmissions, data exchanges between institutions, as well as cloud migrations, may facilitate man-in-the-middle attacks and eavesdropping if end-to-end encryption protocols such as Transport Layer Security (TLS) are not implemented. The risks are very high, especially in federated healthcare networks [37, 46].
- **Data Storage and Processing:** When data is stored in databases, data warehouses, or even cloud repository environments for aggregation, cleansing, and preprocessing for AI model creation and training. Risks include insecure storage configurations, insufficient access controls, and data leakage during processing. The training process itself can be a vulnerability, as models can inadvertently memorize and expose training data, thus hang an overfitted model, which can be a source of membership inference and reconstruction attacks [37, 45].
- **Data Sharing and Utilization:** The sharing of cleaned datasets and/or the deployment of models to collaborators, vendors, or research consortia causes regulatory compliance gaps and insufficient data processing agreements, which in turn lead to a strong secondary misuse as well as cascade failures in supply chains.
- **Data Archiving:** Data that is no longer in active use must be archived securely for legal or research retention purposes. Archived data is often a "soft target" that are often overlooked and might be vulnerable to insider threats or a late discovery of the preexisting compromises, as it may not be monitored as rigorously as active data.
- **Data Destruction:** The end of the life cycle necessitates cryptographically verifiable erasure so as not to allow forensic recovery. It must be securely and permanently destroyed; however, improper disposal can lead to data recovery and breaches long after the data's intended use has ended.

A "Privacy by Design" approach, which is at the core of Article 25 of the EU GDPR, requires that privacy and security controls are not only integrated but also anticipated in all life cycle stages rather than being only implemented as a backup. This way, technology is kept in harmony with patient rights and rules [47]. Figure 3.3 shows data life cycle in AI-enabled healthcare.

### 3.2.3 The Threat Landscape: Why Healthcare Is a Prime Target

The healthcare industry remains a very attractive target for cyber attackers as it exhibits a convergence of various factors that are based on the unique nature of its data assets, operational criticality, and system complexity. Healthcare data that includes personally identifiable information (PII), sensitive clinical histories, and financial identifiers are valued even more than traditional financial data; thus, their

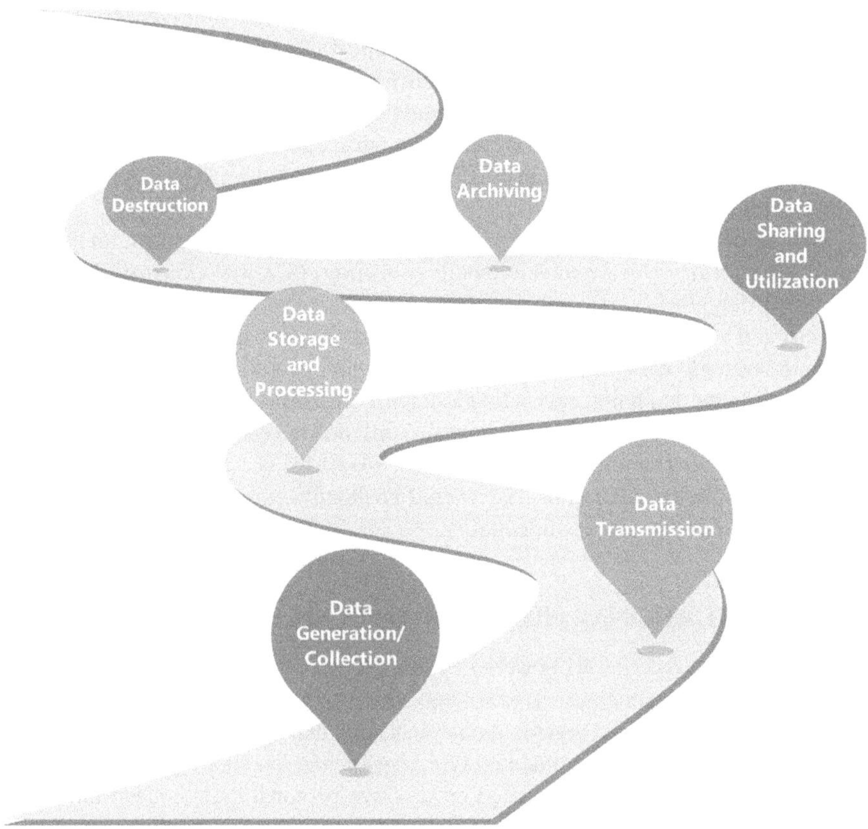


**FIGURE 3.3** Data life cycle in AI-enabled healthcare.

significant illicit demand is what is primarily responsible for the underground markets where healthcare data may cost several times more than the price of a credit card [37, 48]. At the same time, the need for almost 24/7 system availability due to the dependence of healthcare infrastructures on delivering life-sustaining functions increases the vulnerability of the sector to ransomware attacks, which is a dominant modus operandi by which the attackers deliberately encrypt critical data resources such as EHRs and/or imaging archives in order to force the issuing of ransom payments, in this way causing severe damage both to patient safety and organizational resilience [46].

Besides that, the healthcare operational milieus depict the scenarios of the merger of old information technologies with new biomedical devices as well as interconnected IoMT devices, where the majority of the devices were designed before the establishment of rigorous cybersecurity standards and, therefore, have contributed to a persistently and extensively vulnerable attack surface that cannot be adequately secured by traditional patch management and access control methods [46]. Insider threats, which encompass the situation of deciding to take away data intentionally and a scenario of unintentional security breach like social engineering exploit or misconfiguration, to name a few, have been identified as the dominant factor in the occurrence of breach events and thus lift the importance of the development of comprehensive security frameworks that are fully focused on human factors [49]. Also, medical institutions are on the radar of state-sponsored advanced persistent threat (APT) actors, who are mostly driven by economic and strategic intelligence objectives, especially in cases where intellectual property and clinical research can be the assets of interest [50, 51].

The use of adversary techniques is very elaborate and sophisticated, and, among other things, it involves fraudulent emails (phishing) [52], malicious software (malware) [53], denial-of-service attacks, and exploitation of zero-day vulnerabilities [54]. Therefore, it is imperative to have a multilayered security approach with a defense-in-depth strategy, which includes the proactive plot of anticipating threats, having strong perimeter, endpoint, and network defense measures in place, and keeping the healthcare data life cycle under constant surveillance in order to meet this challenge successfully [55]. The implementation of such measures is crucial for the protection of data that is the foundation of AI-powered healthcare ecosystems in terms of their integrity, availability, and confidentiality.

## 3.3 FOUNDATIONAL PILLARS OF DATA SECURITY

To eliminate the risks to AI-powered healthcare systems, a multilayered, defense-in-depth security architecture is absolutely necessary. Such an architecture would include both technical and organizational measures that are implemented in overlapping layers to protect the confidentiality, integrity, and availability of very personal health information, usually regulated or sensitive personal data, under frameworks like HIPAA and GDPR. The methods outlined in this chapter should be considered non-negotiable elements of the core design for any healthcare organization that is involved in the development, deployment, or consumption of AI systems, rather than as optional features.

### 3.3.1 Encryption as a Cornerstone Control: The First Line of Defense

Encryption is the main cryptographic technique used to ensure the confidentiality of data. Technically, it changes the data in readable form into a coded form (ciphertext) with the help of a secret or private key, and, in well-designed cases, it provides a guarantee that an adversary without access to the correct key will not be able to get the original data in a reasonable way. Nowadays, encryption should be done consistently for data in all three states, that is, data at rest, data in transit, and data in use, if it wants to give real protection in complex, distributed health information infrastructures [49].

#### 3.3.1.1 Data-at-Rest Encryption

Data at rest is the information saved on permanent storage devices, such as the local disks, network-attached storage devices, backup tapes, and cloud object storage. In the health sector, there are EHRs, imaging archives, audit logs, and AI training corpora that fall under this category [56]. An effective data-at-rest encryption plan usually consists of the following components:

- **Full-Disk Encryption (FDE):** FDE is a method that works at the block-device level and encrypts the entire storage medium in a way that all data written to the device are automatically encrypted and all reads are transparently decrypted for authorized processes. This method is a powerful tool for physical compromise of endpoints, and it is usually carried out by means of standard algorithms such as AES-256 in XTS mode.
- **Database-level Encryption:** At the database level, elements such as tables, columns, or individual attributes (e.g., patient identifiers, diagnoses, or billing details) can be encrypted. The protection provided by this granularity corresponds to the data sensitivity classes and is used for the separation of duties, for example, application logic operating on non-sensitive attributes, whereas access to cryptographically protected fields is tightly restricted [57].
- **File-Level or Application-Level Encryption:** There are some cases, for instance, document repositories, imaging studies, and exported model artifacts, where the files are encrypted separately. Application-level approaches can associate cryptographic protection with certain workflows or identities, thereby facilitating more accurate access control policies.

Regardless of these methods, the use of well-tested, standard algorithms and key sizes (e.g., AES with 256-bit keys) is of paramount importance. Also, an equally important factor, quite often more than in theory, is the management of cryptographic keys: keys have to be created with high entropy, changed according to a policy, kept in a secure key management system (KMS) or hardware security modules (HSMs), and protected by stringent access control and auditing. Incorrect key management can completely cancel out the advantages of even the strongest cipher.

#### 3.3.1.2 Data-in-Transit Encryption

Information in transit refers to data that are actively moving through communication channels: within hospital networks, between facilities, between on-premises data centers and cloud platforms, or between edge devices and backend services. Since interception and tampering are possible on both internal and external networks, the protection of data in transit is the most basic condition for any AI-enabled health system. The current best practice is the deliberate utilization of modern transport-layer security protocols: TLS, with focus on TLS 1.2+ and TLS 1.3 [58–60]. TLS ensures channel confidentiality, integrity, and server (and, if requested, client) authentication. Especially, TLS 1.3 eliminates old, insecure ciphers and reduces protocol complexity, thereby lessening the attack surface.

An elaborate plan for data-in-transit encryption in the healthcare sector involves the following:

- Making "encryption everywhere" mandatory so that no sensitive medical information is allowed to be sent in clear text over any part of the network, internal VLANs, and "trusted" data center links included.

- Besides that, API traffic must be secure, for instance, microservices communication, clinical applications interfacing with AI backend services, and on-premises systems integrating with cloud-hosted models.
- Moreover, third-party systems and vendors should authenticate and encrypt communications, especially when exchanging deidentified datasets, model artifacts, or decision support outputs.
- Furthermore, strong certificate management (issuing, rotation, and revocation) should be in place to avoid downgrade and impersonation attacks.

After data in transit encryption is set up correctly, the chances of passive eavesdropping and active "man-in-the-middle" attacks are significantly lowered. Such attacks are otherwise quite feasible in Wi-Fi network, remote access, and multi-institutional connectivity environments.

#### 3.3.1.3 Data-in-Use Encryption: The Homomorphic Frontier

Conventional computing models require that data be decrypted before algorithms can process them, whether the operation is a transactional workload or AI training and inference. The sensitive data exposure happens in memory or on temporary storage during this decryption step; thus, if the host, hypervisor, or runtime environment is compromised at that moment, the attacker may get access to plaintext. Since AI workflows often mean that large, sensitive datasets are processed in a centralized manner, sometimes by a third-party service provider, this "data-in-use" exposure has drawn so much attention recently. One possible conceptually elegant solution is Homomorphic Encryption (HE) [61–63]. A (fully) HE scheme is one in which computations of certain classes can be executed over encrypted data; when decrypted, the output is identical to that obtained by performing the computation on the original unencrypted data. Theoretically, it permits such situations as:

- By means of an HE scheme, a hospital encrypts a batch of patient records and transmits the encrypted data to an external AI service.
- The service trains a model or executes inference only on the encrypted data; thus, it doesn't obtain the raw data at any time.
- The service sends back encrypted model parameters or predictions, which only the data owner can decrypt.

From a security and privacy standpoint, the attraction is obvious: encryption is maintained even when a curious or partially compromised processing environment is present; thus, the trust assumptions on external compute infrastructures are significantly lowered. HE is widely regarded as a frontier technology for privacy-preserving AI. In combination with other PETs (secure multiparty computation, trusted execution environments, and federated learning), it offers a credible technical pathway toward collaborative analytics and model training on distributed, sensitive data without exposing raw records to central aggregators or external vendors [64].

#### 3.3.1.4 Taxonomy of Encryption Standards in Healthcare

Selecting the right encryption primitives is an essential healthcare security architectural decision, as various algorithms, depending on their different performance, security, and deployment characteristics, can be more or less suitable for certain use cases.

**Symmetric-key encryption:** symmetric algorithms take advantage of only one secret key that is used for both encryption and decryption. They provide very high throughput and, hence, are the main tools for large data volume protection [65].

- **Advanced Encryption Standard (AES):** AES is the worldwide standard for symmetric encryption in healthcare and other essential areas. It allows key lengths of 128, 192, and 256 bits, where generally AES-256 is advised for the long-term security of SHI due to its strong security margin and effective hardware and software implementations. In this way, FDE, database field encryption, and TLS bulk data encryption can be performed efficiently and effectively [66, 67].
- **Data Encryption Standard (DES) and Triple DES (3DES):** DES, with its 56-bit key, is considered as one that has been cryptographically broken by modern standards, and accordingly, it is not advisable to use it in any healthcare context. The only reason 3DES is still around is that it was made as a temporary solution, but now it is being gradually removed due to its performance limitations and cryptanalytic concerns. It is recommended that existing installations be relocated to AES [68].

**Asymmetric (public-key) encryption:** Asymmetric cryptography utilizes different keys for encryption and decryption: a public key that can be made available to anyone and a private key that should be kept secret. Even now, public-key algorithms remain the primary method for securely establishing keys, digital signatures, and certificate infrastructures, albeit they are computationally less efficient than symmetric ones [69].

- **Rivest–Shamir–Adleman (RSA):** RSA is one of the public-key algorithms that is the most commonly used. It is the base of numerous public key structures, and it is the main protocol that is used for TLS handshakes, digital certificates, and code signing. In healthcare, after RSA establishes the secure channels between clients, servers, and cloud services, AES and other symmetric algorithms are used to encrypt the bulk data [70].
- **Elliptic Curve Cryptography (ECC):** ECC is very important, especially in the case of limited medical and IoT devices, as it provides the same level of security as RSA but with much smaller key sizes, thus cutting down both the bandwidth and computation required. Healthcare architectures that use wearable or implantable devices are most likely to depend on ECC-based key exchange and signatures [71, 72].

**Advanced and application-specific encryption:** Besides the traditional symmetric and asymmetric schemes, there are more specialized primitives that can provide more granular control and more flexible data sharing models, which are particularly relevant to complex healthcare workflows and multi-institutional AI collaborations.

- **Proxy Re-encryption (PRE):** PRE gives the ability to a semi-trusted proxy to change a ciphertext under one key into a ciphertext that can be decrypted under another key, without the proxy ever having access to the plaintext or either of the private keys. A hospital, for instance, may use PRE to let a specialist or an outside researcher have access to some selected encrypted records without revealing to them the hospital's own long-term decryption keys. Besides that, correctly constructed PRE protocols provide a means for implementing revocable, auditable, and minimally trusted data-sharing workflows [73].

- **Ciphertext-Policy Attribute-Based Encryption (CP-ABE):** CP-ABE takes public-key encryption a step further by associating the capabilities of decryption with attributes rather than identities. The users have private keys that are associated with certain attributes. The data owners encrypt the records in accordance with an access policy that is defined by the attributes. If the user's attributes fulfill the policy in the ciphertext, then decryption will be successful [74]. CP-ABE facilitates data-centric access control for healthcare: the enforcement logic is embedded within the encrypted object itself, which is particularly advantageous in multi-tenant cloud environments, cross-organizational registries, and collaborative research infrastructures where traditional perimeter-based controls are inadequate. It allows very fine-grained, context-aware authorization to be implemented while the data are still encrypted at rest and in transit [75].

### 3.3.2 Secure Data Architectures and Storage

The design of the underlying information technology (IT) infrastructure is the main factor that determines the systemic security posture of AI-powered healthcare environments. These environments include heterogeneous deployments that span on-premises, cloud, and hybrid paradigms and need to balance control, scalability, and compliance requirements [76–78]. Modern healthcare systems are gradually merging these models to use their resources more efficiently and at the same time lessen the risks that come with distributed data processing.

#### 3.3.2.1 Deployment Paradigms: On-Premises, Cloud, and Hybrid Architectures

- **On-Premises Deployments:** This model implies that data and computational resources remain physically within the organization's premises; thus, the organization gains maximum control over the hardware, network topology, and access policies. However, this total control comes with the burden of comprehensive responsibility for physical security, software patching, and resilience engineering, which is often beyond the capacity of healthcare IT teams [32].
- **Cloud Deployments:** Utilization of infrastructure as a service (IaaS), platform as a service (PaaS), or software as a service (SaaS) by providers like Amazon Web Services (AWS), Microsoft Azure, or Google Cloud Platform (GCP), can lead to cloud models being more efficient and cost-effective in the areas of automated patching, redundancy, and threat intelligence. In the shared responsibility model, a provider is responsible for the "security of the cloud" while the customer is responsible for the "security in the cloud" (configuration, encryption keys, and identity management). What is very important for the healthcare sector is the implementation of HIPAA

Business Associate Agreements (BAAs) and compliance with FedRAMP Moderate/High or equivalent certifications [77, 79–82].

- **Hybrid:** In reality, most practices operate on a hybrid model that separates workloads based on their sensitivity level; thus, highly regulated data (e.g., PHI) is kept on-premises, whereas the cloud is used for elasticity of analytics, archival, or de-identified datasets. This division allows for the dynamic scheduling of tasks, the isolation of faults, and the migration of different phases, but it requires the establishment of strong trust relationships between different domains [83, 84].

#### 3.3.2.2 Secure Infrastructure and Network Segmentation

Resilient architectures, irrespective of their deployment topology, comply with the established engineering principles [85]:

- **Network Segmentation:** Breaking down into isolated security zones (e.g., through VLANs, micro-segmentation, or software-defined networking [SDN]) limits the extent of a hacker's lateral movement inside a network. The networks of critical care devices (e.g., infusion pumps and ventilators) should either be physically separated by being in different rooms or logically separated by being on different VLANs, thereby ensuring that they do not have direct communication with the administrative/guest segments. This arrangement is in line with NIST SP 800-207 Zero Trust Architecture [86–88].
- **Firewalls and Intrusion Detection/Prevention Systems (IDS/IPS):** With the use of stateful inspection combined with deep packet inspection (DPI) and application layer filtering, next-generation firewalls (NGFWs) are able to locate the source of an intrusion. Anomaly in behavior detection can be supported by host-based IDS/IPS. Security information and event management (SIEM), when coupled with these devices, can be used as a live-time threat correlation tool.
- **Secure Configuration:** It is very important that the least functionality principle is strictly followed, and for this purpose, the unnecessary services need to be turned off, the authentication needs to be strong, and the vulnerabilities need to be fixed in a timely manner [89].

### 3.3.3 Identity and Access Management (IAM)

The IAM systems control the authentication, authorization, and accountability processes. Hence, they are the only systems that can guarantee to allow authorized users to have access to specific resources and only under certain conditions. They represent one of the main means of protection against the most common types of threats to credentials and the insider risks [90].

**The Principle of Least Privilege (PoLP):** PoLP is a rule that states that entities, which may be human users, service accounts, or containers, should be given only the minimum of permissions necessary for them to be able to perform their legitimate functions. In the case of healthcare, a radiologist gets access to the imaging repositories and case-relevant EHRs but cannot get access to the billing ledgers or genomic vaults. The risk of privilege creep is lessened by automated privilege auditing as well as by the just-in-time (JIT) method of privilege elevation [91].

**Advanced Access Control Models:**

- **Role-Based Access Control (RBAC):** Roles are assigned the permissions; thus, the users who fall under a certain role become entitled to the corresponding access rights [92, 93].
- **Attribute-Based Access Control (ABAC):** Dynamic policies make the decision by considering the attributes of the user, attributes of the resource, and factors of the environment through predicates [94].

**Multi-Factor Authentication (MFA):** MFA represents a key instrument in the user's security arsenal by demanding two or even more confirmation factors from the user before the resource access is granted. Usually, a combination of the following is employed: Something you know (a password or PIN); Something you have (a smartphone with an authenticator app, a hardware token); Something you are (a fingerprint, facial scan, or other biometrics). MFA-enabled cybercriminals are put in a situation where it is extremely challenging to break into a system just by a stolen password, which is still one of the most common ways of attacking [95].

Through the use of comprehensive encryption, secure architecture, and rigorous IAM, healthcare entities will be able to build a resilient defense against various cyber threats, thereby ensuring a safe environment for the AI technologies to evolve and be implemented.

## 3.4 AI AS A GUARDIAN: LEVERAGING ARTIFICIAL INTELLIGENCE FOR CYBERSECURITY

Despite the fact that AI systems need a lot of sensitive health data, which in turn creates new vulnerabilities, AI still provides very strong tools to a health system to improve its security. The conventional defenses, which are mainly based on signature matching and static heuristics, have a limited capability against zero-day exploits and polymorphic adversaries. AI and ML can introduce a more dynamic, adaptive, and predictive layer of security, transforming cybersecurity from a reactive to a proactive discipline [77, 96, 97].

### 3.4.1 Intelligent Threat Detection and Response

Modern healthcare networks generate immense volumes of log data from firewalls, servers, applications, and medical devices. Manually analyzing this data for signs of an attack is an impossible task. AI excels at this, using ML algorithms to analyze vast datasets in real-time and identify subtle patterns that may indicate a security incident, far beyond what can be achieved by monitoring threshold-based alerts.

- **Anomaly Detection:** AI-powered security systems first establish a baseline of "normal" network and user behavior. They then continuously monitor the system for deviations from this baseline. Autoencoders and isolation forests model empirical baselines of user entity behavior analytics (UEBA), flagging deviations such as anomalous off-hours bulk record access from anomalous geolocations indicative of insider threats or credential compromise. This behavioral analysis can detect insider threats and compromised accounts far more effectively than rule-based systems [98, 99].

- **Malware and Ransomware Identification:** ML models, the same as convolutional and recurrent neural networks, analyze static and dynamic data, identifying new strains through structural homology; ransomware is identified by encryption cascades and shadow copy deletion, thus the mean time to containment (MTTC) is reduced from days to hours [100].
- **Phishing and Social Engineering Mitigation:** BERT-based NLP classifiers interpret semantic intent, lexical urgency, and sender graphs to detect sophisticated social engineering tactics, such as a sense of urgency, unusual requests, or subtle impersonations of trusted individuals [101].
- **Security Orchestration, Automation, and Response (SOAR):** Security platforms powered by AI can automatically react to detected threats. For instance, if unusual activity on a user account is detected, a SOAR system can automatically revoke the account, isolate the device by disconnecting it from all other devices, and create a high-priority ticket for a human security analyst to check out the situation. This is a major step forward in reducing the "dwell time," the most important time interval between the moment of breach and the moment of detection and solution, thus limiting the possible extent of the attack.

### 3.4.2 Automating Compliance and Policy Enforcement

Continually maintaining compliance with complicated regulations such as HIPAA and GDPR is a heavy and costly process in terms of resources. Many parts of compliance management, with the help of AI, can be automated; human mistakes can lessen, and on top of that, AI can provide a record of the steps taken, showing good management practice.

- **Continuous Compliance Monitoring:** AI tools may be set up to perform the compliance checks unceasingly; they will examine not only systems but also the databases and any cloud environments for any configuration that does not comply with the set rules. For instance, an AI system could automatically detect whether a cloud storage bucket containing SHI has been accidentally made publicly accessible or whether encryption has been disabled on a critical database. After that, the system can either trigger a warning or even take automatic action to solve the problem [102].
- **Automated Data Discovery and Classification:** In a large healthcare organization network full of numerous branches, it is a hard task to be sure that one knows where all of the sensitive data is stored. AI-driven data discovery tools perform this job via NLP and pattern matching to scan structured and unstructured data sources for the purpose of identifying and classifying SHI. Afterward, the right security policies can be deployed automatically,

and this will ensure that the sensitive data will be protected no matter in which place it is stored [103].

- **Access Control Auditing:** AI can go through access logs to verify compliance with the Least Privilege Principle. It may identify some users who have more permission than they actually use and highlight those accounts that are inactive and should thus be removed and also discover various access activities that by themselves are not necessarily malicious but over time may lead to "privilege creep" or violations of the policy [104].

### 3.4.3 Predictive Threat Intelligence

Part of a security strategy that is really proactive is to foresee threats even before they happen. An AI can do this by processing numerous data points from all over the world about threat intelligence, for example, from security forums, reports, and even the dark web. In this way, they can identify the new phishing campaigns, new malware, and vulnerabilities that are actively being exploited in the wild [105].

- **Vulnerability Prioritization:** Organizations are confronted with the discovery of new software vulnerabilities very often. It is impossible to patch everything immediately. AI models can thus play a role in the patching process by figuring out which patches need to be implemented first. They do so by checking the exploitability of a vulnerability, the criticality of the asset in the hospital network, and whether the threat intelligence is indicating that the vulnerability is being targeted. With such information, security teams can decide and concentrate their energies on the areas where they can have the greatest impact with the fewest resources at hand [106].
- **Predicting Attacker Behavior:** Utilizing the data of previous attacks to create the model, AI systems can infer the most likely next steps of an attacker who is already inside the network. Using this "attack path modeling," the security team can decide which defenses to strengthen around the most probable targets, thus effectively staying one step ahead of the adversary.

### 3.4.4 The Caveats: Challenges and Limitations of AI in Cybersecurity

Despite the capability of AI to radically change cybersecurity, putting it into use raises limitations that are inherent and produces new attack vectors that require the employment of stringent mitigation measures. For instance, adversarial ML is a great example of such a dual system: as AI defense becomes stronger, issues can arise if a sophisticated actor is able to trick the model to undermine it. Evasion attacks, which were first introduced by Szegedy et al.[107], subtly modify malicious inputs in industries such as malware binaries or network payloads in such a way that classifiers label them as harmless while in reality they are harmful. Poisoning attacks cause training data to be polluted with provocatively abnormal samples, thereby inserting dormant backdoors that can later be activated by the attacker, whereas model extraction (or stealing) allows one to get a model by smartly querying and thus creating the needed evasion [108, 109]. Moreover, difficulties in operations limit the effectiveness of the methods to that extent. Even though anomaly detection mechanisms are very sensitive, they tend to produce too many false alarms, thus causing analysts to become fatigued with the alerts and therefore losing their ability to distinguish real threats, a phenomenon that has been empirically observed in different enterprises [110, 111]. In addition to this, the problem of deep neural networks being referred to as "black boxes" that limit the possibilities of forensic interpretation still remains: these systems can identify intrusions but cannot offer rationales that are understandable to humans, which leads to a decrease in trust and makes validation difficult in regulated sectors such as healthcare [112, 113]. Thus, the best use of AI goes together with a human-in-the-loop model, wherein machine intelligence supports rather than replaces judgment by experts. What AI is good at is telemetry distillation, threat prioritization, and routine automation; hence, analysts are free to focus on strategic orchestration, hypothesis-driven investigations, and countering the adaptive cunning of human adversaries.

## 3.5 THE ANONYMIZATION TIGHTROPE: BALANCING DATA UTILITY AND REIDENTIFICATION RISK

In order to build strong AI models, the teams behind the research and development require large and varied datasets. But it is against the law and morally wrong to share raw patient data. Data anonymization has been the conventional way out of this problem; it is the method of extracting or changing the parts of the data that can directly identify a person (PII) so as not to be able to link the data to an individual. Nevertheless, with the advent of big data and sophisticated analytics, the idea of "anonymous" data has been questioned very intensely. It is almost difficult to find a dataset that is truly non-identifiable and can still be used for complicated AI operations.

### 3.5.1 Traditional Deidentification Techniques and Their Shortcomings

The HIPAA Privacy Rule sets out two models, both based on the reduction of quasi-identifiers and thus both being susceptible to linkage attacks.

1. **Safe Harbor:** This is a prescriptive method that requires the removal of a specific list of 18 identifiers, including personal names, geographic subdivisions smaller than a state, all elements of dates directly related to an individual, telephone numbers, and Social Security numbers [114].
2. **Expert Determination:** This method involves a qualified statistician or data scientist applying accepted statistical principles and methods to determine that the risk of reidentification is "very small" [115].

Additional methods are: Pseudonymization (Consistent token substitution) [116], Generalization (Coarsening; age→bands, ZIP→3-digits) [117], Suppression

(Omission of high-risk fields/records) [118], Perturbation/Shuffling (Noise addition/permutation) [119].

These methods have been the standard for decades, but they have been less and less reliable with the modern data ecosystem. The risk becomes extremely high with high-dimensional data such as genomic sequences or continuous data streams from wearables.

Usually, these kinds of data are intrinsically unique to an individual; therefore, traditional suppression and generalization techniques become ineffective. An attacker with access to an external dataset can carry out a linkage attack whereby they essentially "reidentify" the anonymized data.

### 3.5.2 The Re-Identification Risk in AI Models

The risk does not just stop at the raw data but also includes the AI models that have been trained using that data. Attacks that are sophisticated in nature can be directed against the models that have been trained in order to obtain information about the data that was used for the training.

- **Membership Inference Attacks:** An attacker who can make use of a model's predictions (e.g., through a public API) and also has some limited information about an individual can determine with a very high probability whether the data of that individual was included in the model's training set [108]. In a healthcare context, this could reveal that a specific person has a certain disease, a highly sensitive piece of information.
- **Model Inversion and Attribute Inference Attacks:** The purpose of these attacks is to recover the fragments of the training data or to infer the sensitive attributes of the training subjects. For instance, an attacker may use the facial recognition model to create the face of a person in the training set by the model or use a predictive model to get a sensitive diagnosis of a patient based on other easily available attributes of the patient [120].
- **Memorization:** DL models, particularly those with a very large number of parameters, are prone to "memorizing" the unique or rare examples in their training data. A group of researchers has proved that one can take out these memorized data points, like the text of a particular person's medical record, right from the trained model [121].

These are examples of how vulnerabilities may be implemented to show that just de-identifying the input data is far from being enough to ensure privacy. The privacy concerns related to the AI model should be taken into account all the way through its life cycle.

### 3.5.3 Advanced Privacy-Preserving Data Analysis

In order to overcome the limitations of traditional anonymization, there is a new generation of PETs that can provide more rigorous, mathematically provable privacy guarantees.

#### 3.5.3.1 k-Anonymity, l-Diversity, and t-Closeness

These techniques are much more complex than simple suppression, and they also include altering data so that it is less detailed.

- **k-Anonymity:** Makes sure that an individual cannot be identified in a dataset among at least *k-1* other individuals. This is achieved by generalizing or suppressing quasi-identifiers. As an illustration, a certain age may be converted into an age range (e.g., 30–35), and a 5-digit ZIP code may be converted into the first three digits [117].
- **l-Diversity:** A concept of k-anonymity that solves the problem of homogeneity attacks (where all individuals in a k-anonymous group have the same sensitive attribute) by ensuring that each equivalence class (set of indistinguishable records) contains at least l "well-represented" values for the sensitive attribute [122].
- **t-Closeness:** A subsequent enhancement that demands the closeness (within a threshold t) of the distribution of a sensitive attribute in an equivalence class to that in the entire dataset. This prevents the attacker from inferring the overall distribution of values, thus preventing inference attacks.

Although these methods offer more stringent assurances than a simple de-identification, there is a trade-off. The granularity and utility of the data are inherently lowered by the processes of generalization and suppression, which means that AI models trained on such data may have their performance negatively affected. It is quite a challenge to find the right balance between k, l, t, and data utility.

#### 3.5.3.2 Differential Privacy: A Gold Standard

Differential Privacy (DP) is a way of thinking that moves away from the norm of anonymizing data and instead anonymizes the output of a query or an analysis. Using a formal mathematical model, it guarantees that the inclusion or exclusion of any single individual's data in a dataset will not significantly variate the result of the analysis [123]. DP adds the so-called statistical "noise" to the results of a query or the training process of an ML model, and this noise is meticulously calibrated. The noise size is determined by a privacy parameter, epsilon ($\varepsilon$), that is, the privacy "budget." More privacy comes from a smaller epsilon at the expense of a larger noise, which can even cause less accuracy. If the epsilon is larger, then the privacy is weaker, but the accuracy is higher [124, 125]. The most attractive feature of DP is the list of the attacks, from which it, provably, provides protection, and these include linkage attacks and membership inference attacks. It allows organizations to share in aggregate the statistical results or to train AI models with a quantifiable privacy assurance. DP is the preferred route for data collection and analysis by Apple, Google, and the U.S. Census Bureau. In the healthcare sector, it can be used for federated learning (FL) (differentially private federated learning) or for aggregate research data release, thus building a much stronger privacy basis than conventional methods [126]. Nevertheless, it takes a lot of expertise to put DP into effect properly and to select a suitable epsilon for a specific use case.

The move from simple de-identification to provable DP tells a story of the data privacy concept that changes along the way. It points out that there is no perfect privacy solution, but rather a set of compromises between data utility, analytical accuracy, and the fundamental right of patients to privacy.

## 3.6 THE REGULATORY AND ETHICAL MAZE: COMPLIANCE, CONSENT, AND GOVERNANCE

AI utilization in the medical domain is linked with a legal network of regulations, moral principles, and governance structures that aim to shield patients and ensure the ethically correct deployment of the technology. The healthcare providers', technology developers', and policymakers' dilemma is the problem of navigating this rulebook labyrinth. If these provisions are not observed, there can be a substantial monetary penalty, legal actions, and, most importantly, an irrevocable decrease in the public trust.

### 3.6.1 Key Regulatory Frameworks

There exists a considerable number of local and regional laws; however, two frameworks have set the global standards for the protection of health data: HIPAA in the USA and GDPR in the EU.

#### 3.6.1.1 The Health Insurance Portability and Accountability Act (HIPAA)

In the U.S., HIPAA was primarily intended to reform the healthcare information flow and make it more secure. The Privacy Rule and the Security Rule are the major components of this act that are of relevance to AI.

- **The Privacy Rule:** It sets out the protection standards for PHI on a national level. Firstly, the rule describes the types of information to be protected, those who are covered by the law, and the situations in which PHI can be used and disclosed. In relation to AI creation, the significant point is that health data may be used for "healthcare operations" without patient consent, a category that sometimes might include activities like quality assessment and improvement. However, in the case of commercial AI product development, the use of PHI would require either a clear patient authorization or strong de-identification of the data in compliance with HIPAA regulations.
- **The Security Rule:** It changes the Privacy Rule by fixing requirements for the security of electronic PHI. The rule requires that certain administrative, physical, and technical measures be taken. The technical aspects of AI systems that are at issue here can include the steps needed to control who has access to a system, audit controls, integrity controls, and transmission security.

The HITECH Act of 2009 has made HIPAA a stricter law by giving more power to the authorities to enforce it and making the penalties heavier. It also introduced a breach notification rule requiring organizations to notify both the individuals whose data have been compromised and the government. In case of signing with a healthcare provider, it is necessary that AI vendors obtain a BAA. This document is a legal obligation that requires the vendor to follow HIPAA regulations on the protection of PHI [127].

#### 3.6.1.2 The General Data Protection Regulation (GDPR)

GDPR [128] is considered to be one of the most comprehensive and strict data privacy laws worldwide. Any company that uses the personal data of people living in the EU must comply with the law, no matter where it is located. "Data relating to health" has been classified as a "special category" of personal data, which benefits from the highest security level. The primary principles of GDPR, which can have a substantial impact on the use of AI in healthcare, are:

- **Lawful Basis for Processing:** The handling of health data must never be carried out under any condition without a certain lawful basis being applicable, for example, an explicit consent of the data subject, a necessity for a medical diagnosis, or a vital public interest in the area of public health.
- **Data Minimization:** Data shall be adequate, relevant, and limited to the necessary minimum for the specified purpose. AI model developers may find this provision challenging as their models are usually more efficient with larger datasets.
- **Purpose Limitation:** Information gathered for a specific goal should not be used for a different incompatible goal without a legal basis.
- **Rights of the Data Subject:** According to GDPR, individuals are entitled to a range of rights, including the right to access their data, the right to correction (in case of errors), the right to deletion ("right to be forgotten"), and the right to data portability. Moreover, the regulation provides a right to receive an explanation for decisions made by an automated system and a right not to be subjected to a decision that is based solely on automated processing, which has legal or similarly significant effects.
- **Privacy by Design and by Default:** As mentioned earlier, this implies that organizations have to build in data protection into the construction of their systems and processes from the very start.

### 3.6.2 The Centrality of Patient Consent

Both HIPAA and GDPR, along with fundamental ethical principles, place enormous weight on patient consent. For AI development, the traditional model of broad, one-time consent given at the beginning of a patient relationship is often inadequate. The secondary use of data for training AI models that may be commercialized or used for purposes beyond the patient's direct care raises complex ethical questions. A more robust approach is dynamic consent. This model uses digital platforms to enable an ongoing dialogue between patients and the data controllers. Thus, patients may be made aware of novel data utilization scenarios and can decide to opt in or opt out at a detailed level. They can find out who is accessing their data and for what reason and can alter their preferences whenever they want [129]. Although it is more difficult to implement, dynamic consent enhances transparency and gives patients the power, thereby creating the trust that is essential for a sustainable data sharing ecosystem.

### 3.6.3 Data Governance and Accountability

Robust data governance is the operating system that adjust the legal and ethical principles into practice. It defines the policies, roles, and responsibilities as well as the procedures for managing and safeguarding data throughout its life cycle. A strong governance framework for AI-enabled healthcare should feature the following [130]:

- **Clear Data Ownership and Stewardship:** Determining who has the ultimate accountability for the data. Although patients "own" their data in theory, the healthcare organization acts as a "steward," with a fiduciary obligation to protect it.
- **Data Use Agreements (DUAs):** These are binding legal agreements that detail the conditions under which the data can be shared with and be used by third parties, including AI developers. Such agreements should indicate the degree of use, the security measures, and privacy commitments.
- **AI Model Governance:** The measures that very specifically control the AI life cycle, tracing the origin of the data, model validation procedures, bias detection and removal strategies, and, finally, monitoring after the deployment.
- **Institutional Review Boards (IRBs) and Ethics Committees:** These entities should be provided the necessary expertise to assess the ethical dimensions of AI research and its application. Apart from supervising traditional clinical trials, they should also be involved in issues of algorithmic fairness, privacy, and the impact on society.

## 3.7 FAIRNESS, ACCOUNTABILITY, AND TRANSPARENCY: THE ROLE OF EXPLAINABLE AI (XAI)

One of the ethical and safety issues that go beyond the usual data security arise when AI is integrated into clinical decision-making. The encryption of data and controlled access can make an AI system appear perfectly secure, and yet if the internal logic of the AI is biased, flawed, or totally unexplainable, it may actually lead to tragic consequences. Therefore, the implementation of these three principles, fairness, accountability, and transparency, is a must along with the other goals of data privacy and security. Besides ensuring the protection of data, they also guarantee that data is used in a fair, comprehensible, and accountable way by AI systems [131].

### 3.7.1 The Specter of Algorithmic Bias in Healthcare

Algorithmic bias is when AI systems unfairly target certain groups due to the wrong assumptions made during ML. This means that such systems give outputs that are additionally discriminative in nature. In the area of healthcare, this results in the occurrence of discriminatory outcomes that contribute to the widening of health inequalities. Bias may originate from different sources, such as:

- **Biased Data:** This is the predominant cause of bias. This is because if the data employed for the training of an AI model reflects biases that are historical or societal, then the model will learn based on those biases, and most of the time it will amplify them. For instance, if a particular demographic group has had less access to healthcare over time, their conditions may be less represented or recorded differently in EHR data. Therefore, an AI model trained on this data may not work well for this group; thus, it may cause wrong diagnoses or inappropriate treatment recommendations [132, 133].
- **Flawed Model Design:** A model's features selection, target variable definition, and model optimization goals can easily bring in bias unintentionally [134, 135].
- **Unfair Privacy Outcomes:** Bias interacts with privacy as well. For instance, an anomaly detection system that is intended to raise the flag of fraudulent insurance claims may be more probable to charge the specific socioeconomic group making these claims if the patterns in the training data are from this group, thus subjecting people from that group to more observation and potential privacy violations [136].

Dealing with bias in AI is not only a matter of fixing the technology but also an ethical requirement. The process entails choosing the data with a lot of care, employing fair ML algorithms, and continuously checking that the models do not have any kinds of biases toward certain demographic groups [137, 138].

### 3.7.2 The "Black Box" Problem and the Need for Accountability

Most highly advanced AI models, especially deep neural networks, are inherently black boxes. In principle, they can take a complex input (such as a medical image) and produce a very accurate output (a diagnosis), but the factor behind the decision is, in most cases, not accessible. The problem of a lack of interpretability stands in the way of social dialogue and, hence, trust, as a very significant issue. In the case of AI systems issuing recommendations with a significant impact on human lives, it is essential for clinicians, patients, and regulators to know why [113, 139–141].

- **For Clinicians:** A recommendation that is not substantiated with any explanation is not a candidate for a doctor's trust. It is the doctor's obligation to verify that the AI's reasoning correlates with their clinical knowledge to be sure that it is medically accurate and not an artifact of a random correlation in the dataset.
- **For Patients:** Respect for patients' rights implies providing them with the basis of a decision that has an impact on their health. This is an integral part of regulations like GDPR that grants a "right to an explanation" for automated decisions.

- **For Accountability:** In the case where an AI model makes a mistake, it is very important to have the capability of performing a "digital autopsy" to figure out the mistake. Without interpretability, figuring out the person responsible, fixing the error, and stopping it from happening again is almost infeasible.

### 3.7.3 Explainable AI (XAI) as a Pathway to Transparency

XAI is a novel scientific and practical domain that aims to keep AI models minimally complicated while still maintaining the performance of the system at a high level. A key point of XAI is to open the "black box," providing a transparent and verifiable model decision [142]. XAI methods can be generally categorized based on two axes:

- **Scope (Local vs. Global):**
  - **Local Explanations:** The explanation is narrowed down to a single instance or prediction made by the system. For instance, "Why did the model predict a high risk of stroke for this particular patient?"
  - **Global Explanations:** They have the goal of explaining how the system behaves in general. For instance, "What are the most important features the model considers in general when predicting stroke risk?"
- **Applicability (Model Specific vs. Model Agnostic):**
  - **Model Specific:** These methods are designed for a specific group of models that are interpretable by nature, for example, decision trees or linear regression.
  - **Model Agnostic:** These methods have a wider range of application and can be used with any ML model. They analyze the model by providing it with various inputs and looking at the outputs. LIME and SHAP are two major model-agnostic methods.

Other possible categories for XAI:

**Model Interpretability Frameworks (Post-hoc):** These techniques are applied after the creation of a black box model to explain the results obtained from it [143].

**Local Interpretable Model-agnostic Explanations (LIME):** Interprets the prediction that is made from any black box model by approximating it locally with a simpler, more understandable model around the specific instance that is being explained [144, 145].

**SHapley Additive exPlanations (SHAP):** This is a method based on cooperative game theory that SHAP uses to give each feature an "importance value" (Shapley value) in a particular prediction, thus fairly attributing the credit among features [146, 147].

**Saliency Maps and Attention Mechanisms:** For image-based AI, saliency maps visually highlight the specific regions of an input image (e.g., pixels in an X-ray) that were most influential in the model's decision [148]. In Transformer models (e.g., for NLP), attention mechanisms explicitly show which parts of the input sequence the model focused on [149].

**Inherently Interpretable Models:** When suitable, intrinsically interpretable models such as decision trees, rule-based systems, or Generalized Additive Models (GAMs) might be utilized.

**"Glass-Box" Deep Learning Architectures:** Exploring deep neural network designs that come with built-in interpretability, where certain layers or components are deliberately designed to have a more understandable function or where the model's internal representations can be directly interpretable.

**Comprehensive Documentation and Auditing:** Thorough documentation of the whole AI model development life cycle, covering data sources, preprocessing steps, model architecture, training parameters, validation metrics (including fairness metrics), and known limitations. Regular, independent algorithmic auditing for transparency, bias, and robustness [150].

**User Centric Explanation Design:** Creating explanations that are contextually relevant and are specifically made for the technical understanding and informational needs of the particular end users.

**Counterfactual Explanations:** Generating explanations that describe "what would have to be different for the prediction to change" (e.g., if the patient's cholesterol level was X instead of Y, the AI would have predicted low risk instead of high risk) [151].

## 3.8 THE FUTURE FRONTIER: ADVANCED PRIVACY-ENHANCING TECHNOLOGIES

While methods such as DP offer strong guarantees, these usually involve a central trusted entity that collects and adds noise to the data. In addition, the trade-off between privacy and the usefulness of the data is still an issue. To overcome these drawbacks, researchers are developing a new frontier of PETs that aim to enable secure and private AI by changing how data is accessed and processed. Although these methods require more computation, they envision a scenario where state-of-the-art AI models can be developed using sensitive health data without revealing the data.

### 3.8.1 Federated Learning: Training Models without Moving Data

Federated Learning (FL) is a decentralized ML paradigm that enables model training on data distributed across multiple devices or institutions without the need to share their raw data [152–154]. Unlike a conventional centralized learning setup, where all training data are collected in one place, FL only communicates the model parameters or updates (e.g., gradients or weights) and not the actual records. This architecture is in line with the ideas of data minimization and locality that form the core of modern data protection regulations like GDPR and sectoral frameworks in healthcare.

This feature is what makes healthcare a field where AI can be very useful. Healthcare is a sector that is heavily regulated by laws, ethics, and organizational rules, which makes it very difficult to consolidate sensitive clinical data in one place. Nevertheless, for the purpose of creating strong and generalizable AI models, multicenter collaboration is required. FL, in its standard configuration, is an iterative client-server operation.

Typically, the very first step of the operation is the initialization phase: a coordinating server (a health system, vendor, or research consortium) defines and builds a global model, and thereafter, it sends the current parameters to a group of participants, for example, hospitals, imaging centers, or edge devices. While training locally, each institution trains this model duplicate on its own confidential dataset for one or more local epochs, thereby generating an update. Most of the time, this is in the form of gradients or updated weights that summarize how local data would change the model. Importantly, it is only these updates that are sent out; raw patient-level data are never shared outside the institution.

During the aggregation phase, each participant is required to send their model update to the coordinator. To protect against interception or inspection of individual updates, the coordinator may apply cryptographic protections (e.g., encryption in transit, secure aggregation). Subsequently, the server executes a global model update, which involves merging the client contributions, typically by a weighted averaging method such as Federated Averaging (FedAvg), where updates are weighted according to the relative size of each client's local dataset to obtain a new global parameter set.

The updated global model is shared with the clients, and thus the cycle is repeated over several communication rounds until convergence, at which time the resultant model is close to a centrally trained model on the union of all participating datasets, yet none of those datasets have been combined. Such a structure presents two key advantages to healthcare. Firstly, it allows learning from different, multi-institutional datasets, thus reflecting demographic patterns and equipment changes, which in turn make clinical AI systems more externally valid and robust. Secondly, it keeps data locality and institutional sovereignty intact: SHI is kept under the governance and security measures of the organization from which it originated. This can be very important for compliance with various frameworks like HIPAA and GDPR, as well as local ethics and data use agreements.

Nonetheless, FL should not be considered as a privacy solution on its own. Even in cases where raw data are stored locally, model updates alone can disclose information about the original data used for training, thus enabling attacks like gradient inversion or membership inference, where an adversary attempts to reconstruct or infer features of local data from shared updates. In order to lessen these risks, cutting-edge FL implementations are being gradually combined with PETs. Secure aggregation protocols employ cryptographic techniques to guarantee that the coordinator can only see an aggregate of client updates, but never any individual contribution in isolation. DP methods, performed either at the client side (local DP) or on aggregated updates (central DP), introduce calibrated noise to gradients or model parameters to offer mathematically quantifiable privacy guarantees that any single patient's data have only a limited impact on the final model, even when auxiliary information and adaptive adversaries are taken into account. By this means, that is, federated optimization for data locality, secure aggregation for update confidentiality, and DP for formal leakage bounds, the aim of FL can be a door to the privacy-preserving ML concept in healthcare to create a highly robust privacy-preserving ML framework [155–160].

### 3.8.2 Homomorphic Encryption: Computing on Encrypted Data

As introduced in Section 3.3, HE is a game-changing cryptographic primitive that allows any computations to be done directly on encrypted ciphertexts, without the need for decryption. The outputs are also encrypted, and they, upon decryption, are the same as if the operations were carried out on the original unencrypted data. In simple terms, this makes secure outsourced computations possible in the field of AI. For instance, a healthcare provider can keep the patient data encrypted by itself under its private key. It sends the ciphertext to a cloud-based AI service. The latter trains the model or performs inference entirely on ciphertext and returns an encrypted result. Only the data owner with the decryption key can get the plaintext outcome. The computation service provider never sees the data in the clear; thus, breach risks at the compute endpoint are removed altogether [61, 64].

This paradigm enables "secure AI as a service" to be used in the healthcare sector, where institutions with limited resources can take advantage of a high-capacity cloud infrastructure for different tasks like risk stratification, diagnostic imaging analysis, or genomic modeling without losing control over their data or compromising regulatory compliance (e.g., HIPAA BAA exemptions for encrypted processing). A hospital, for example, might encrypt EHRs or DICOM images and send out logistic regression for disease prediction or CNN inference for radiology while the cloud is computing gradients on ciphertexts [161]. The service delivers encrypted model parameters or predictions, which can only be decrypted by the provider.

HE schemes are differentiated by their level of expressiveness:

- Partially Homomorphic Encryption (PHE): Allows unlimited operations of one type only [162].
- Somewhat Homomorphic Encryption (SHE): Limited depth circuits through a small number of bootstrapping operations [163].
- Fully Homomorphic Encryption (FHE): Computation of arbitrary depth by "bootstrapping" to refresh ciphertexts, thus enabling Turing-complete evaluation [61, 164].

The overheads of the first generation of FHE were very high per operation for the security parameter, but the second and third generation schemes [164–166] have ring learning with errors (RLWE) lattices as a common element [167], and they achieve less computation for linear/logistic regression and shallow CNN inference ML workloads that are still practical. As hardware and algorithms continue to improve, HE is poised to become a cornerstone of secure data outsourcing and collaboration.

### 3.8.2 Secure Multiparty Computation (SMPC)

SMPC is a cryptography paradigm, which allows multiple parties that do not trust each other to cooperate to jointly compute any function and get the correct result over their inputs while keeping those inputs private. SMPC is a perfect example of how AI can be used in a collaborative fashion in different healthcare institutions without the need for data centralization. As a result, several research hospitals might cooperatively create a predictive model based on the fusion of their EHRs or imaging datasets: Hospital A sends encrypted versions of its patient cohorts, and Hospital B provides its local features, and via interactive cryptographic protocols, they obtain a shared model just as if the data had been pooled. Still, no hospital has access to the other's raw records. It is only the final model parameters or aggregate statistics that are disclosed; thus, patient confidentiality is maintained, and data localization mandates can be met [168, 169]. SMPC works alongside FL to solve the problem of update leakage in FL: while FL shares gradients (which can be inverted), SMPC obtains exact aggregates or full models through encrypted shares, thus offering information theoretic or computational security against honest but curious/malicious adversaries.

### 3.8.3 Synthetic Data Generation: High-Fidelity Proxies for Privacy-Preserving

Synthetic data generation is one of the generative modeling paradigms in which an ML system, a system trained only on private real-world datasets, produces data samples that are completely artificial but statistically imitate the original distribution and are free from authentic records [170]. Major architectures are: Generative Adversarial Networks (GANs), which align a generator against a discriminator to reduce Jensen Shannon divergence between real and synthetic distributions [171, 172]; Variational Autoencoders (VAEs), which obtain latent representations through evidence lower bound (ELBO) optimization to generate viable reconstructions [173]; and denoising diffusion probabilistic models (DDPMs), which gradually move Gaussian noise toward data manifold using reverse diffusion processes [174].

Such a synthetic dataset may subsequently be shared with less restrictions with researchers or developers for the purpose of training AI models in a way that does not reveal any real patient information. In order to be really efficient, the synthetic data production should be inherently linked with privacy assurances, such as DP, so as not to allow the generative model to simply memorize and reproduce the patient data. Excellent synthetic data have the potential to democratize the access to realistic health data, thus speeding up the process of research and innovation, while at the same time ensuring the privacy of patients.

These advanced techniques are at the forefront of privacy research. Even though some of them are still in the developmental stage, they indicate a clear direction toward a future where the conflict between data-driven innovation and individual privacy can be solved more efficiently, thus making it possible to harness the full power of AI in healthcare in a safe and ethical way.

## 3.9 CONCLUSION: TOWARD A COLLABORATIVE FRAMEWORK FOR TRUSTWORTHY AI IN HEALTHCARE

The integration of AI in the medical field is not a future concept; it is the present, already altering how diagnostics, treatment, and clinical operations are conducted. Powered by vast amounts of highly personal medical data, this transformation constitutes a unique proposition to improve the human condition. Nevertheless, as this chapter has shown, the promise accompanies an immense obligation: unwavering support for patient data confidentiality and protection. We have explored the intricate healthcare data environment, uncovering its distinct value and weaknesses. We argued that a robust defense depends on essential pillars: thorough encryption in all data states, secure and compartmentalized architectures, and strict IAM following the principle of least privilege. Such a defense-in-depth plan is no longer a matter of choice but a fundamental prerequisite for any organization operating in this high-stakes field.

Besides that, AI is a long way from being the only factor that increases the risks. Measures secured by AI can change the organization's reaction from a quick and reactive one to a proactive one. Therefore, the company will be able to intelligently detect threats, monitor compliance automatically, and have the ability to defend itself predictively, which are capabilities that far exceed human scale. However, this innovation should be carefully managed since it is susceptible to being exploited by the adversaries, and it also requires human supervision.

The heart of the challenge lies in balancing the immense utility of health data with the non-negotiable right to privacy. Traditional anonymization techniques, while once sufficient, have proven fragile in the face of modern data linkage attacks. Consequently, this has caused a shift toward adopting PETs that are more secure. The accuracy of DP, the advantages of decentralized FL, the cryptographic charm of HE, and the capability of synthetic data are very essential elements of trustable AI systems. Regulatory and ethical considerations are as important as the technical ones. Compliance with regulations such as HIPAA and GDPR should not be viewed as bureaucratic burdens but rather as an indication of the moral values of the community. This reality necessitates efficient data governance, adherence to the "Privacy by Design" principle, and a shift toward patient consent models that are both dynamic and transparent. Moreover, privacy and security should be considered together while also handling other issues such as fairness, accountability, and transparency. An AI system that discriminates certain groups or works as an unexplainable "black box" loses the trust of the users, even if it handles data securely. The development of XAI is a significant step to make sure that AI is a transparent and reliable assistant to healthcare professionals.

In the end, ensuring strong data privacy and security in healthcare powered by AI is not a single stakeholder's problem. This issue calls for a collaborative, multi-layered approach that involves different players. By upgrading to modern security structures and creating a culture of security consciousness through which protection of data is regarded as one of the fundamental elements of patient safety, Healthcare Providers can play their part. The Technology Developers and AI researchers should incorporate privacy and ethics aspects in their design processes from the very beginning. They should move from only considering model accuracy toward also taking into account fairness, interpretability, and privacy engineering. Regulators and policymakers must keep modifying the laws to reflect the real-world AI situation, thus providing precisely regulatory guidelines that are friendly to innovations and free from the risk of suffocating the development by strictly prescriptive rules. Patients should be enabled to be one of the main actors in the data ecosystem and be given a clear explanation, as well as instruments with which they can decide how their information is used.

The way out is cooperation between these groups. As one, they have the power to create a future where health AI is not just an amazing technological advancement but also a system that is safe due to strong technical, ethical, and governance provisions.

## REFERENCES

1. Esteva, A., et al., *Dermatologist-level classification of skin cancer with deep neural networks*. Nature, 2017. **542**(7639): p. 115–118.
2. Oyeniyi, J. and Oluwaseyi, P., *Emerging trends in AI-powered medical imaging: enhancing diagnostic accuracy and treatment decisions*. International Journal of Enhanced Research in Science Technology & Engineering, 2024. **13**(4): p. 81–94.
3. Bragazzi, N.L. and Mahroum, N., *Google trends predicts present and future plague cases during the plague outbreak in Madagascar: infodemiological study*. JMIR Public Health and Surveillance, 2019. **5**(1): p. e13142.
4. Gala, D., Behl, H., Shah, M., and Makaryus, A.N., *The role of artificial intelligence in improving patient outcomes and future of healthcare delivery in cardiology: a narrative review of the literature*. Healthcare, 2024. **12**(4): p. 481.
5. Adeghe, E.P., Okolo, C.A., and Ojeyinka, O.T., *The role of big data in healthcare: a review of implications for patient outcomes and treatment personalization*. World Journal of Biology Pharmacy and Health Sciences, 2024. **17**(3): p. 198–204.
6. Maleki Varnosfaderani, S. and Forouzanfar, M., *The role of AI in hospitals and clinics: transforming healthcare in the 21st century*. Bioengineering, 2024. **11**(4): p. 337.
7. Wang, D.Q., et al., *Accelerating the integration of ChatGPT and other large-scale AI models into biomedical research and healthcare*. MedComm–Future Medicine, 2023. **2**(2): p. e43.
8. Evans, R.S., *Electronic health records: then, now, and in the future*. Yearbook of Medical Informatics, 2016. **25**(S 01): p. S48–S61.
9. Bagabir, S.A., Ibrahim, N.K., Bagabir, H.A., and Ateeq, R.H., *Covid-19 and artificial intelligence: genome sequencing, drug development and vaccine discovery*. Journal of Infection and Public Health, 2022. **15**(2): p. 289–296.
10. Wan, J., et al., *Wearable IoT enabled real-time health monitoring system*. EURASIP Journal on Wireless Communications and Networking, 2018. **2018**(1): p. 1–10.
11. Byerly, K., et al., *Real-time big data processing and wearable internet of medical things sensor devices for health monitoring*. American Journal of Medical Research, 2019. **6**(2): p. 67–72.
12. Adeghe, E.P., Okolo, C.A., and Ojeyinka, O.T., *A review of wearable technology in healthcare: monitoring patient health and enhancing outcomes*. OARJ of Multidisciplinary Studies, 2024. **7**(01): p. 142–148.
13. Topol, E.J., *High-performance medicine: the convergence of human and artificial intelligence*. Nature Medicine, 2019. **25**(1): p. 44–56.
14. Liu, X., et al., *A comparison of deep learning performance against health-care professionals in detecting diseases from medical imaging: a systematic review and meta-analysis*. The Lancet Digital Health, 2019. **1**(6): p. e271–e297.
15. Alum, E. and Ugwu, O.P.-C., *Artificial intelligence in personalized medicine: transforming diagnosis and treatment*. Discover Applied Sciences, 2025. **7**(3): p. 193.
16. Li, Y.-H., Li, Y.-L., Wei, M.-Y., and Li, G.-Y., *Innovation and challenges of artificial intelligence technology in personalized healthcare*. Scientific Reports, 2024. **14**(1): p. 18994.
17. Poweleit, E.A., Vinks, A.A., and Mizuno, T., *Artificial intelligence and machine learning approaches to facilitate therapeutic drug management and model-informed precision dosing*. Therapeutic Drug Monitoring, 2023. **45**(2): p. 143–150.

18. Rashidieranjbar, F., Farhadi, A., and Zamanifar, A., *Revolutionizing healthcare with generative artificial intelligence technologies*, in *Generative artificial intelligence (AI) approaches for industrial applications*. 2025, Springer. p. 189–221.
19. Askin, S., Burkhalter, D., Calado, G., and El Dakrouni, S., *Artificial intelligence applied to clinical trials: opportunities and challenges*. Health and Technology, 2023. **13**(2): p. 203–213.
20. Haddad, T., et al., *Accuracy of an artificial intelligence system for cancer clinical trial eligibility screening: retrospective pilot study*. JMIR Medical Informatics, 2021. **9**(3): p. e27767.
21. Marques, L., et al., *Advancing precision medicine: a review of innovative in Silico approaches for drug development, clinical pharmacology and personalized healthcare*. Pharmaceutics, 2024. **16**(3): p. 332.
22. Serrano, D.R., et al., *Artificial intelligence (AI) applications in drug discovery and drug delivery: revolutionizing personalized medicine*. Pharmaceutics, 2024. **16**(10): p. 1328.
23. Ordu, M., Demir, E., Tofallis, C., and Gunal, M.M., *A novel healthcare resource allocation decision support tool: a forecasting-simulation-optimization approach*. Journal of the Operational Research Society, 2021. **72**(3): p. 485–500.
24. Yazdani, M., Shahriari, S., and Haghani, M., *Real-time decision support model for logistics of emergency patient transfers from hospitals via an integrated optimisation and machine learning approach*. Progress in Disaster Science, 2025. **25**: p. 100397.
25. Murdoch, B., *Privacy and artificial intelligence: challenges for protecting health information in a new era*. BMC Medical Ethics, 2021. **22**(1): p. 122.
26. Seh, A.H., et al., *Healthcare data breaches: insights and implications*. Healthcare. 2020. **8**(2): p. 133.
27. Li, S., Surineni, K., and Prabhakaran, N., *Cyber-attacks on Hospital systems: a narrative review*. The American Journal of Geriatric Psychiatry: Open Science, Education, and Practice, 2025.
28. Aldosari, B., *Cybersecurity in healthcare: new threat to patient safety*. Cureus, 2025. 17(5).
29. Di Palma, G., et al., *AI-induced cybersecurity risks in healthcare: a narrative review of blockchain-based solutions within a clinical risk management framework*. Risk Management and Healthcare Policy, 2025: p. 3479–3497.
30. Yadav, N., et al., *Data privacy in healthcare: in the era of artificial intelligence*. Indian Dermatology Online Journal, 2023. **14**(6): p. 788–792.
31. Khan, M.M., et al., *Towards secure and trusted AI in healthcare: a systematic review of emerging innovations and ethical challenges*. International Journal of Medical Informatics, 2025. **195**: p. 105780.
32. Fernández-Alemán, J.L., Señor, I.C., Lozoya, P.Á.O., and Toval, A., *Security and privacy in electronic health records: a systematic literature review*. Journal of Biomedical Informatics, 2013. **46**(3): p. 541–562.
33. Bernal, J. and Mazo, C., *Transparency of artificial intelligence in healthcare: insights from professionals in computing and healthcare worldwide*. Applied Sciences, 2022. **12**(20): p. 10228.
34. Janssen, A., Donnelly, C., and Shaw, T., *A taxonomy for health information systems*. Journal of Medical Internet Research, 2024. **26**: p. e47682.
35. An, D., Lim, M., and Lee, S., *Challenges for data quality in the clinical data life cycle: systematic review*. Journal of Medical Internet Research, 2025. **27**: p. e60709.
36. Lerner-Ellis, J.P., et al., *The evolution of health data ecosystems: an international survey*. The American Journal of Human Genetics, 2025. **112**(8): p. 1769–1777.
37. Khaloufi, H., Abouelmehdi, K., Beni-hssane, A., and Saadi, M., *Security model for big healthcare data lifecycle*. Procedia Computer Science, 2018. **141**: p. 294–301.

38. Nickerson, R.C., Varshney, U., and Muntermann, J., *A method for taxonomy development and its application in information systems.* European Journal of Information Systems, 2013. **22**(3): p. 336–359.
39. Shickel, B., Tighe, P.J., Bihorac, A., and Rashidi, P., *Deep EHR: a survey of recent advances in deep learning techniques for electronic health record (EHR) analysis.* IEEE Journal of Biomedical and Health Informatics, 2017. **22**(5): p. 1589–1604.
40. Onken, M., Eichelberg, M., Riesmeier, J., and Jensch, P., *Digital imaging and communications in medicine*, in *Biomedical image processing.* 2010, Springer. p. 427–454.
41. Erlich, Y. and Narayanan, A., *Routes for breaching and protecting genetic privacy.* Nature Reviews Genetics, 2014. **15**(6): p. 409–421.
42. Naghib, A., Gharehchopogh, F.S., and Zamanifar, A., *The role of large language models in delivering artificial intelligence-based psychological interventions and therapies*, in *Applications of large language models (LLM) in healthcare systems.* 2025, Chapman and Hall/CRC. p. 142–178.
43. Khatiwada, P., Yang, B., Lin, J.-C., and Blobel, B., *Patient-generated health data (PGHD): understanding, requirements, challenges, and existing techniques for data security and privacy.* Journal of Personalized Medicine, 2024. **14**(3): p. 282.
44. Cohen, I.G. and Mello, M. M., *HIPAA and protecting health information in the 21st century.* Jama, 2018. **320**(3): p. 231–232.
45. Madhusudhanan, S. and Jose, A.C., *Privacy preservation techniques through data lifecycle: a comprehensive literature survey.* Computers & Security, 2025: p. 104473.
46. Thantilage, R.D., Le-Khac, N.-A., and Kechadi, M.-T., *Healthcare data security and privacy in data warehouse architectures.* Informatics in Medicine Unlocked, 2023. **39**: p. 101270.
47. Cavoukian, A., *Privacy by design: the 7 foundational principles.* Information and Privacy Commissioner of Ontario, Canada, 2009. **5**(2009): p. 12.
48. Coventry, L. and Branley, D., *Cybersecurity in healthcare: a narrative review of trends, threats and ways forward.* Maturitas, 2018. **113**: p. 48–52.
49. Nadhan, A.S. and Jacob, I.J., *Enhancing healthcare security in the digital era: safeguarding medical images with lightweight cryptographic techniques in IoT healthcare applications.* Biomedical Signal Processing and Control, 2024. **88**: p. 105511.
50. Sharma, A., Gupta, B.B., Singh, A.K., and Saraswat, V., *Advanced persistent threats (apt): evolution, anatomy, attribution and countermeasures.* Journal of Ambient Intelligence and Humanized Computing, 2023. **14**(7): p. 9355–9381.
51. Gambo, M.D. and Alkharobi, T.M., *Modeling of APT actors targeting healthcare sector.* International Journal of Computer Science & Network Security, 2025: p. 155–168.
52. Priestman, W., et al., *Phishing in healthcare organisations: threats, mitigation and approaches.* BMJ Health & Care Informatics, 2019. **26**(1): p. e100031.
53. Chowdhury, M., Jahan, S., Islam, R., and Gao, J., *Malware detection for healthcare data security*, in *International Conference on Security and Privacy in Communication Systems.* 2018. Springer.
54. Karaca, K.N. and Çetin, A., *Systematic review of current approaches and innovative solutions for combating zero-day vulnerabilities and zero-day attacks.* IEEE Access, 2025.
55. Al-Karaki, J.N., *Defense in depth: a multilayered approach.* Defense in Depth: Modern Cybersecurity Strategies and Evolving Threats, 2025: p. 51–72.
56. Arora, A., *Analyzing best practices and strategies for encrypting data at rest (Stored) and data in transit (transmitted) in cloud environments.* Available at SSRN 5268190, 2025.
57. Basharat, I., Azam, F., and Muzaffar, A.W., *Database security and encryption: a survey study.* International Journal of Computer Applications, 2012. **47**(12).

58. Dierks, T. and Rescorla, E., *The transport layer security (TLS) protocol version 1.2.* 2008.
59. Rescorla, E., *The transport layer security (TLS) protocol version 1.3.* 2018.
60. Jangam, S.K., *Importance of encrypting data in transit and at rest using TLS and other security protocols and API security Best practices.* International Journal of AI, BigData, Computational and Management Studies, 2023. **4**(3): p. 82–91.
61. Gentry, C., *Fully homomorphic encryption using ideal lattices*, in *Proceedings of the forty-first annual ACM symposium on theory of computing.* 2009.
62. Gentry, C., *A fully homomorphic encryption scheme.* 2009, Stanford University.
63. Aslett, L.J., Esperança, P.M., and Holmes, C.C., *A review of homomorphic encryption and software tools for encrypted statistical machine learning.* arXiv preprint arXiv:1508.06574, 2015.
64. Acar, A., Aksu, H., Uluagac, A.S., and Conti, M., *A survey on homomorphic encryption schemes: theory and implementation.* ACM Computing Surveys (Csur), 2018. **51**(4): p. 1–35.
65. Agrawal, M. and Mishra, P., *A comparative survey on symmetric key encryption techniques.* International Journal on Computer Science and Engineering, 2012. **4**(5): p. 877.
66. Abdullah, A.M., *Advanced encryption standard (AES) algorithm to encrypt and decrypt data.* Cryptography and Network Security, 2017. **16**(1): p. 11.
67. Mohammed, Z.K., et al., *A metaverse framework for IoT-based remote patient monitoring and virtual consultations using AES-256 encryption.* Applied Soft Computing, 2024. **158**: p. 111588.
68. Alanazi, H., et al., *New comparative study between DES, 3DES and AES within nine factors.* arXiv preprint arXiv:1003.4085, 2010.
69. Banoth, R. and Regar, R., *Asymmetric key cryptography*, in *Classical and modern cryptography for beginners.* 2023, Springer. p. 109–165.
70. Sihotang, H.T., Efendi, S., Zamzami, E.M., and Mawengkang, H., *Design and implementation of Rivest Shamir Adleman's (RSA) cryptography algorithm in text file data security*, in *Journal of Physics: Conference Series.* 2020. IOP Publishing.
71. Yan, Y., *The overview of elliptic curve cryptography (ECC)*, in *Journal of Physics: Conference Series.* 2022. IOP Publishing.
72. He, D. and Zeadally, S., *An analysis of RFID authentication schemes for internet of things in healthcare environment using elliptic curve cryptography.* IEEE Internet of Things Journal, 2014. **2**(1): p. 72–83.
73. Green, M. and Ateniese, G., *Identity-based proxy re-encryption*, in *International Conference on Applied Cryptography and Network Security.* 2007. Springer.
74. Bethencourt, J., Sahai, A., and Waters, B., *Ciphertext-policy attribute-based encryption*, in *2007 IEEE Symposium on Security and Privacy (SP'07).* 2007. IEEE.
75. Satar, S.D.M., Hussin, M., Hanapi, Z.M., and Mohamed, M.A., *Cloud-based secure healthcare framework by using enhanced ciphertext policy attribute-based encryption scheme.* International Journal of Advanced Computer Science and Applications, 2021. **12**(6): p. 393–399.
76. Kruse, C.S., et al., *Telehealth and patient satisfaction: a systematic review and narrative analysis.* BMJ Open, 2017. **7**(8): p. e016242.
77. Kruse, C.S., Frederick, B., Jacobson, T., and Monticone, D.K., *Cybersecurity in healthcare: a systematic review of modern threats and trends.* Technology and Health Care, 2017. **25**(1): p. 1–10.
78. Al Kuwaiti, A., et al., *A review of the role of artificial intelligence in healthcare.* Journal of Personalized Medicine, 2023. **13**(6): p. 951.
79. Bamiah, M., Brohi, S., and Chuprat, S., *A study on significance of adopting cloud computing paradigm in healthcare sector*, in *2012 International Conference on Cloud Computing Technologies, Applications and Management (ICCCTAM).* 2012. IEEE.

80. Manvi, S.S. and Shyam, G.K., *Resource management for infrastructure as a service (IaaS) in cloud computing: a survey.* Journal of Network and Computer Applications, 2014. **41**: p. 424–440.
81. Faridi, F., Sarwar, H., Ahtisham, M., and Jamal, K., *Cloud computing approaches in health care.* Materials Today: Proceedings, 2022. **51**: p. 1217–1223.
82. Younis, R., et al., *A comprehensive analysis of cloud service models: IaaS, PaaS, and SaaS in the context of emerging technologies and trend*, in *2024 International Conference on Electrical, Communication and Computer Engineering (ICECCE).* 2024. IEEE.
83. Hussein, S., et al., *Recent developments in antibiotic resistance: an increasing threat to public health – a review.* Annals of Animal Science, 2025. **25**(3): p. 981–998.
84. Deb, M. and Choudhury, A., *Hybrid cloud: a new paradigm in cloud computing.* Machine Learning Techniques and Analytics for Cloud Security, 2021: p. 1–23.
85. Al-Ofeishat, H.A. and Alshorman, R., *Build a secure network using segmentation and micro-segmentation techniques.* International Journal of Computing and Digital Systems, 2023. **14**(1): p. 1–16.
86. Kallatsa, M., *Strategies for network segmentation: a systematic literature review.* 2024.
87. Halman, L.M. and Alenazi, M.J., *MCAD: a machine learning based cyberattacks detector in Software-Defined Networking (SDN) for healthcare systems.* IEEE Access, 2023. **11**: p. 37052–37067.
88. Alsuwaidi, N., Alharmoodi, N., and Al Hamadi, H., *The transformative impact of zero-trust architecture on healthcare security*, in *2024 2nd International Conference on Cyber Resilience (ICCR).* 2024. IEEE.
89. Deshpande, S. and Damle, M., *Enhancing IoT security: A pursuit of excellence through the NIST 800-53 cybersecurity framework*, in *2025 Seventh International Conference on Computational Intelligence and Communication Technologies (CCICT).* 2025. IEEE.
90. Sutradhar, S., et al., *Enhancing identity and access management using hyperledger fabric and OAuth 2.0: a block-chain-based approach for security and scalability for healthcare industry.* Internet of Things and Cyber-Physical Systems, 2024. **4**: p. 49–67.
91. Sammartino, V. and Baiardi, F., *Database decomposition to satisfy the least privilege principle in healthcare.* ARIS2-Advanced Research on Information Systems Security, 2024. **4**(1): p. 47–69.
92. Butt, A.U.R., et al., *An optimized role-based access control using trust mechanism in e-health cloud environment.* IEEE Access, 2023. **11**: p. 138813–138826.
93. de Carvalho Junior, M.A. and Bandiera-Paiva, P., *Health information system role-based access control current security trends and challenges.* Journal of Healthcare Engineering, 2018. **2018**(1): p. 6510249.
94. Barhoun, R., Ed-Daibouni, M., and Namir, A., *An extended attribute-based access control (ABAC) model for distributed collaborative healthcare system.* International journal of service science, Management, Engineering, and Technology (IJSSMET), 2019. **10**(4): p. 81–94.
95. Ometov, A., et al., *Multi-factor authentication: a survey.* Cryptography, 2018. **2**(1): p. 1.
96. Jimmy, F., *Emerging threats: the latest cybersecurity risks and the role of artificial intelligence in enhancing cybersecurity defenses.* Valley International Journal Digital Library, 2021. **1**: p. 564–74.
97. Sultan, M.S. and Sultan, M.S., *Leveraging artificial intelligence for enhanced cybersecurity: a systematic approach.* International Journal of Science and Research (IJSR), 2024. **13**(8): p. 832–839.

98. Chandola, V., Banerjee, A., and Kumar, V., *Anomaly detection: a survey.* ACM Computing Surveys (CSUR), 2009. **41**(3): p. 1–58.
99. Pang, G., Shen, C., Cao, L., and Hengel, A.V.D., *Deep learning for anomaly detection: a review.* ACM Computing Surveys (CSUR), 2021. **54**(2): p. 1–38.
100. Ucci, D., Aniello, L., and Baldoni, R., *Survey of machine learning techniques for malware analysis.* Computers & Security, 2019. **81**: p. 123–147.
101. Fakhouri, H. N., et al., *Ai-driven solutions for social engineering attacks: Detection, prevention, and response*, in *2024 2nd International Conference on Cyber Resilience (ICCR).* 2024. IEEE.
102. Boda, V.V.R. and Allam, H., *Automating compliance in healthcare: tools and techniques you need.* International Journal of Emerging Trends in Computer Science and Information Technology, 2021. **2**(3): p. 38–48.
103. Gkoulalas-Divanis, A. and Loukides, G., *Medical data privacy handbook.* 2015, Springer.
104. Sandhu, R.S. and Samarati, P., *Access control: principle and practice.* IEEE Communications Magazine, 2002. **32**(9): p. 40–48.
105. Adesokan-Imran, T.O., et al., *Predictive cybersecurity risk modeling in healthcare by leveraging AI and machine learning for proactive threat detection.* Journal of Engineering Research and Reports, 2025. **27**(4): p. 144–165.
106. Jacobs, J., Romanosky, S., Adjerid, I., and Baker, W., *Improving vulnerability remediation through better exploit prediction.* Journal of Cybersecurity, 2020. **6**(1): p. tyaa015.
107. Szegedy, C., et al., *Intriguing properties of neural networks.* arXiv preprint arXiv: 1312.6199, 2013.
108. Shokri, R., Stronati, M., Song, C., and Shmatikov, V., *Membership inference attacks against machine learning models*, in *2017 IEEE Symposium on Security and Privacy (SP).* 2017. IEEE.
109. Tramèr, F., et al., *Stealing machine learning models via prediction (APIs)*, in *25th USENIX security symposium (USENIX Security 16).* 2016.
110. Rajora, K., *Reviews research on applying machine learning techniques to reduce false positives for network intrusion detection systems.* Babylonian Journal of Machine Learning, 2023. **2023**: p. 26–30.
111. Pietraszek, T., *Using adaptive alert classification to reduce false positives in intrusion detection*, in *International workshop on recent advances in intrusion detection.* 2004, Springer.
112. Castelvecchi, D., *Can we open the black box of AI?* Nature News, 2016. **538**(7623): p. 20.
113. Von Eschenbach, W.J., *Transparency and the black box problem: why we do not trust AI.* Philosophy & Technology, 2021. **34**(4): p. 1607–1622.
114. Sweeney, L., *k-anonymity: a model for protecting privacy.* International Journal of Uncertainty, Fuzziness and Knowledge-Based Systems, 2002. **10**(05): p. 557–570.
115. Rocher, L., Hendrickx, J.M., and De Montjoye, Y.-A., *Estimating the success of re-identifications in incomplete datasets using generative models.* Nature Communications, 2019. **10**(1): p. 3069.
116. Zimmer, E., Burkert, C., Petersen, T., and Federrath, H., *PEEPLL: privacy-enhanced event pseudonymisation with limited linkability*, in *Proceedings of the 35th annual ACM symposium on applied computing.* 2020.
117. Samarati, P. and Sweeney, L., *Protecting privacy when disclosing information: k-anonymity and its enforcement through generalization and suppression.* 1998.
118. Iyengar, V.S., *Transforming data to satisfy privacy constraints*, in *Proceedings of the eighth ACM SIGKDD international conference on Knowledge discovery and data mining.* 2002.
119. Kargupta, H., Datta, S., Wang, Q., and Sivakumar, K., *On the privacy preserving properties of random data perturbation techniques*, in *Third IEEE International Conference on Data Mining.* 2003. IEEE.

120. Fredrikson, M., Jha, S., and Ristenpart, T., *Model inversion attacks that exploit confidence information and basic countermeasures*, in *Proceedings of the 22nd ACM SIGSAC conference on computer and communications security*. 2015.
121. Carlini, N., et al., *The secret sharer: evaluating and testing unintended memorization in neural networks*, in *28th USENIX security symposium (USENIX security 19)*. 2019.
122. Machanavajjhala, A., Kifer, D., Gehrke, J., and Venkitasubramaniam, M., l-diversity: privacy *beyond k-anonymity*. ACM Transactions on Knowledge Discovery from Data (tkdd), 2007. **1**(1): p. 3-es.
123. Dwork, C., *Differential privacy*, in *International colloquium on automata, languages, and programming*. 2006, Springer.
124. Dwork, C., McSherry, F., Nissim, K., and Smith, A., *Calibrating noise to sensitivity in private data analysis*, in *Theory of Cryptography Conference*. 2006. Springer.
125. Dwork, C., *Differential privacy: A survey of results*, in *International Conference on Theory and Applications of Models of Computation*. 2008. Springer.
126. Abadi, M., et al., *Deep learning with differential privacy*, in *Proceedings of the 2016 ACM SIGSAC conference on computer and communications security*. 2016.
127. Adler-Milstein, J. and Jha, A.K., *HITECH act drove large gains in hospital electronic health record adoption*. Health Affairs, 2017. **36**(8): p. 1416–1422.
128. Regulation, P., *General data protection regulation*. Intouch, 2018. **25**: p. 1–5.
129. Kaye, J., et al., *Dynamic consent: a patient interface for twenty-first century research networks*. European Journal of Human Genetics, 2015. **23**(2): p. 141–146.
130. Khatri, V. and Brown, C.V., *Designing data governance*. Communications of the ACM, 2010. **53**(1): p. 148–152.
131. Chamola, V., et al., *A review of trustworthy and explainable artificial intelligence (XAI)*. IEEe Access, 2023. **11**: p. 78994–79015.
132. Obermeyer, Z., Powers, B., Vogeli, C., and Mullainathan, S., *Dissecting racial bias in an algorithm used to manage the health of populations*. Science, 2019. **366**(6464): p. 447–453.
133. Panch, T., Mattie, H., and Atun, R., *Artificial intelligence and algorithmic bias: implications for health systems*. Journal of Global Health, 2019. **9**(2): p. 020318.
134. Giovanola, B. and Tiribelli, S., *Beyond bias and discrimination: redefining the AI ethics principle of fairness in healthcare machine-learning algorithms*. AI & Society, 2023. **38**(2): p. 549–563.
135. Althubaiti, A., *Information bias in health research: definition, pitfalls, and adjustment methods*. Journal of Multidisciplinary Healthcare, 2016: p. 211–217.
136. Ueda, D., et al., *Fairness of artificial intelligence in healthcare: review and recommendations*. Japanese Journal of Radiology, 2024. **42**(1): p. 3–15.
137. Chen, I.Y., et al., *Ethical machine learning in healthcare*. Annual Review of Biomedical Data Science, 2021. **4**(1): p. 123–144.
138. Gerke, S., Minssen, T., and Cohen, G., *Ethical and legal challenges of artificial intelligence-driven healthcare*, in *Artificial intelligence in healthcare*. 2020, Elsevier. p. 295–336.
139. Price, W.N., *Big data and black-box medical algorithms*. Science Translational Medicine, 2018. **10**(471): p. eaao5333.
140. Hassija, V., et al., *Interpreting black-box models: a review on explainable artificial intelligence*. Cognitive Computation, 2024. **16**(1): p. 45–74.
141. Ghassemi, M., Oakden-Rayner, L., and Beam, A.L., *The false hope of current approaches to explainable artificial intelligence in health care*. The Lancet Digital Health, 2021. **3**(11): p. e745–e750.
142. Hulsen, T., *Explainable artificial intelligence (XAI): concepts and challenges in healthcare*. AI, 2023. **4**(3): p. 652–666.

143. Madsen, A., Reddy, S., and Chandar, S., *Post-hoc interpretability for neural NLP: a survey*. ACM Computing Surveys, 2022. **55**(8): p. 1–42.
144. Zafar, M.R. and Khan N.M., *DLIME: A deterministic local interpretable model-agnostic explanations approach for computer-aided diagnosis systems*. arXiv preprint arXiv:1906.10263, 2019.
145. Ribeiro, M.T., Singh,S., and Guestrin, C., *Model-agnostic interpretability of machine learning*. arXiv preprint arXiv:1606.05386, 2016.
146. Nohara, Y., Matsumoto, K., Soejima, H., and Nakashima, N., *Explanation of machine learning models using shapley additive explanation and application for real data in hospital*. Computer Methods and Programs in Biomedicine, 2022. **214**: p. 106584.
147. Lundberg, S.M. and Lee, S.-I., *A unified approach to interpreting model predictions*. Advances in Neural Information Processing Systems, 2017.
148. Arun, N., et al., *Assessing the trustworthiness of saliency maps for localizing abnormalities in medical imaging*. Radiology: Artificial Intelligence, 2021. **3**(6): p. e200267.
149. Lai, T., *Interpretable medical imagery diagnosis with self-attentive transformers: a review of explainable AI for health care*. BioMedInformatics, 2024. **4**(1): p. 113–126.
150. Zhang, C.A., Cho, S., and Vasarhelyi, M., *Explainable artificial intelligence (XAI) in auditing*. International Journal of Accounting Information Systems, 2022. **46**: p. 100572.
151. Mittelstadt, B., Russell, C., and Wachter, S., *Explaining explanations in AI*, in Proceedings of the conference on fairness, accountability, and transparency. 2019.
152. McMahan, B., et al., *Communication-efficient learning of deep networks from decentralized data*, in *Artificial intelligence and statistics*. 2017, PMLR.
153. Li, L., Fan, Y., Tse, M., and Lin, K.-Y., *A review of applications in federated learning*. Computers & Industrial Engineering, 2020. **149**: p. 106854.
154. Zhang, C., et al., *A survey on federated learning*. Knowledge-Based Systems, 2021. **216**: p. 106775.
155. Bonawitz, K., et al., *Practical secure aggregation for privacy-preserving machine learning*, in *Proceedings of the 2017 ACM SIGSAC conference on computer and communications security*. 2017.
156. Konečný, J., et al., *Federated learning: strategies for improving communication efficiency*. arXiv preprint arXiv:1610.05492, 2016.
157. Rieke, N., et al., *The future of digital health with federated learning*. NPJ Digital Medicine, 2020. **3**(1): p. 119.
158. Dayan, I., et al., *Federated learning for predicting clinical outcomes in patients with COVID-19*. Nature Medicine, 2021. **27**(10): p. 1735–1743.
159. Sohan, M.F. and Basalamah, A., *A systematic review on federated learning in medical image analysis*. IEEE Access, 2023. **11**: p. 28628–28644.
160. Xu, J., et al., *Federated learning for healthcare informatics*. Journal of Healthcare Informatics Research, 2021. **5**(1): p. 1–19.
161. Hesamifard, E., Takabi, H., and Ghasemi, M., *Cryptodl: deep neural networks over encrypted data*. arXiv preprint arXiv:1711.05189, 2017.
162. Ryu, J., Kim, K., and Won, D., *A study on partially homomorphic encryption*, in *2023 17th International Conference on Ubiquitous Information Management and Communication (IMCOM)*. 2023. IEEE.
163. Subramaniyaswamy, V., et al., *Somewhat homomorphic encryption: ring learning with error algorithm for faster encryption of IoT sensor signal-based edge devices*. Security and Communication Networks, 2022. **2022**(1): p. 2793998.
164. Fan, J. and Vercauteren, F., *Somewhat practical fully homomorphic encryption*. Cryptology ePrint Archive, 2012.

165. Brakerski, Z. and Vaikuntanathan, V., *Fully homomorphic encryption from ring-LWE and security for key dependent messages*, in *Annual Cryptology Conference*. 2011. Springer.
166. Cheon, J.H., Kim,A., Kim, M., and Song, Y., *Homomorphic encryption for arithmetic of approximate numbers*, in *International Conference on the Theory and Application of Cryptology and Information Security*. 2017. Springer.
167. Lyubashevsky, V., Peikert, C., and Regev, O., *On ideal lattices and learning with errors over rings*, in *Annual International Conference on the Theory and Applications of Cryptographic Techniques*. 2010. Springer.
168. Zhao, C., et al., *Secure multi-party computation: theory, practice and applications*. Information Sciences, 2019. **476**: p. 357–372.
169. Zhou, I., et al., *Secure multi-party computation for machine learning: a survey*. IEEE Access, 2024. **12**: p. 53881–53899.
170. Beaulieu-Jones, B.K., et al., *Privacy-preserving generative deep neural networks support clinical data sharing*. Circulation: Cardiovascular Quality and Outcomes, 2019. **12**(7): p. e005122.
171. Goodfellow, I.J., et al., *Generative adversarial nets*. Advances in Neural Information Processing Systems, 2014.
172. Goodfellow, I., et al., *Generative adversarial networks*. Communications of the ACM, 2020. **63**(11): p. 139–144.
173. Kingma, D. and Welling, M., *Auto-encoding variational bayes*. arXiv preprint arXiv:1312.6114, 2013.
174. Ho, J., Jain, A., and Abbeel, P., *Denoising diffusion probabilistic models*. Advances in Neural Information Processing Systems, 2020. **33**: p. 6840–6851.

# 4 Risk Management and Safety Protocols for AI Systems

*Mohammad Zareinejad and Parisa Tavana*

## 4.1 INTRODUCTION

Healthcare systems are complex and dynamic structures in which human factors, the physical environment, medical technologies, and quality of care interact within an interconnected network [1]. Any disruption in this network can jeopardize patient safety [2]. Patient safety—defined as "the avoidance of preventable harm and the reduction of unnecessary risks associated with healthcare to an acceptable level" [3]—is one of the fundamental principles of healthcare and a basic right of patients. According to the World Health Organization (WHO), the likelihood of a patient being harmed during treatment is approximately 1 in 300, whereas the probability of an aviation accident is only 1 in 1,000,000 [3]. This comparison clearly highlights that even the smallest error in a clinical environment can lead to irreversible consequences.

In the past decade, the emergence of artificial intelligence (AI) and machine learning (ML) has opened new horizons in diagnosis and clinical decision support (CDS) [4]. Leveraging large-scale data and statistical methods, these technologies have demonstrated remarkable effectiveness in areas such as medical image interpretation, analysis of electronic health records (EHRs), and treatment optimization [5]. However, as AI becomes increasingly pervasive in healthcare systems, its potential risks are also becoming more apparent [6]. Model errors or malfunctions may result in physical harm or even death. Likewise, the leakage of sensitive data or biased decision-making can severely undermine public trust. Therefore, the need for structured frameworks for risk management and ensuring the safety of AI systems is now more critical than ever.

One of the key pillars of quality of care is clinical risk management, a structured process that encompasses tools, procedures, and both preventive and corrective actions to identify, monitor, and mitigate potential hazards in the clinical environment [7]. Common tools include incident reporting [8], clinical record reviews [9], safety walk-arounds [3], and analysis of administrative data or patient complaints [10]. These methods enable the early detection of issues that may lead to adverse events affecting patients or healthcare staff.

In this context, AI can serve both as a tool for enhancing safety and as a source of new risks. In clinical applications, AI systems—particularly through CDS systems—can integrate and analyze patient data to assist physicians in making complex decisions [11]. This functionality has been facilitated by the expansion of electronic medical records (EMR) and computerized physician order entry (CPOE) systems [12]. Moreover, natural

DOI: 10.1201/9781003743422-4

language processing (NLP) can prepare unstructured data, such as clinical notes, for analysis by ML models [13], while Internet of Medical Things (IoMT) networks provide a continuous flow of biometric data [14].

Numerous studies have demonstrated that the use of AI can enhance the quality of care [15], although significant technical, regulatory, and ethical limitations remain [16]. Consequently, while much of future innovation will occur in industry and healthcare services, academic research has yet to establish standardized frameworks for the safety and validation of such systems [17]. As a result, developers may produce intelligent systems that are technically advanced but potentially hazardous from a safety standpoint.

To bridge this gap, scientific findings and field experiences must be translated into practical guidelines for designers, regulators, and users of AI systems. In this regard, lessons can be drawn from safety-critical industries such as medical device manufacturing or aerospace [18]. Formal frameworks like the NIST[1] AI Risk Management Framework provide practical tools for identifying, prioritizing, and mitigating risks [19]. These frameworks are structured around the system life cycle and offer clear guidance for design, evaluation, and continuous monitoring. Similarly, international documents—such as the WHO's guidance on the ethics and governance of AI—emphasize the fundamental principles of fairness, transparency, accountability, and data protection.

Despite these advancements, the increasing use of AI in real-world environments introduces new types of risks [20]. Recent reports of incidents caused by autonomous decision-making in intelligent systems (including fatal accidents involving self-driving cars [21]) demonstrate that AI safety remains an open and challenging issue. Therefore, developing safe AI systems requires a deep understanding of the components of trustworthy AI [22, 23] and alignment of risk management strategies with their unique nature. Identifying emerging risks and analyzing how AI's distinctive features affect risk models represent the first steps toward the design of effective health policy frameworks.

Currently, international standards related to AI are still evolving and often address only specific aspects such as explainability [24] or controllability [25], while many of these guidelines remain incompatible with high-sensitivity clinical environments [26]. On the other hand, legal instruments such as the EU AI Act define broader requirements for high-risk systems, including medical applications [27]. From a policy perspective, the adoption of the AI Act in the European Union marks a major step toward transparent regulation of high-risk systems, particularly in the medical domain. These developments illustrate that the implementation of AI in healthcare is not merely a technical challenge but a multifaceted process requiring deep risk awareness, scientific validation, and robust governance mechanisms.

Therefore, the aim of this chapter is to provide a comprehensive framework of technical, operational, and policy solutions that developers, clinical specialists, healthcare managers, and regulators can use to mitigate risks and ensure patient safety in the implementation of clinical AI. The outcomes of these efforts would lay the foundation for establishing a permanent institution dedicated to the development, evaluation, and dissemination of AI safety standards in healthcare. In this chapter, the nature and various dimensions of AI-related risks in healthcare systems are first examined, including clinical, technical, security, legal, and social risks. Then, by leveraging modern risk management frameworks and international standards such as ISO 14971[2] and NIST's AI RMF[3], solutions are proposed for identifying, assessing, and mitigating these risks. Next, methodologies for clinical risk assessment and validation mechanisms for AI-based systems are discussed. Finally, the chapter concludes with a set of safety protocols and operational strategies to ensure safe, transparent, and reliable performance of AI systems in clinical environments.

## 4.2 CLASSIFICATION OF AI-RELATED RISKS IN HEALTHCARE

The implementation of AI in healthcare promises to improve the quality of care and reduce costs [28]. Alongside these significant opportunities, a diverse set of risks also emerges. Errors in diagnosis, data deficiencies, and cyberattacks can all jeopardize patient safety [29]. Therefore, a comprehensive classification and assessment of risks is a prerequisite for the responsible development and deployment of AI technologies in healthcare systems. In this section, to create a coherent understanding of the threats that AI systems face in healthcare, five main categories are proposed. These categories include clinical/patient safety risks, technical risks, security risks, legal/compliance risks, and social/ethical risks, as illustrated in Figure 4.1. Each of these domains presents unique challenges and opportunities, and neglecting one domain can undermine the effectiveness of the others.

### 4.2.1 Clinical and Patient Safety Risks

AI systems, through ML algorithms, can exhibit more complex behaviors than conventional diagnostic tools [30]; however, diagnostic errors and adverse outcomes

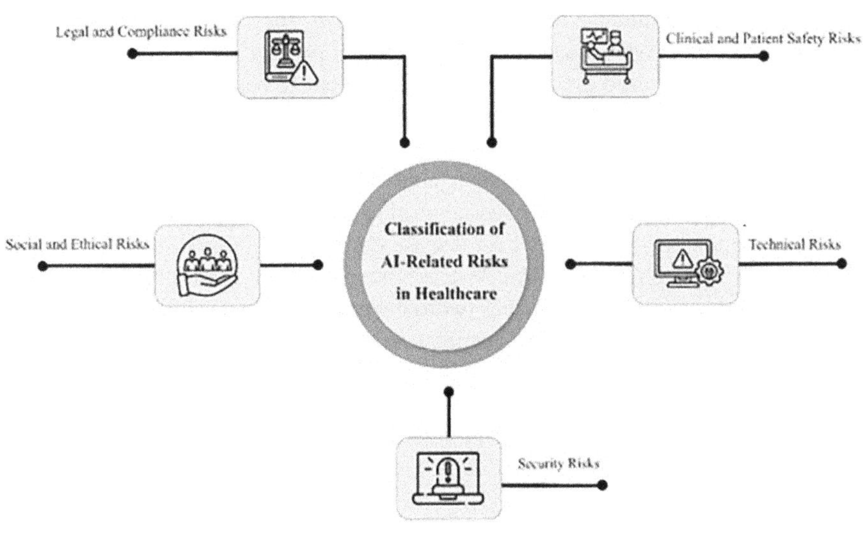


**FIGURE 4.1** Classification of AI-related risks in healthcare, including clinical, technical, security, legal/compliance, and social/ethical categories.

remain a primary concern [31]. AI systems may suffer from overfitting due to deficiencies in training data or insufficient generalizability [32], meaning they learn patterns that exist only in the training dataset. Such models can perform unpredictably when encountering new patients, potentially leading to incorrect predictions.

Additionally, reports of serious errors, such as "hallucinations" or the generation of unfounded outputs in language models, have been documented. These errors can result in incorrect medical recommendations, and if deployed without human oversight, they pose a risk to patient safety [33].

Currently, AI is applied in clinical practice to stratify risk in patients undergoing coronary CT angiography (CTCA), integrating prognostic models with information on coronary plaques and clinical risk factors [34, 35]. Recent evidence indicates that guiding preventive treatments based on this AI-based risk assessment strategy—applied in routine CTCA—has led to changes in management decisions in approximately 45% of patients undergoing this test. This approach is particularly useful for patients with no or minimal coronary atherosclerosis [36].

Alongside cardiovascular applications, microbiological studies have shown that risk management in AI is not limited to computational errors but also relates to the interpretation of genetic and infectious disease data [37]. In a recent study [38] conducted in the intensive care units (ICU) of a university hospital in China, patterns of antifungal resistance in *Candida glabrata* were examined. The results indicated that among *C. glabrata* isolates, cross-resistance to multiple antifungal drugs exists, posing a significant challenge for treating critically ill patients. The study found that the sequence type (ST type) did not show a meaningful association with drug resistance patterns, but it was correlated with the geographical distribution of samples. Furthermore, researchers identified novel mutations in the FKS1 and FKS2 genes, which are associated with high-level resistance to echinocandins. The authors emphasized that these findings highlight the need for continuous and systematic monitoring in ICU and provide valuable information for improving the management of infectious risks in hospitals. From a clinical risk management perspective, such data can serve as the basis for AI-based predictive models that analyze patterns of drug resistance and genetic mutations, playing an important role in preventing the spread of resistant infections [39].

In another recent study [40] aiming to apply Ensemble Learning methods in clinical risk assessment, the SuperLearner algorithm was used to predict liver fibrosis in patients with non-alcoholic fatty liver disease (NAFLD). In this research, data from 648 patients in the NASH Clinical Research Network were used to train the model, and validation was performed using two independent datasets: the FLINT clinical trial (270 patients) and the NHANES database (1,244 NAFLD patients). The model was trained using 23 clinical and demographic variables. The results demonstrated that the SuperLearner model outperformed conventional models such as FIB-4, APRI, Forns, BARD, and NAFLD Fibrosis Score in detecting significant fibrosis. The AUC values were reported as 0.79 for FLINT and 0.74 for NHANES, indicating high discriminative power. Additionally, the SAFE[4] model showed similar performance to SuperLearner, and both models outperformed other existing approaches. Overall, this study suggests that the SuperLearner algorithm can serve as a reference tool for evaluating and comparing risk prediction models in clinical settings, contributing to improved diagnostic accuracy and clinical decision-making, particularly in patients with NAFLD.

Clinical risks are also related to fatigue and over-reliance on automated systems. Automation bias occurs when a clinician accepts a system's recommendation without considering clinical context, even when other evidence contradicts it [41]. Conversely, algorithmic aversion can lead to ignoring correct system recommendations due to user distrust, potentially harming the patient. These two extremes highlight that striking a balance between human oversight and technology use is critical.

### 4.2.2 Technical Risks

Technical risks pertain to infrastructure, data quality, model stability, and generalizability. If training data are incomplete, biased, or lack diversity, the model cannot perform reliably in real-world settings [42]. Predictive models may also be optimized for the conditions of a specific hospital or population; applying them in a different context—e.g., a model trained on cardiac patients in a heart hospital being used in a cancer center—can lead to generalization errors. A recent review of AI's role in managing technical risks has shown that AI can act as a transformative tool for predicting and mitigating potential hazards across various industries [43–45]. By leveraging ML algorithms, data analysis, and predictive modeling, AI enables the identification, assessment, and mitigation of technical failures with unprecedented accuracy and efficiency.

A review of the research literature on AI-related risks shows that quality assurance measures for AI systems focus heavily on identifying and addressing fundamental system issues [46]. The study [47] serves as a notable example, presenting a comprehensive set of measures to ensure the safety and integrity of AI systems. These measures align with risk sources identified in prior studies and address key technical challenges. Furthermore, an examination of legal documents and international standards—including the draft EU regulations, ISO/IEC standards, and reports from the European Commission's high-level expert group—indicates that the requirements outlined in these documents correspond closely with the identified technical risks. Comparing these sources allows for an assessment of the completeness of risk coverage.

Regarding infrastructure issues, attacks occur when malicious actors manipulate medical devices to produce fake medical data, potentially endangering patient safety. To address this security concern, study [48] investigated a vulnerability in the design flow of biochip devices, where attackers could manipulate samples via DoS attacks, hardware malware, and forgery. They developed a user-defined algorithm that efficiently allocates review points for error recovery, thereby enhancing the security of microfluidic biochips. The results demonstrated that this algorithm outperformed baseline methods in terms of computational complexity and error detection rate. Additionally, authors [49, 50] examined security issues related to IoT device attacks in healthcare systems and proposed a multilayered framework in which hardware-based cryptographic algorithms are integrated to optimize security and ensure privacy. The results showed that this framework outperforms other methods in energy consumption, computation time, and processing rate.

In another study [51], a recent review of ML software development projects revealed that these projects face new technical risks rarely or never observed in traditional software projects. The study methodology included a literature review to compile an initial list of technical risk factors, followed by two rounds of a modified Delphi process involving 17 ML experts to assess the completeness and validity of these factors. Based on this review, a hierarchical structure consisting of five categories of technical risks and 22 technical risk factors was developed for analytic hierarchy process (AHP) analysis. Three rounds of online AHP questionnaires were conducted, and consistency ratio (CR) and quartile deviation (QD) were used to evaluate the validity of responses and the level of agreement among participants. The results indicated that the category "Data Availability and Quality" had the highest priority in terms of severity, probability, and impact compared to other technical risk categories. Furthermore, all four technical risk factors associated with this category ranked in the top four positions for impact.

Overall, preventing data drift or distribution drift requires continuous monitoring and model updates. Guideline frameworks such as FUTURE-AI recommend that developers maintain a risk management dossier for each AI product, identify risks, assess their probability and severity, define mitigation measures, and periodically monitor their effectiveness. This process includes repeated performance testing, retraining models when patient populations change, and logging unexpected events to ensure the accuracy and reliability of the algorithm.

### 4.2.3 Security Risks

Today, most traditional healthcare systems are connected to each other via the Internet to provide widespread medical services such as telemedicine, remote diagnostics, and patient information systems [52]. This connectivity has saved many lives before conditions worsen, reduced global healthcare costs, and consequently improved people's quality of life. However, connecting medical services or devices to open-access networks, that is, the Internet, carries inevitable security and privacy implications, as these devices are exposed to various attacks, including denial-of-service (DoS) attacks, tampering with patient information systems, and malware intrusions that can disrupt entire healthcare networks. Healthcare AI systems rely on large volumes of patient data, making these data highly attractive targets for cyberattacks [53]. Data breaches or database theft can cause irreparable damage to patient privacy and erode public trust. According to the HIPAA[5] Journal, the number of major security breaches in healthcare has increased significantly in recent years, with 168 million records compromised in 2023 [54]. In 2024, a ransomware attack on Change Healthcare led to unauthorized access to the data of 190 million individuals, further increasing the number of stolen records [55].

In study [56], a comprehensive review of the latest security challenges and mitigation strategies in smart healthcare environments is presented. Additionally, a secure AI- and blockchain-based architecture is proposed to analyze malware and network attacks on wearable devices. The performance of this architecture was evaluated using metrics such as blockchain scalability, accuracy, and dynamic malware analysis. Finally, the study highlights open issues and research challenges facing AI-driven healthcare systems.

In addition, healthcare systems possess numerous physical assets, such as oxygen cylinders, nebulizers, wheelchairs, oxygen measurement devices, cardiac monitors, personal protective equipment, and surgical instruments, which must be properly managed to allow easy tracking of their quantity and location during emergencies [57]. IoT-based healthcare asset management enables rapid tracking of these assets. For example, in a study [58] conducted during the global COVID-19 pandemic, the need for advanced medical facilities within a short timeframe was examined. To address this, an IoT-based monitoring architecture was proposed, incorporating hybrid communications, large-scale medical screening, and cloud data centers to support hospitals, emergency teams, and first aid units. Furthermore, study [59] developed an IoT-based healthcare management system with edge capabilities aimed at improving patient data monitoring, diagnosis, and management. This system monitors various medical tasks and manages diverse care activities using database systems; however, due to its centralized storage, it remains vulnerable to intrusion by attackers.

Therefore, given that the healthcare domain is constantly exposed to threats and malicious activity, the use of blockchain technology facilitates secure patient data exchange, prevention of disruptions, and effective management of medical resources. In study [60], a blockchain-based smart healthcare system was proposed to protect the privacy of users across healthcare systems. This system employs various types of smart contracts for data transaction validation, access control, and decision-making within an open network. Additionally, differential privacy (DP) mechanisms are used to preserve user privacy. The results indicate that this proposed framework outperforms other methods in terms of system reliability, stability, and traceability.

Recent legal proposals to strengthen HIPAA security law include requirements for data encryption at rest and in transit, conducting comprehensive risk analyses, and implementing periodic audits to ensure organizational readiness against cyber threats. In addition, some reports emphasize that AI models may retain sensitive inputs in memory, and without proper safeguards, this information could leak [61]. The use of federated learning and DP techniques can render data untraceable and reduce the risk of leaks. Furthermore, study [62] proposed a secure and trustworthy blockchain-based framework to address security attacks in EHR systems, employing private blockchain and swarm intelligence methods to ensure safe data exchange in IoT networks. The study [63] also examined the use of blockchain in managing diabetes care, especially during the COVID-19 pandemic. Through blockchain, healthcare resources—including hospital beds, oxygen, insulin pumps, telemedicine services, and continuous monitoring systems for diabetic patients most affected by the pandemic—were prioritized. They used blockchain-based technologies such as InterPlanetary File Systems (IPFS), smart contracts, and modern economic approaches for encrypting and authenticating patient data and developed a Proof-of-Concept model. The proposed system demonstrated notable performance in terms of transaction speed, transaction cost, and energy consumption.

### 4.2.4 Legal and Compliance Risks

For responsible use of AI in compliance, organizations must take preventive measures, including establishing transparent governance frameworks, implementing AI ethical guidelines, and adhering to data protection laws [64]. These actions not only prevent fines and legal claims but also enhance trust in AI technologies in sensitive environments. The deployment of AI in healthcare is governed by a set of international and national regulations. In the European Union, the AI Act classifies medical systems as high-risk, including medical software, remote diagnostic tools, and insurance risk assessment systems [27]. Providers of high-risk systems must establish a risk management system throughout their life cycle, ensure data quality and proper representation, provide technical documentation, maintain records for risk identification, and design systems to allow human oversight. These requirements also emphasize accuracy, robustness, and cybersecurity. In the United States, regulations such as HIPAA mandate the protection of health data privacy. If companies fail to update models or monitor potential errors, they may be held legally liable. Many states have also enacted requirements for disclosure, bias mitigation, and transparency in AI usage [65].

In study [66], the use of AI within health governance frameworks is presented as an innovative approach for risk management and compliance monitoring. The research shows that traditional health governance frameworks are struggling to keep pace with increasing regulatory complexity, growing data volumes, and operational risk reduction in rapidly evolving technology environments. In this study, a novel computational architecture is proposed for dynamic risk classification and compliance monitoring, utilizing multilayer neural networks combined with reinforcement learning mechanisms. The proposed framework also employs advanced probabilistic reasoning systems that continuously evaluate governance indicators against compliance thresholds while simultaneously adapting to emerging regulatory requirements. Empirical validation across 17 healthcare systems demonstrated that this approach significantly outperformed traditional monitoring methods in predicting compliance violations (sensitivity 87.3%, specificity 92.1% vs. sensitivity 64.5%, specificity 71.8%). Implementation of this system led to a 42.6% reduction in governance-related adverse events and a 31.4% reduction in regulatory fines among participating institutions.

A legal review of AI in healthcare reveals that existing legal frameworks are adapting slowly to emerging AI technologies and often cannot fully address the unique challenges posed by these systems. One key issue is the ambiguity of liability for AI-driven clinical decisions. In traditional healthcare systems, decisions are generally made by humans, and responsibility is clear. However, when AI is involved in decision-making or supports medical decisions, it is uncertain who is responsible for the outcomes. Moreover, healthcare organizations must simultaneously navigate these legal ambiguities while complying with existing regulations, including data protection laws such as HIPAA in the United States and the AI Act in the European Union, which impose strict requirements for managing personal health information. Compliance with these regulations is essential, but given the rapidly evolving nature of AI technologies and potential gaps in legal frameworks, it remains a challenging task.

### 4.2.5 Social and Ethical Risks

In addition to technical and legal threats, AI faces profound social and ethical questions. If training data are not representative of diverse populations, discriminatory patterns can emerge [67]. For example, triage and resource allocation systems trained on historical data may place minority patients or patients with socioeconomic disadvantages lower in treatment priority. Speech recognition algorithms may fail to correctly interpret different accents, resulting in errors. Hidden biases may appear "scientific," suggesting fair decisions, but in reality, they reproduce structural inequalities.

A review of AI applications in digital health revealed that while this technology has significant potential to improve medical services, it also raises privacy concerns and ethical considerations that necessitate the development of a responsible AI framework [68]. According to this framework, AI systems should be considered as part of socio-technical systems, and their development should be managed with attention to social and ethical consequences. In study [69], a two-pronged systematic review (SR) was employed: one part (SR1) involved an extensive review of recent scientific literature (2021–2023) to capture the latest developments and debates. The second part (SR2) involved a focused review of previous systematic and scoping reviews on AI ethics in healthcare over a longer timeframe (2014–2024) to identify recurring trends and issues. This approach enabled a comprehensive analysis, examining both the depth and evolution of the literature. Results show that SR1 highlights the diversity of audiences, medical contexts, and social and ethical issues raised by AI systems, as well as conflicts among them, while SR2 provides a broader view of how scoping reviews conceptualize AI ethics and social issues, identifying trends and gaps in the field. Overall, our analysis indicates that the commonly used approach based solely on general ethical principles is insufficient to fully capture the complexity and specific characteristics of social and ethical issues arising from AI in healthcare, especially when technology moves from theoretical discussion to real-world clinical application.

In summary, AI in healthcare has the potential to improve medical services, but without human oversight and responsible AI frameworks, the risk of reproducing discrimination and social inequities remains. Systematic review findings indicate that current ethical approaches are insufficient, and the development of AI systems must simultaneously consider social impacts and real-world clinical applications.

To summarize the risk classification in Section 2, Table 4.1 presents the types of risks, along with descriptions, clinical examples, and proposed risk mitigation strategies.

## 4.3 CLINICAL RISK ASSESSMENT METHODOLOGY FOR AI

Every diagnostic or predictive algorithm should be used based on scientific criteria, alongside human supervision and ethical frameworks, to prevent unintended harm. International standards such as ISO 14971 define risk as a combination of the likelihood of occurrence and the severity of consequences, emphasizing the integration of risk management throughout the entire product life cycle. This section introduces the key steps for clinical risk assessment in AI systems, performance-sensitive criteria, scoring tools, and reporting templates.

### 4.3.1 Identification of Clinical Hazards

The first step in risk assessment is to define precisely the clinical process in which the AI system will be used [70]. The "Healthcare Failure Mode and Effects Analysis"

**TABLE 4.1**
**Summary of Major Risk Categories Associated with AI Deployment in Healthcare, Their Descriptions, Clinical Examples, and Corresponding Mitigation Strategies**

| Risk Categories | Description and Source | Clinical Examples | Risk Mitigation Strategies |
|---|---|---|---|
| Clinical/ Patient Safety | Diagnostic or treatment errors due to overfitting or concept drift; overreliance on algorithmic recommendations; hallucinations; and generation of unfounded outputs. | An AI-based triage system trained on data from a specialized cardiac hospital, when used in a cancer center, may underestimate the severity of cancer patients' conditions. | Human oversight of AI recommendations<br>Use of explainable algorithms<br>Continuous staff training<br>Performance monitoring and model retraining |
| Technical | Poor-quality or non-representative data; lack of model generalizability; hardware failures; or software updates affecting system stability. | An early cancer detection model whose accuracy drops significantly after a change in the MRI device. | Implementation of data quality standards<br>Continuous monitoring<br>Collection of diverse data |
| Security | Unauthorized access, ransomware attacks, data breaches, misuse of data, adversarial attacks, and input manipulation to mislead the algorithm. | A ransomware attack on a health insurance platform causing system disruption and exposure of millions of patient records.<br>Intrusion into a radiology system and alteration of a CT image to hide a tumor. | Strengthening security protocols (data encryption at rest and in transit, multi-factor authentication, firewalls)<br>Staff training on phishing and cyberattacks<br>Deployment of incident response teams and penetration testing |
| Legal/ Compliance | Compliance with regulations such as the EU AI Act, HIPAA, data ownership rights, and informed consent. | Failure to inform patients about AI use in diagnosis, constituting a violation of informed consent.<br>GDPR fines for collecting patient data without proper authorization. | Design of risk management systems in compliance with the AI Act<br>Complete documentation and record-keeping |
| Social/ Ethical | Algorithmic bias, discrimination, and inequality in access. | A skin disease diagnosis app trained on light skin, which is ineffective at detecting lesions on darker skin tones. | Ensuring data diversity and representativeness<br>Inclusion of vulnerable groups in design and evaluation<br>Development of clear guidelines to maintain fairness and prevent discrimination |

(HFMEA) guideline recommends mapping the scope and main steps of the process as a flowchart to reveal potential error points [71]. In study [72], the HFMEA model was applied in four stages to identify vulnerabilities and design an appropriate workflow for risk control. Matrix risk analyses and decision trees were also used to prioritize control actions. The results showed that in four main processes and nine subprocesses related to the entry of companions and contractual caregivers, 26 potential failure modes and 42 possible causes of errors were identified. After implementing corrective actions and risk mitigation strategies, the number of errors decreased from 42 to 13. Compliance with the permissible body temperature threshold increased from 53.1% to 90.8%, and hand hygiene adherence rose from 89.5% to 100%. Based on these results, the HFMEA model proves to be an efficient approach for proactive risk assessment and management of high-risk processes in healthcare services. This model enables effective monitoring of hospital patients' health during a pandemic, enhances preventive training, and improves awareness of infection control principles.

In study [73], an integrated framework was developed that combines qualitative and quantitative methods to enable the identification, prioritization, and optimization of problems at the hospital-wide level. In the qualitative phase, the Fishbone Diagram and HFMEA were used to identify root causes of issues and determine priorities based on expert knowledge. In the quantitative phase, mathematical models, discrete event simulation (DES), and the non-dominated sorting genetic algorithm II (NSGA-II) were applied to provide optimal solutions for selected problems. In a case study conducted at a reputable public hospital, this model was able to identify the most significant organizational challenges and simulate the impact of various improvement plans before actual implementation. The results showed that the proposed model is not only effective in more accurately diagnosing problems but also, through a simulation-based multi-objective optimization approach, can substantially support data-driven decision-making and enhance the overall efficiency of the hospital system.

The combination of qualitative methods such as HFMEA and Fishbone with quantitative tools (DES and multi-objective algorithms like NSGA-II) provides a powerful framework for identifying, prioritizing, and optimizing clinical risks. Empirical evidence indicates that this approach can significantly reduce failure modes and improve operational compliance metrics, thereby enhancing the efficiency and safety of clinical processes.

### 4.3.2 Determining Severity and Probability

After listing the failure modes, the team must determine the potential severity of harm and the likelihood of each failure occurring. ISO 14971 guidance specifies that there is no single standard for levels of severity and probability, and organizations should define appropriate levels based on empirical evidence. Severity can include physical patient outcomes (e.g., death, hospitalization, or temporary injury) as well as social and economic consequences [74]. Probability can be estimated using historical data, error reports, test trials, and expert experience. In medical risk management standards, the risk score is often defined by multiplying severity and probability. Both parameters are usually measured on a multi-level scale (e.g., 1–5) to better reflect relative differences. For example, if the severity of a failure is "4" (serious harm) and the probability is "3" (occasional occurrence), the resulting risk score is 12, which may be classified as "moderate." This semi-quantitative approach allows the team to compare and prioritize different risks. After calculating the score, the team must decide whether the risk is acceptable. ISO 14971 guidelines suggest that high levels require immediate mitigation, medium levels should be reduced as much as possible, and low levels may be accepted. In some countries, the concept of ALARP (As Low As Reasonably Practicable) is applied, meaning the risk should be reduced as much as possible, even if still acceptable [75].

In study [76], the authors emphasize that in emergencies such as accidents, heart attacks, or sudden incidents, clinicians often make decisions based solely on initial vital parameters, while supplementary information becomes available later. This delay in accessing comprehensive data can increase risk to patient safety. To address this challenge, the study employed a multimodal IoT (MMIoT) system that allows simultaneous monitoring of health data from multiple parts of the body. Collected data include vital signals and medical images, which are automatically processed by two deep learning models: U-Net (for image data analysis) and LSTM (for temporal data analysis). Data processing occurs on a server connected to the MMIoT network, using a 5G communication platform for fast and stable data transfer. Subsequently, the outputs of both models are combined through a Dense Layer and used for accurate detection of health anomalies. Results indicate that this approach not only assists clinicians in making faster and more precise decisions but also serves as a learning and professional empowerment tool, preparing specialists for rare and complex cases. Overall, the proposed system can improve healthcare quality, enhance diagnostic accuracy, and reduce patient mortality in critical conditions.

In study [77], the authors addressed the growing incidence of spinal deformities caused by modern lifestyle factors. They proposed an improved U-Net deep neural network for the automated segmentation of spinal vertebrae in radiographic images. By modifying the network architecture and loss function, the model achieved higher segmentation accuracy and enhanced interpretability compared to traditional approaches. This study highlights the critical role of advanced deep learning models in supporting clinicians during diagnosis and treatment planning. Automated segmentation not only reduces analysis time but also minimizes human error, contributing to safer and more consistent clinical outcomes.

Another study [78] provides valuable insight into the application of deep learning for scoliosis detection and classification. What stands out is the authors' use of transfer learning to overcome data limitations, which reflects a practical and well-grounded approach often required in medical imaging research. By evaluating multiple pre-trained architectures such as MobileNetV2, Xception, and ResNet152, the study demonstrates that even with a relatively small dataset, meaningful diagnostic accuracy can be achieved.

Study [79] addresses one of the most fundamental challenges in healthcare risk management: the resilience of healthcare supply chains. Given that human life and quality of care depend on the stability of this supply chain, identifying and prioritizing resilience strategies is of critical importance. Since multiple measures have been proposed to enhance resilience, this study was designed to prioritize key resilience strategies by considering severity, likelihood, and recovery time of major risks. Methodologically, the research employed a multi-criteria decision-making (MCDM) approach. In the first step, risk evaluation criteria were weighted using the Fuzzy AHP. These weights were then applied in Fuzzy TOPSIS analysis to rank the identified risks. Subsequently, the identified risks were linked to appropriate resilience strategies using Fuzzy quality function deployment (Fuzzy QFD). The results indicated that strategies such as the adoption of Industry 4.0 technologies, diversification of supply sources, increased risk awareness, organizational agility, and supply chain globalization are among the most effective measures for enhancing resilience in healthcare supply chains.

In another study [80], the authors examined the concept of "disease severity" within healthcare prioritization systems and aimed to analyze, from a normative perspective, the role of severity sensitivity to risk and time. The central question of the research is whether, in assessing disease severity, the probability of occurrence (risk) and the time of disease onset (time sensitivity) should be considered. The study employs a Reflective Equilibrium approach, meaning that judgments and reasoning related to severity in preventive contexts are compared with background theories and general principles of fairness in resource allocation to achieve conceptual coherence. For theoretical purposes, severity is assumed to vary from 0 to 100, where 100 represents the worst possible health state, and 0 corresponds to full health. In the first part of the analysis, the authors explore arguments for and against risk-sensitive severity. They argue that, ethically, the risk of disease can be factored into severity assessment, just as the risk of death is considered in mortality risk evaluation. However, if severity is reduced in proportion to risk, this may "dilute" the concept of severity, particularly when the boundaries of at-risk populations are not precisely defined. Such an approach could lower the priority of preventive measures (e.g., vaccination or screening) relative to acute and less effective treatments. In the next step, arguments related to time-sensitive severity are examined. The strongest rationale for reducing severity over time is potential future medical advances, as more effective treatments for the same disease may become available. Consequently, the authors propose a middle-ground approach: severity can be partially adjusted based on risk and time, but this adjustment should be limited and proportionate to the current level of knowledge. For instance, if the probability of disease occurrence is low, a higher discount rate (e.g., 5–6%) could be applied, whereas a lower, more general rate (e.g., 3%) could be used for higher probabilities. However, because there is no clear empirical basis for the actual levels of these rates, any decision-making should be approached cautiously and grounded in careful normative analysis.

Overall, determining severity and probability is a key step in clinical risk management and should be conducted based on both empirical evidence (error reports, historical data, simulation results) and expert judgment. Multimodal approaches, such as MMIoT, can reduce delays in data collection and improve the accuracy of risk estimation, while multi-criteria and fuzzy decision-making methods assist in prioritizing resilience strategies.

### 4.3.3 Clinical Risk Assessment Report Template

After performing the analysis and calculating the risk score, the team must document the results using a standardized template. An example HFMEA report template includes columns for sub-process, failure mode, cause, severity, probability, risk score, risk level, proposed action, and outcome metric. The team should explain how severity and probability were determined based on evidence and what actions are proposed to reduce or eliminate the risk. Table 4.2 presents an example of such a report for a hypothetical AI system.

In this example, three sub-processes—"Test Sampling," "Algorithm Analysis," and "Report Delivery"—are reviewed. For each failure mode (e.g., "mislabeled sample" or "data bias"), severity and probability are rated on a 1–5 scale, and the risk score is calculated by multiplying these two values. Actions such as "control and training" or "retraining and data augmentation" are proposed, and metrics to measure the success of these actions (e.g., "reduction in sampling errors" or "reduction in test bias") are defined. Such a report allows the safety committee to make informed decisions regarding acceptance, modification, or suspension of the system's use.

### 4.3.4 Risk Management Processes

The use of risk management processes is a common approach to addressing hazards. These processes consist of two main stages:

1. Risk Assessment: Identifying sources of risk and examining risks related to normal use as well as potential misuse of a system or product [81].
2. Risk Reduction: Reducing risks to an acceptable level, meaning a level of risk that is tolerated under current technological conditions [81].

**TABLE 4.2**
**Risk Assessment Matrix Presenting Key Process Failures, Their Causes, Associated Risk Levels, and Proposed Mitigation Actions within the Healthcare Data Analysis Workflow**

| Process Step | Failure Mode | Cause | Severity (1–5) | Prob (1–5) | Risk Score | Risk Level | Proposed Action | Outcome Metric |
|---|---|---|---|---|---|---|---|---|
| Test Sampling | Mistake in labeling samples | User Error | 4 | 3 | 12 | Medium | Data quality control and user training | Reduce Sampling Error |
| Algorithm Analysis | Data Bias | Lack of Representative Data | 3 | 4 | 12 | Medium | Review sampling methods and augment representative data | Regular backups, monitoring, and automatic alerts |
| Report Submission | Delay in Report | Communication Disruption | 2 | 3 | 6 | Low | Reduce Data Bias | Reduce Report Delay |

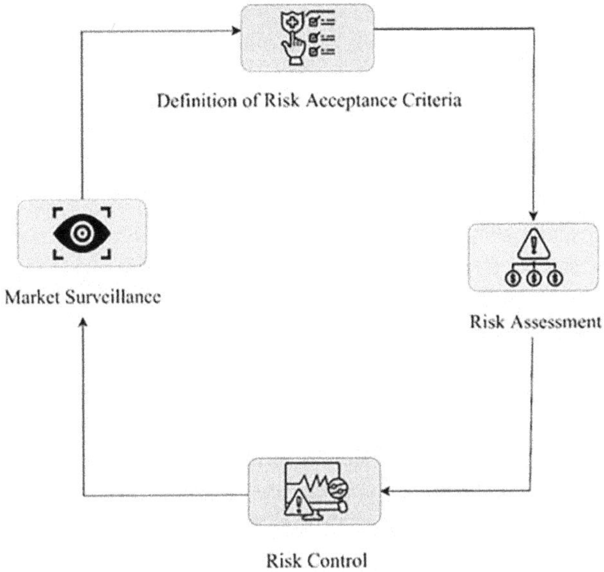


**FIGURE 4.2** Conceptual framework illustrating the main strategies for privacy and data protection in smart healthcare systems, including data minimization and obfuscation, differential privacy mechanisms, and adherence to ethical and regulatory standards.

To establish a risk management process for AI systems in occupational safety and health, familiarity with existing standards is useful [82]. ISO 12100 describes the risk management process for machinery, but AI systems are typically used for complex tasks in complex environments, and deep learning models are highly intricate [83]. Therefore, the ISO 12100 process needs to be slightly adapted to account for the specific characteristics of AI systems.

ISO 14971 is helpful in this context, as active medical devices often interact with complex systems, here represented by the human body. Thus, this measure can be considered a useful complement to the ISO 12100 process. A potential risk management process, both general and partially detailed, can include the steps shown in Figure 4.2. These steps will be discussed in the following section.

#### 4.3.4.1 Defining Risk Acceptance Criteria

The first step in the risk management process is to define risk acceptance criteria. In this stage, the level of residual risk that is still acceptable or tolerable is determined [84]. This residual risk is primarily based on factors such as:

- Extent of harm
- Benefits
- Voluntary use
- Costs
- Secondary effects
- Delay in the occurrence of a harmful event

Currently, only a few social positions regarding AI are clearly recognized. Many applications are implicitly accepted, while others have gradually emerged and are increasingly discussed. In areas where applications directly affect individuals or their health, the European market remains cautious about adopting AI technologies [85]. The main reason is the lack of comprehensive regulations and relevant technical standards. In cases where such systems are used, they are often misused, stemming from a lack of true understanding of the technology's capabilities. Public perception is usually shaped by either idealized or apocalyptic scenarios, both arising from misconceptions about the technology and its portrayal in the media [86].

#### 4.3.4.2 Risk Assessment

Risk assessment consists of two main components: risk identification and risk analysis. First, in the risk identification phase, the precise purpose of the application and its limitations are defined (similar to defining the scope of machinery, intended use in ISO 12100, and identifying safety-related features in medical devices according to ISO 14971). This phase is particularly important for AI, but it is challenging to implement because the technology is mainly used in highly complex environments. A specific characteristic of these environments is that their boundaries usually cannot be fully defined, which introduces uncertainty. Therefore, a key question regarding the use of AI is how extensively this technology can be applied in safety-critical environments and how these uncertainties can be mitigated. Answers to these questions are usually found in relevant regulations and standards; however, these standards are still under development and must evolve simultaneously with efforts to address these questions.

Next, in the risk analysis phase, the likelihood of occurrence and the actual exposure to each identified hazard are assessed (compared with hazard identification and risk assessment in ISO 12100 and ISO 14971). Since there is limited experience in developing and applying AI-based solutions, and the management of associated risks is often unknown, small and medium-sized enterprises that have not yet entered the domain of Trusted AI require extensive support. In assessing risk in a work environment, three main factors determine risk [87]:

- Degree of exposure to the hazard
- Occurrence of the hazardous event
- Possibility of preventing or mitigating harm

#### 4.3.4.3 Risk Control

After the first iteration of the previous steps, the preliminary risk assessment results are determined. If it is found that the tolerable risk threshold has been exceeded, risk control measures must be applied. After analyzing risk control options, measures should be implemented, and residual risk should be reassessed (compared with risk reduction in ISO 12100 and risk control in ISO 14971).

Risk control measures are typically prioritized hierarchically. For example, ISO IEC Guide 51 [88] defines three levels of priority:

1. Inherently safe design
2. Protective devices and safety measures
3. Provision of information to end users

In general, efforts should always focus on achieving an inherently safe design; if this is not feasible, protective devices and safety measures are used. If these measures are also not possible, providing information to end users is mandatory. The challenge lies in transferring an existing idea or product to a safety-related application, which requires extensive experience. Existing regulations and standards are not the only obstacles; practical implementation of these measures also presents significant challenges.

The authors in study [89] demonstrated that employing generative AI can play a key role in strengthening the relationship between patients and healthcare providers and personalizing the treatment experience for each individual. Specifically, the use of generative models helps improve patient–physician interactions, increase accuracy in predicting treatment outcomes, and ultimately reduce clinical risks arising from impersonal decision-making or inefficient communication. In this context, generative AI, by analyzing patient data and providing personalized recommendations, can identify current patient needs and prevent human errors in treatment decisions. This not only contributes to the continuous improvement of patients' quality of life but is also critically important from a clinical risk management perspective, as it reduces the likelihood of diagnostic or therapeutic errors and enhances patient safety.

In another study [90], the authors stated that the use of generative models for predicting epidemiological trends and simulating disease spread scenarios can play a decisive role in reducing health risks and enhancing the preparedness of the healthcare system. This technology, through the analysis of complex data and the generation of predictive patterns, enables the early identification of potential threats and the design of effective preventive strategies. From a risk management perspective, generative AI, by improving prediction accuracy, can help reduce uncertainty in high-level public health decision-making and, consequently, minimize the economic and clinical impacts of health crises. Moreover, generative model-based simulations provide a useful tool for evaluating the effectiveness of different interventions before an actual crisis occurs, allowing decision-makers to select lower-risk and more efficient options.

In study [91], the authors, focusing on risk management in crisis and emergency situations, examine the role of emerging technologies, particularly AI, in reducing the vulnerability of healthcare systems. As natural disasters such as earthquakes, floods, and fires or human-induced crises such as wars, environmental pollution, and virus outbreaks have shown, insufficient preparedness at national and regional levels can have widespread consequences for public health. Therefore, gap analysis, risk assessment, and the design of proactive preventive programs are essential to mitigate destructive outcomes. In this context, the study emphasizes that AI can be effectively employed as a tool to enhance resilience and risk management in healthcare systems. Key applications include optimizing triage and resource allocation processes, inventory management, forecasting hospital needs, and facilitating rapid decision-making in crisis situations. Additionally, using AI models in image-based diagnostics, gene therapy design, and early disease detection helps reduce the burden on healthcare staff and improves the accuracy of clinical decisions.

In study [92], from the perspective of clinical risk management, findings confirm that applying AI models for early diabetes detection can play a significant role in reducing health risks and optimizing therapeutic interventions. Early detection using accurate models enables the prevention of secondary complications and reduces the economic burden on the healthcare system. The aim of the study was to evaluate the effectiveness of various ML models in identifying individuals at risk of developing diabetes early. For this purpose, four algorithms—logistic regression, k-nearest neighbors (KNN), decision tree, and random forest—were trained on a comprehensive diabetes diagnosis dataset. Analysis results showed that the random forest model performed best, achieving an overall accuracy of 96%. This model had a precision of 0.94 and a recall of 0.69 for positive cases, showing the highest alignment with real-world data. The KNN model also performed acceptably (precision = 0.91, recall = 0.62), while logistic regression and decision tree models, although providing useful insights into data structure, performed less effectively on some evaluation metrics.

Study [93] examines the application of ML in predicting the clinical deterioration of patients in ICU and emphasizes the importance of external validation of models to reduce the risk of errors in clinical decision-making. Many ML algorithms, although performing well on initial datasets, show lower performance when applied in new hospitals or patient populations. This discrepancy can lead to a high risk of misdiagnosis or inaccurate predictions in real-world settings. In models that underwent external validation, the average AUROC decreased by 0.037, and in nearly half of the studies, the drop exceeded 0.05. The authors note that without external validation, ML predictions may be dangerous and lead to incorrect clinical decisions. Therefore, to improve patient safety and ensure the reliability of risk scores in real-world environments, external validation and the use of diverse data are essential.

#### 4.3.4.4 Market Surveillance

In AI systems, market surveillance refers to the process of continuously collecting, analyzing, and providing feedback on performance data after system deployment. The goal of this stage is to identify performance deviations, unexpected model behaviors, and new risks arising from environmental or data changes. This monitoring is typically conducted through automated performance metric tracking, user reports, and analysis of adverse events. The resulting data forms the basis for corrective actions such as algorithm updates, parameter adjustments, or limiting use under specific conditions. In fact, market surveillance creates a closed-loop cycle between development, evaluation, and continuous improvement of AI systems, ensuring that system safety and reliability are maintained throughout their life cycle [94].

Therefore, the risk management process in AI systems should integrate traditional safety standards (such as ISO 12100) with requirements specific to data-driven technologies. Precisely defining risk acceptance criteria, conducting comprehensive risk identification and analysis, and implementing hierarchical controls are core components of this process. Given the dynamic nature of AI-based environments, risk assessment should be performed cyclically and iteratively. Ultimately, continuous monitoring of system performance in real-world settings and analysis of operational data (market surveillance) play a key role in ensuring the ongoing safety and reliability of the system.

## 4.4 PRIVACY, DATA PROTECTION, AND ETHICAL CONSIDERATIONS IN HEALTHCARE

Protecting patients' sensitive data is not merely a technical concern; it is a fundamental component of public trust and professional ethics in healthcare. According to recent studies, de-identification and data anonymization are essential methods for safeguarding patient privacy [95]. Similarly, the fair information practice principles (FIPPs) state that organizations should collect or disclose only personal information that is relevant and necessary to achieve a legally permitted purpose and should retain personal data only as long as required to fulfill that purpose [96]. This emphasis on data minimization is also reflected in legal frameworks such as the European Union general data protection regulation (GDPR). Article 5(1)(c) of the GDPR mandates that personal data should be limited to what is necessary for the processing purposes, thereby reinforcing the principle of data minimization [97]. As shown in Figure 4.3, the protection of patient data in healthcare environments is grounded in three fundamental approaches: data minimization and obfuscation, DP mechanisms, and compliance with established legal and ethical frameworks.

Various technical and procedural methods have been proposed to protect health data. Some of the most important approaches include:

### 4.4.1 Data Minimization and Obfuscation

Data minimization is a core principle of privacy protection, reflected in several fundamental privacy frameworks and privacy laws [98]. Instead of retaining exact values (e.g., age in years or full date of birth), these values can be grouped into broader ranges or rounded. This reduces the "identifiability" of individuals.

Study [99] addresses a modern challenge in generative AI, namely the unintentional disclosure of personal information when interacting with large language models (LLMs). To tackle this issue, the authors introduced Rescriber, a browser extension that helps users identify and remove personal information before sending messages to language models. Rescriber is designed with a user-centered approach and uses LLMs such as Llama3-8B and GPT-4o to implement the principle of data minimization in user interactions with AI systems. The experimental study, involving 12 participants, showed that Rescriber significantly reduced unnecessary disclosure of personal information and increased users' sense of security and trust.

**FIGURE 4.3** Conceptual representation of key approaches to privacy and data protection in healthcare systems, including data minimization, differential privacy, and adherence to standard regulatory frameworks.

Evaluations indicated that the lighter model (Llama3-8B) performed comparably to GPT-4o and was also satisfactory in terms of user experience.

In another study [100], the authors introduce an innovative protocol called DtMin, designed to effectively implement the principle of data minimization in the process of sharing medical information between healthcare providers (HCPs) and electronic health record providers (EHRPs). The DtMin protocol uses a multilayered and hybrid encryption approach, which includes attribute-based encryption (ABE) and Hybrid Encryption. In this method, patient data attributes are divided into six categories based on sensitivity, patient consent status, and type of sharing request. The system then allows only the sharing of data that intersects both patient consent and the healthcare provider's information needs, while all other information remains unreadable. The authors formally analyzed and verified the security of DtMin under the ICR-DB[6] and ICR-IS[7] security models. Performance tests show that the protocol is highly efficient across various data volumes and a diverse patient population. The article also explores the potential integration of DtMin with more advanced encryption methods, including lattice-based ABE and lightweight ABE versions, which could further enhance security and efficiency in complex and large-scale healthcare environments.

### 4.4.2 Adding Random Noise (Differential Privacy)

Differential privacy (DP) is an approach that, instead of modifying the database itself, adjusts the data access process by adding random noise to statistical outputs to prevent the identification of individuals [101]. For example, a study in intensive care demonstrated that combining ML algorithms with DP mechanisms (e.g., Gaussian or Laplace noise) can enhance patient data protection while preserving the utility of the data analysis.

In study [102], the authors analytically examine various methods of applying DP to medical data. They show that adding Laplace-distributed noise can preserve privacy in categorical and numerical data, whereas for continuous data, noisy values must be rounded to meet masking requirements. In datasets with correlations between variables, noise should be added to only one variable to maintain a balance between accuracy and confidentiality. The study's findings indicate that while adding noise slightly reduces the accuracy of analytical parameters, such as slopes, increasing the value of $\epsilon$ (representing the allowable disclosure level) and having higher variance in the independent variable significantly improve the accuracy of statistical results.

In study [103], the authors, focusing on reducing the risk of sensitive data leakage in federated learning, introduce a new algorithm called federated learning with sparsified model perturbation (Fed-SMP). They note that although federated learning seemingly protects data privacy, sensitive information can still be inferred from the shared model parameters. To address this issue, DP is used as a defensive mechanism. The main innovation of this paper is the application of sparsified model perturbation (SMP); that is, before adding Gaussian noise for privacy preservation, local models are first compressed or "sparsified" so that less noise is required, thereby maintaining model accuracy. The authors then provide a rigorous privacy analysis using Rényi DP, demonstrating that their algorithm ensures client-level DP, preserves model accuracy, and reduces communication costs.

In study [104], the authors systematically examine the challenges in real-world applications of DP in ML and attempt to provide a comprehensive, step-by-step guide for researchers and practitioners. They explain that while DP is theoretically accepted and adopted as a standard for data anonymization in some industries, practical implementation faces obstacles such as the lack of clear guidelines for choosing privacy parameters, difficulty in tuning hyperparameters, and challenges in balancing privacy, accuracy, and computational cost. To address these, the authors review existing literature, explain how to fine-tune parameters, and provide recommendations for adapting model architectures to meet DP requirements. In addition to reviewing theoretical advances in privacy accounting and analyzing the convergence of DP algorithms, the article proposes a set of best practices for transparent reporting of privacy guarantees, facilitating the evaluation of research and comparison of models.

### 4.4.3 Use of Standard Frameworks

Many organizations are developing various projects and, to reduce regulatory risks and comply with legal requirements, need well-defined frameworks aligned with global standards. International organizations and institutions (e.g., ISO/IEC 20889) have provided guidelines for performing de-identification processes to ensure that data is shared in accordance with legal and ethical privacy principles. Overall, maintaining privacy and adhering to ethical considerations in smart healthcare systems requires a combination of technological and managerial strategies. The use of privacy-preserving methods (such as de-identification and DP) alongside legal frameworks (e.g., GDPR and HIPAA, which mandate explicit consent, encryption, and breach notification) can ensure the security of patient data.

## 4.5 DISCUSSION

Although the proposed solutions for risk management and ensuring the safety of AI systems in healthcare appear innovative and efficient, their practical implementation in real healthcare environments faces multiple challenges and limitations. From a technical perspective, many advanced ML models, especially deep learning, are inherently "black boxes" and lack sufficient transparency in explaining their decision-making. This lack of explainability hinders clinicians and technical supervisors from fully understanding model outputs, reducing clinical trust. Developing advanced XAI methods and providing explanatory tools to physicians and general users is essential. Studies show that the more explainable an AI system is, the higher both system safety and public trust become.

On the other hand, standardization processes and risk assessment metrics in AI are still incomplete. Current medical device standards, such as ISO 14971, primarily focus on managing physical or general risks in medical systems and do not specifically address AI-related aspects (e.g., continuous learning, model variability). Therefore, new guidance documents, such as the AAMI CR34971 report, have been developed to address AI/ML-specific gaps. At the international level, structural differences between frameworks and key regulations are evident: for example, the NIST AI risk management framework (NIST AI RMF) is a voluntary, global guide for improving trustworthiness in AI, whereas the EU AI Act is a binding legal framework based on risk classification, imposing stringent requirements on "high-risk" systems, including many medical tools.

Legal and ethical dimensions also create significant constraints. Gaps in liability, regulatory records, and privacy protection lead to uncertainty. Practically, broad adoption of AI in healthcare requires several operational preconditions. Without them, advanced technological innovations cannot be easily integrated into routine clinical processes. Thus, technological limitations (e.g., insufficient explainability and data bias), inconsistencies in reference standards, research gaps, and legal-organizational challenges collectively delay the operational implementation of AI safety protocols in healthcare systems.

## 4.6 CONCLUSION

In conclusion, ensuring the safety of AI systems in healthcare requires a systemic and multifaceted approach. This approach must go beyond mere algorithmic performance and encompass managerial, legal, educational, and standardization aspects. Research and deployment of AI in healthcare will succeed only if strong governance frameworks are established—from national and international macro levels down to the operational level of hospitals. Standardizing processes and complying with international regulations (such as the EU AI Act, the NIST framework, and ISO standards related to medical devices) ensures that AI systems align with scientific and ethical standards.

Furthermore, equipping human resources with proper training in AI and risk management is vital for the responsible handling of these technologies. Ultimately, all efforts should focus on the noble goal of safeguarding and enhancing patient safety. If the development and deployment of AI technologies prioritize patient health and adhere to ethical principles, there is hope that these technologies will improve healthcare through more accurate diagnoses, personalized treatments, and optimized care processes, ultimately enhancing patient welfare.

## NOTES

1 National Institute of Standards and Technology.
2 Medical devices—Application of risk management to medical devices (International Organization for Standardization).
3 Artificial Intelligence Risk Management Framework (National Institute of Standards and Technology).
4 Steatosis-Associated Fibrosis Estimator.
5 Health Insurance Portability and Accountability Act.
6 Identity concealment and revocation under data-based model defines a security framework that focuses on protecting data-level identity attributes and ensuring revocation capabilities in distributed healthcare databases.
7 Identity concealment and revocation under identity-based model emphasizes the concealment and controlled revocation of user identities within identity-centric security infrastructures.

## REFERENCES


1. Nifakos S, Chandramouli K, Nikolaou CK, Papachristou P, Koch S, Panaousis E, et al. Influence of human factors on cyber security within healthcare organisations: A systematic review. Sensors 2021;21:5119.
2. Berdida DJE, Alhudaib N. Linking patient safety, caring behaviours and professional self-efficacy with missed nursing care among Filipino emergency room nurses: a structural equation model study. Journal of Clinical Nursing 2025;34:2181–93.
3. Ferrara M, Bertozzi G, Di Fazio N, Aquila I, Di Fazio A, Maiese A, et al. Risk management and patient safety in the artificial intelligence era: a systematic review. Healthcare (Basel) 2024;12:549.
4. Zamanifar A, Faezipour M. Application of Generative AI in Healthcare Systems. Springer; 2025.
5. Mullankandy S, Mukherjee S, Ingole BS. Applications of AI in electronic health records, challenges, and mitigation strategies. In: 2024 International Conference on Computer and Applications (ICCA). IEEE; 2024, page 1–7.
6. Hirani R, Noruzi K, Khuram H, Hussaini AS, Aifuwa EI, Ely KE, et al. Artificial intelligence and healthcare: a journey through history, present innovations, and future possibilities. Life 2024;14:557.
7. Montella L, Ayokunle O V, Salvi F. Healthcare System Approach for Implementing Risk Management Models Oriented to Patient Safety. In: International Conference Logistics & Lean Engineering for Advanced Healthcare Methodologies Modelling. Springer; 2024, page 411–9.
8. Sufi F. An innovative GPT-based open-source intelligence using historical cyber incident reports. Natural Language Processing Journal 2024;7:100074.
9. Finkelstein J, Gabriel A, Schmer S, Truong TT, Dunn A. Identifying facilitators and barriers to implementation of AI-assisted clinical decision support in an electronic health record system. Journal of Medical Systems 2024;48:89.
10. Al Khatib I, Ndiaye M. Examining the role of AI in changing the role of nurses in patient care: systematic review. JMIR Nursing 2025;8:e63335.
11. Hanna MG, Pantanowitz L, Dash R, Harrison JH, Deebajah M, Pantanowitz J, et al. Future of artificial intelligence (AI)-machine learning (ML) trends in pathology and medicine. Modern Pathology 2025;100705.
12. Ruutiainen H, Holmström AR, Kunnola E, Kuitunen S. Use of computerized physician order entry with clinical decision support to prevent dose errors in pediatric medication orders: a systematic review. Pediatric Drugs 2024;26:127–43.
13. Lakshmipriya B, Jayalakshmy S, Ajagbe SA, Ogie PI, Awotunde JB, Adigun MO. COPD scope: smart clinical pathways for respiratory illness diagnosis and management. Annals of Data Science 2025;1–33.
14. El-Saleh AA, Sheikh AM, Albreem MAM, Honnurvali MS. The internet of medical things (IoMT): opportunities and challenges. Wireless Networks 2025;31:327–44.
15. Gala D, Behl H, Shah M, Makaryus AN. The role of artificial intelligence in improving patient outcomes and future of healthcare delivery in cardiology: a narrative review of the literature. Healthcare (Basel) 2024;12:481.
16. Papyshev G, Yarime M. The limitation of ethics-based approaches to regulating artificial intelligence: regulatory gifting in the context of Russia. Artificial Intelligence Security Operations Center 2024;39:1381–96.
17. Ranjitsingh LM, Rao TVS. Establish legal and regulatory standards for the testing and validation of AI systems to ensure their reliability and safety in operational environments. International Journal of System Assurance Engineering and Management 2025;1–16.

18. Perez-Cerrolaza J, Abella J, Borg M, Donzella C, Cerquides J, Cazorla FJ, et al. Artificial intelligence for safety-critical systems in industrial and transportation domains: a survey. ACM Computing Surveys 2024;56:1–40.
19. Swaminathan N, Danks D. Application of the NIST AI risk management framework to surveillance technology. arXiv preprint arXiv:2403.15646 2024.
20. Zhang X, Chan FTS, Yan C, Bose I. Towards risk-aware artificial intelligence and machine learning systems: an overview. Decision Support System 2022;159:113800.
21. Wen H, Sajid Z, Arunthavanathan R. Risk perception in complex systems: a comparative analysis of process control and autonomous vehicle failures. AI 2025;6:164.
22. Liang W, Tadesse GA, Ho D, Fei-Fei L, Zaharia M, Zhang C, et al. Advances, challenges and opportunities in creating data for trustworthy AI. Natural Machine Intelligence 2022;4:669–77.
23. Kaur D, Uslu S, Rittichier KJ, Durresi A. Trustworthy artificial intelligence: a review. ACM Computing Surveys (CSUR) 2022;55:1–38.
24. Reddy S. Explainability and artificial intelligence in medicine. Lancet Digit Health 2022;4:e214–5.
25. Kieseberg P, Weippl E, Tjoa AM, Cabitza F, Campagner A, Holzinger A. Controllable AI-an alternative to trustworthiness in complex AI systems? In: International Cross-Domain Conference for Machine Learning and Knowledge Extraction. Springer; 2023, page 1–12.
26. Veleanovici AC, Oncioiu AE, Baryla-Matejczuk M. The influence of the work environment on hypersensitive employees. In: Science and Education: New Approaches and Perspectives. 2023, page 201–8.
27. Fraser AG, Biasin E, Bijnens B, Bruining N, Caiani EG, Cobbaert K, et al. Artificial intelligence in medical device software and high-risk medical devices—a review of definitions, expert recommendations and regulatory initiatives. Expert Review of Medical Devices 2023;20:467–91.
28. El Arab RA, Abu-Mahfouz MS, Abuadas FH, Alzghoul H, Almari M, Ghannam A, et al. Bridging the gap: from AI success in clinical trials to real-world healthcare implementation—a narrative review. Healthcare (Basel) 2025;12:701.
29. Gupta S, Kapoor M, Debnath SK. Cybersecurity risks and threats in healthcare. In: Artificial Intelligence-Enabled Security for Healthcare Systems: Safeguarding Patient Data and Improving Services. Springer; 2025. page 39–64.
30. Iqbal MJ, Javed Z, Sadia H, Qureshi IA, Irshad A, Ahmed R, et al. Clinical applications of artificial intelligence and machine learning in cancer diagnosis: looking into the future. Cancer Cell International 2021;21:270.
31. Rubinger L, Gazendam A, Ekhtiari S, Bhandari M. Machine learning and artificial intelligence in research and healthcare. Injury 2023;54:S69–73.
32. Aliferis C, Simon G. Overfitting, underfitting and general model overconfidence and under-performance pitfalls and best practices in machine learning and AI. Artificial intelligence and machine learning in health care and medical sciences. Best Practices and Pitfalls 2024;477–524.
33. Ahmad MA, Yaramis I, Roy TD. Creating trustworthy llms: Dealing with hallucinations in healthcare AI. arXiv preprint arXiv:2311.01463 2023.
34. Jaltotage B, Sukudom S, Ihdayhid AR, Dwivedi G. Enhancing risk stratification on coronary computed tomography angiography: the role of artificial intelligence. Clinical Therapeutics 2023;45:1023–8.
35. Irannejad K, Krishnan S, Iskander B, Kambalapalli S, Punanithinont N, Ichikawa K, et al. Advancements in coronary CT angiography: innovations in diagnosis, risk stratification, and prognosis in atherosclerosis. Current Treatment Options in Cardiovascular Medicine 2025;27:34.

36. Eldesouky M, Jaiswal S, Badra A, De-Silva S, Naeem H, Khurram A, et al. Clinical outcomes of computed tomography coronary angiography (CTCA) in patients with suspected coronary artery disease: a single-center experience. Catheterization and Cardiovascular Interventions 2025;106:2850–8
37. Tsitou VM, Rallis D, Tsekova M, Yanev N. Microbiology in the era of artificial intelligence: transforming medical and pharmaceutical microbiology. Biotechnology & Biotechnological Equipment 2024;38:2349587.
38. Huang SJ, Lv G, Song YH, Zhao JT, Liu JY, Wang LL, et al. Antifungal susceptibility, molecular epidemiology, and clinical risk factors of *Candida glabrata* in intensive care unit in a Chinese Tertiary Hospital. Frontiers in Cellular and Infection Microbiology 2024;14:1455145.
39. Branda F, Scarpa F. Implications of artificial intelligence in addressing antimicrobial resistance: innovations, global challenges, and healthcare's future. Antibiotics 2024;13:502.
40. Charu V, Liang JW, Mannalithara A, Kwong A, Tian L, Kim WR. Benchmarking clinical risk prediction algorithms with ensemble machine learning for the noninvasive diagnosis of liver fibrosis in NAFLD. Hepatology 2024;80:1184–95.
41. Abdelwanis M, Alarafati HK, Tammam MMS, Simsekler MCE. Exploring the risks of automation bias in healthcare artificial intelligence applications: a Bowtie analysis. Journal of Safety Science and Resilience 2024;5:460–9.
42. Liu F, Panagiotakos D. Real-world data: a brief review of the methods, applications, challenges and opportunities. BMC Medical Research Methodology 2022;22:287.
43. Zong Z, Guan Y. AI-driven intelligent data analytics and predictive analysis in Industry 4.0: transforming knowledge, innovation, and efficiency. Journal of the Knowledge Economy 2025;16:864–903.
44. Li H, Yazdi M, Nedjati A, Moradi R, Adumene S, Dao U, et al. Harnessing AI for project risk management: a paradigm shift. In: Progressive Decision-making Tools and Applications in Project and Operation Management: Approaches, Case Studies, Multi-criteria Decision-making, Multi-objective Decision-making, Decision under Uncertainty. Springer; 2024. page 253–72.
45. Majka M. Revolutionizing Risk Management: The Role of AI in Identifying, Mitigating, and Managing Risks. 2025.
46. Steimers A, Schneider M. Sources of risk of AI systems. International Journal of Environmental Research and Public Health. 2022;19:3641.
47. Houben S, Abrecht S, Akila M, Bär A, Brockherde F, Feifel P, et al. Inspect, understand, overcome: a survey of practical methods for AI safety. In: Deep neural Networks and Data for Automated Driving: Robustness, Uncertainty Quantification, and Insights towards Safety. Springer International Publishing Cham; 2022. page 3–78.
48. Gountia D, Behera RR, Bal PR, Pati SL. Trojan detection in digital microfluidic biochips via image classification: a deep-learning based approach. IEEE Transactions on Dependable and Secure Computing 2025;1–13.
49. Nasiri S, Sadoughi F, Dehnad A, Tadayon MH, Ahmadi H. Layered architecture for internet of things-based healthcare system. Informatica (Slovenia) 2021;45.
50. Qi K. Advancing hospital healthcare: achieving IoT-based secure health monitoring through multilayer machine learning. J Big Data 2025;12:1.
51. Qin X, Gao X, Yang Y, Ou S, Luo J, Wei H, et al. Developing a risk assessment tool for cancer-related venous thrombosis in China: a modified Delphi-analytic hierarchy process study. BMC Cancer 2024;24:120.
52. Dubey A, Verma AS. Effective remote healthcare and telemedicine approaches for improving digital healthcare systems. In: Digital Health Transformation with Blockchain and Artificial Intelligence. CRC Press; 2022. page 273–97.

53. Acuña EGA. Healthcare cybersecurity: data poisoning in the age of AI. Journal of Comprehensive Business Administration Research 2024.
54. Balogun AY. Strengthening compliance with data privacy regulations in US healthcare cybersecurity. Asian Journal of Research in Computer Science 2025;18:154–73.
55. Al-Najjar Y. Cybersecurity in healthcare industry. Global Scientific Journals 2024.
56. Xie Y, Lu L, Gao F, He S jiang, Zhao H juan, Fang Y, et al. Integration of artificial intelligence, blockchain, and wearable technology for chronic disease management: a new paradigm in smart healthcare. Current Medical Science 2021;41:1123–33.
57. Finkenstadt DJ, Handfield R. Blurry vision: supply chain visibility for personal protective equipment during COVID-19. Journal of Purchasing and Supply Management 2021;27:100689.
58. Søreide K, Hallet J, Matthews JB, Schnitzbauer AA, Line PD, Lai PBS, et al. Immediate and long-term impact of the COVID-19 pandemic on delivery of surgical services. Journal of British Surgery 2020;107:1250–61.
59. Subahi AF. Edge-based IoT medical record system: requirements, recommendations and conceptual design. IEEE Access 2019;7:94150–9.
60. Zaabar B, Cheikhrouhou O, Jamil F, Ammi M, Abid M. HealthBlock: a secure blockchain-based healthcare data management system. Computer Networks 2021; 200:108500.
61. Singh H. Building Secure Generative AI Models to Prevent Data Leakage and Ethical Misuse. Available at SSRN 5267908 2025.
62. Ray PP, Chowhan B, Kumar N, Almogren A. BIoTHR: electronic health record servicing scheme in IoT-blockchain ecosystem. IEEE Internet Things J 2021;8:10857–72.
63. Subramanian G, Thampy AS. Implementation of blockchain consortium to prioritize diabetes patients' healthcare in pandemic situations. Ieee Access 2021;9:162459–75.
64. Kumar D, Suthar N. Ethical and legal challenges of AI in marketing: an exploration of solutions. Journal of Information, Communication and Ethics in Society 2024; 22:124–44.
65. Lund B, Orhan Z, Mannuru NR, Bevara RVK, Porter B, Vinaih MK, et al. Standards, frameworks, and legislation for artificial intelligence (AI) transparency. AI and Ethics 2025;1–17.
66. En-Naaoui A, Kaicer M, Aguezzoul A. A novel decision support system for proactive risk management in healthcare based on fuzzy inference, neural network and support vector machine. International Journal of Medical Informatics 2024;186:105442.
67. D. Almeida S, Norajitra T, Lüth CT, Wald T, Weru V, Nolden M, et al. How do deep-learning models generalize across populations? Cross-ethnicity generalization of COPD detection. Insights Imaging 2024;15:198.
68. Gupta S, Kamboj S, Bag S. Role of risks in the development of responsible artificial intelligence in the digital healthcare domain. Information Systems Frontiers 2023; 25:2257–74.
69. Ratti E, Morrison M, Jakab I. Ethical and social considerations of applying artificial intelligence in healthcare—a two-pronged scoping review. BMC Medical Ethics 2025; 26:68.
70. Moghadasi N, Valdez RS, Piran M, Moghaddasi N, Linkov I, Polmateer TL, et al. Risk analysis of artificial intelligence in medicine with a multilayer concept of system order. Systems 2024;12:47.
71. Cheng CH, Chou CJ, Wang PC, Lin HY, Kao CL, Su CT. Applying HFMEA to prevent chemotherapy errors. Journal of Medical Systems 2012;36:1543–51.
72. Tiao CH, Tsai LC, Chen LC, Liao YM, Sun LC. Healthcare failure mode and effect analysis (HFMEA) as an effective mechanism in preventing infection caused by accompanying caregivers during COVID-19—experience of a city medical center in Taiwan. Quality Management in Healthcare 2021;30:61–8.

73. Rahimi Rise Z, Ershadi MM. An integrated HFMEA simulation-based multi-objective optimisation model to improve the performances of hospitals: a case study. Journal of Simulation 2023;17:422–43.
74. Sweis JJG, Alnaimat F, Esparza V, Prasad S, Azam A, Modi Z, et al. From acute infection to prolonged health consequences: understanding health disparities and economic implications in long COVID worldwide. International Journal of Environmental Research and Public Health 2024;21:325.
75. Maselli G, Macchiaroli M, Nestico A. ALARP criteria to estimate acceptability and tolerability thresholds of the investment risk. Applied Sciences 2021;11:9086.
76. Raza A, Mehmood R, Albeshri A, Alzahrani A. Multimodal IoT-based healthcare monitoring using deep learning and 5G networks. IEEE Access 2021;9:146932–146943.
77. Tavana P, Akraminia M, Koochari A, Bagherifard A. Rethinking U-net deep neural network for spine radiographic images-based spine vertebrae segmentation. Journal of Medical and Biological Engineering [Internet] 2023;43:574–84. Available from: https://doi.org/10.1007/s40846-023-00828-6
78. Tavana P, Akraminia M, Koochari A, Bagherifard A. An efficient ensemble method for detecting spinal curvature type using deep transfer learning and soft voting classifier. Expert Systems Applications [Internet] 2023;213:119290. Available from: https://www.sciencedirect.com/science/article/pii/S0957417422023089
79. Goker N, Karsak EE, Dursun M. An integrated QFD and common weight DEA-based fuzzy MCDM framework for performance ranking of countries. Social Indicators Research 2022;159:409–30.
80. Sandman L, Liliemark J. Should severity assessments in healthcare priority setting be risk-and time-sensitive? Health Care Analysis 2023;31:169–85.
81. Settembre-Blundo D, González-Sánchez R, Medina-Salgado S, García-Muiña FE. Flexibility and resilience in corporate decision making: a new sustainability-based risk management system in uncertain times. Global Journal of Flexible Systems Management 2021;22:107–32.
82. Jarota M. Artificial intelligence in the work process. A reflection on the proposed European Union regulations on artificial intelligence from an occupational health and safety perspective. Computer Law & Security Review 2023;49:105825.
83. Hu X, Chu L, Pei J, Liu W, Bian J. Model complexity of deep learning: a survey. Knowledge and Information Systems 2021;63:2585–619.
84. Zwietering MH, Garre A, Wiedmann M, Buchanan RL. All food processes have a residual risk, some are small, some very small and some are extremely small: zero risk does not exist. Current Opinion in Food Science 2021;39:83–92.
85. Chew HSJ, Achananuparp P. Perceptions and needs of artificial intelligence in health care to increase adoption: scoping review. Journal of Medical Internet Research 2022; 24:e32939.
86. Kuai J. Navigating the AI hype: Chinese journalists' algorithmic imaginaries and role perceptions in reporting emerging technologies. Digital Journalism 2025;1–20.
87. Lukan J, Bolliger L, Pauwels NS, Luštrek M, Bacquer D De, Clays E. Work environment risk factors causing day-to-day stress in occupational settings: a systematic review. BMC Public Health 2022;22:240.
88. International Organization for Standardization (ISO), International Electrotechnical Commission (IEC). ISO/IEC Guide 51:2014. Safety aspects—guidelines for their inclusion in standards. ISO; 2014.
89. ZareiNejad M, Tavana P. Application of generative AI in patient engagement. In: Application of Generative AI in Healthcare Systems. Springer; 2025. page 119–54.
90. Tavana P, ZareiNejad M. Generative AI in Pandemic Prediction. In: Application of Generative AI in Healthcare Systems. Springer; 2025. page 35–66.

91. Bari LF, Ahmed I, Ahamed R, Zihan TA, Sharmin S, Pranto AH, et al. Potential use of artificial intelligence (AI) in disaster risk and emergency health management: a critical appraisal on environmental health. Environ Health Insights 2023;17:11786302231217808.
92. Wang J, Rao C, Goh M, Xiao X. Risk assessment of coronary heart disease based on cloud-random forest. Artificial Intelligence Review 2023;56:203–32.
93. Aldhoayan MD, Aljubran Y, Aljubran YA. Prediction of ICU patients' deterioration using machine learning techniques. Cureus 2023;15.
94. Schöning J, Pfisterer HJ. Safe and trustful AI for closed-loop control systems. Electronics (Basel) 2023;12:3489.
95. Lulamba TE, Mutemaringa T, Tiffin N. Ten quick tips for protecting health data using de-identification and perturbation of structured datasets. PLoS Computational Biology 2025;21:e1013507.
96. Gellman R. Fair Information Practices: A Basic History. Available at SSRN 5348107 2025.
97. Bharanitharan K, Kaur G. A Comparative Analysis of Data Minimization Principles: Evaluating GDPR and India's DPDP Act 2023. In: International Conference on Data Mining and Information Security. Springer; 2024, page 41–55.
98. Ganesh P, Tran C, Shokri R, Fioretto F. The data minimization principle in machine learning. In: Proceedings of the 2025 ACM Conference on Fairness, Accountability, and Transparency. 2025, page 3075–93.
99. Zhou J, Xu E, Wu Y, Li T. Rescriber: Smaller-LLM-Powered User-Led Data Minimization for LLM-Based Chatbots. In: Proceedings of the 2025 CHI Conference on Human Factors in Computing Systems. 2025, page 1–28.
100. Park HA. The DtMin protocol: implementing data minimization principles in medical information sharing. Electronics (2079-9292) 2025;14.
101. Kenny CT, Kuriwaki S, McCartan C, Rosenman ETR, Simko T, Imai K. The use of differential privacy for census data and its impact on redistricting: the case of the 2020 US Census. Science Advances 2021;7:eabk3283.
102. Shahmiri AM, Ling CW, Li CT. Communication-efficient Laplace mechanism for differential privacy via random quantization. In: ICASSP 2024-2024 IEEE International Conference on Acoustics, Speech and Signal Processing (ICASSP). IEEE; 2024, page 4550–4.
103. Hu R, Guo Y, Gong Y. Federated learning with sparsified model perturbation: Improving accuracy under client-level differential privacy. IEEE Transactions on Mobile Computing 2023;23:8242–55.
104. Blanco-Justicia A, Sánchez D, Domingo-Ferrer J, Muralidhar K. A critical review on the use (and misuse) of differential privacy in machine learning. ACM Computing Surveys 2022;55:1–16.

# 5 AI Model Transparency in Healthcare

*Amirfarhad Farhadi, Moein Hedayati, Azadeh Zamanifar, and Nasser Mozayani*

## 5.1 INTRODUCTION

Artificial intelligence has been able to help solve problems or make processes easier in various industries in recent years, especially through more complex models such as machine learning and deep learning [1]. One area where artificial intelligence can be beneficial is healthcare [2]. Artificial intelligence models can analyze large amounts of medical data and identify new patterns in diagnosing diseases or identify people susceptible to the disease long before [3]. These models can also be useful in drug discovery and personalizing the treatment process [4–6]. In general, the applications and potential of artificial intelligence in medicine are numerous and can completely change traditional treatment methods.

With the rapid development of artificial intelligence in the field of medicine, given the sensitivity of this field and the importance of accuracy and error prevention in medical operations, there is a need to create protocols to control risk and prevent errors and build trust for artificial intelligence models [2]. One of the important concepts around this issue is transparency. Transparency in artificial intelligence models means that information related to artificial intelligence, from how it makes decisions to the risks and its accuracy, is shared clearly with all people who are involved in the system [7]. In this chapter, we will examine how transparency in AI-based devices in healthcare can lead to greater acceptance of these devices, gain people's trust, and make them perform better and more accurately.

Modern artificial intelligence has been able to achieve very high accuracy with the help of advanced structures such as deep neural networks. However, an important challenge that still exists is the difficulty of interpreting these models and their decision-making process. The internal structure of deep learning models is hidden from our view, and this opacity has led them to be called "black-box" models [1, 8]. Such complexity and ambiguity bring many problems in medical science. A high-accuracy output is not enough for a doctor to decide for various reasons. First, any artificial intelligence system can make an error, even if it has very high accuracy. This is unacceptable in a clinical environment where people's lives are at stake. Therefore, it is not possible to make a decision based on it without examining the reasons for producing an output, considering the accountability of the clinicians. Second, if the results of an artificial intelligence model can be verified, it is possible to eliminate its hidden errors, such as biases. Third, the trust of doctors and patients in such models can only be achieved if the output of these devices can be interpreted and medically justified [1, 2].

DOI: 10.1201/9781003743422-5

To solve the problems related to the opacity of artificial intelligence models, a field called Explainable AI (XAI) was created, and methods were designed to analyze the decision-making logic of a model. With the help of these methods, the interpretability, transparency, and explainability of these models can be improved [9]. Explainability through these methods can result from the structure of the model itself, which is known as intrinsic method, that is, the model is inherently explainable, such as simple models, such as decision trees, or the structure of the model is ambiguous, and an explanation can be generated for it with the help of another algorithm after the original model has been trained, which is known as post-hoc method, such as deep neural networks [8]. Important post-hoc methods include LIME and SHAP, which can give us information about the importance of features and describe individual outputs [10]. Another helpful post-hoc method is Grad-CAM, which is particularly helpful in generating explanations through heatmaps that overlay the original input, which can be an X-ray image, and helps clinicians to find out which regions in the image have led the AI model to produce the result [11].

With the emergence of artificial intelligence in medicine, many questions have arisen regarding ethical issues. For example, if an AI model produces an incorrect output that leads to a medical error, who is responsible for this error and compensation? The developers who were responsible for designing and preventing such errors, the regulatory bodies that were involved in approving and monitoring the operation of such a system, or the doctor who ultimately made the decision based on this model? [12] Also, most AI systems are prone to bias in producing output due to the imbalance of data in different medical datasets. According to a study, most medical datasets used by AI models are made up of information from Europeans, who make up only 20% of the world's population. This makes AI-based systems perform poorly in identifying diseases of minorities, and it is necessary to improve data balance and remove biases to improve the fairness of the model [13].

Another prerequisite for the widespread use of AI in treatment is that patients are informed about the treatment method and obtain their consent. Transparency in providing the patient with the information they need about the treatment method, risks, costs, and limitations of the system is essential to gain their trust [10]. Informed patient consent should be achieved through clear communication and explicit disclosure of the use of patient information. AI models should also have documentation that provides a summary of the tool's performance, source data, and limitations in plain language [14, 15].

Regulatory bodies play an important role in creating transparency in AI tools. Various laws have been enacted for AI so far. Laws such as the US FDA's software as a medical device framework and the EU AI Act allow for performance evaluation and risk assessment at the time of model registration, but they have limitations. Given the structure of AI models and their changes over time, there is a need for constant monitoring and periodic testing to ensure the safety of these systems [2, 7]. Using artificial intelligence in healthcare without transparency also poses challenges related to patient privacy. Given the extensive use of AI by individuals, there is a risk of leakage or misuse of patient information. To this end, there are laws that prohibit the collection and use of personal information without the consent of individuals [2]. In addition to the fact that patients must be satisfied with the use of their information, the diversity of privacy protection frameworks has complicated the process of training models. The existence of a harmonized and global framework for data protection can help produce diverse and representative datasets and unbiased models [2]. One useful thing that can be done to improve patient privacy is to use privacy-preserving techniques such as federated learning, in which patient data remains in the original data source, and only the model features are shared with other institutions [3].

We will examine the reasons for the need for transparency and review the needs of stakeholders separately. Then, we will review the methods of explainability of artificial intelligence and their applications. We will explain the ethical issues surrounding artificial intelligence and how they can be resolved with the help of transparency. Finally, we will examine the role of regulatory bodies and legal frameworks in creating transparency in artificial intelligence models in the following sections of this chapter.

## 5.2 THE NEED FOR TRANSPARENCY

First, we need to understand why there is a need for transparency in AI models in medicine, and why, despite these models achieving remarkable performance, there are still challenges in operationalizing them. Transparency of AI models in healthcare is necessary due to concerns about trust, safety, accountability, bias, and fairness [9, 16].

- **Building trust among stakeholders:** Transparency in AI systems plays an important role in building trust among doctors and specialists. The lack of the ability to analyze the logic of an AI system leads to a lack of trust among doctors and patients in the results obtained through these systems [1, 14].
- **Ensuring the safety of results:** AI models have not been as widely used by professionals as conventional medical equipment because medical decisions are so sensitive, and any wrong decision can be fatal. The use of AI systems requires the creation of a safe environment. Transparency can play an important role in making the use of AI in medical decisions safer by clarifying how the system makes decisions [15].
- **Addressing accountability issues:** Making decisions based on the results of an AI system without understanding the logic behind it can lead to incidents for which responsibility cannot be properly assigned. This responsibility can lie with many people, including the developers of the model, the organization that licensed it, or the doctors who ultimately decided to use the model's results. Transparency about why the model made the decision helps medical professionals make more responsible decisions [10, 12, 17].
- **Eliminating bias and ensuring the fairness of models:** AI models may have biases that lead to wrong decisions. These biases can occur due to the lack of data on a particular population in the dataset, which affects the fairness of the system [18], without the developers or clinicians realizing it. Transparency helps identify and eliminate these biases, ultimately leading to fairer outcomes for these systems [19].

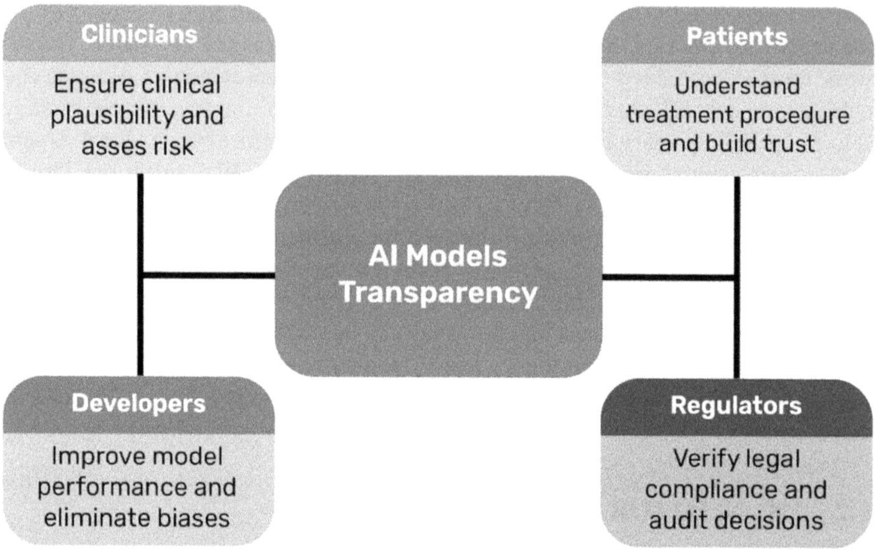


**FIGURE 5.1** An overview of stakeholders' needs for transparency in AI models.

The stakeholders of AI models in the medical field have different needs according to their goals. Figure 5.1 shows an overview of stakeholders' needs for transparency in AI models. The explanation provided to each user should be tailored to their expectations to lead to optimal use of these systems [20].

In the medical field, AI systems stakeholders can be divided into four categories, including clinicians, patients, developers, and regulators.

**Clinicians** are the primary users of AI-based decision-making systems, and they are responsible for making treatment decisions based on these systems. Their priority for using these systems is the clinical plausibility of the results. While developers focus on the mathematical interpretability of the models, physicians believe that, in some cases, this information does not help them make the right decisions. Physicians will better understand how these systems work by integrating patient-specific medical information, such as lab results or their medical history, rather than mathematically interpreting the system's decision-making process [16]. Also, knowing the level of uncertainty of the model's recommendations helps physicians greatly in assessing the risk of using these recommendations [21]. Time is of the essence in medicine. AI recommendations in this field must be fast and understandable. If the physician has to spend a lot of time to ensure that these results are correct, it may lead to medical accidents, and as a result, physicians prefer not to use these models in critical situations. And the question arises: has AI made the doctor's job easier or harder? [22].

**Developers** need transparency in AI systems to examine the internal structure of the model and the flow of information to improve the accuracy and performance of the model and to more easily identify and eliminate potential biases [16, 23]. This transparency also allows for collaboration with medical experts to examine the system's performance more accurately and to verify the results [5].

**Patients** who are directly affected by medical decisions based on AI models need to be aware of and consent to the use of AI in their treatment. The potential risks, limitations, and costs of using these models should be made clear to patients. Information about decisions made through AI should be explained to them in a simple, non-technical way. As a result, explanations directly generated by AI methods should be transformed into a form that is understandable to patients. In one study, patients stated that they preferred to have AI results explained to them by their treating physician [14]. Patients should also be informed of the laws governing the use of AI and data ownership and how their information is used in these systems [7, 14].

**Regulators** need transparency in AI models so that they can verify their legal compliance by reviewing their general specifications and decision logs and so that they can track violations if legal issues arise [15]. They can also identify and manage potential biases by knowing the demographic information in the training data of these models [7]. Regulators need measurable indicators to monitor and manage the level of compliance of AI models with ethical and legal rules, or the level of interpretability of these models [2, 24].

Finally, it is worth noting that the need for transparency of artificial intelligence models in medicine is not limited to creating technical explanations, and necessary measures must be taken according to the needs of each stakeholder in terms of transparency to provide a basis for their trust and make this technology more practical.

## 5.3 IMPACT OF EXPLAINABILITY ON TRANSPARENCY

Artificial intelligence has transformed the field of medicine, particularly through deep learning techniques. Research on this topic has helped healthcare experts to diagnose, treat, or even predict diseases [9, 25]. These systems have become more accurate over time, making them more reliable in practical scenarios, but their accuracy is a result of their complexity, which makes them less interpretable. This problem makes physicians and health experts hesitant to trust AI systems in making life-critical decisions [9, 26]. Ultimately, the reliable use of these systems requires a foundation of transparency and interpretability [2].

### 5.3.1 Definition of Transparency and Explainability

AI models, specifically those using deep learning methods, often operate with limited or no transparency, making them be called "black boxes" [9]. These "black boxes" produce outputs without any explanation or stating the logic behind them. This problem leads to ethical and liability concerns among professionals [9, 19].

To solve this problem, two concepts need to be examined: transparency and explainability.

**Transparency** of AI systems refers to the degree to which information about the system's lifecycle and operations is clearly communicated to the stakeholders. This information includes intended usage, development process, performance metrics, and underlying logic [7].

In [19], multiple dimensions for transparency have been stated:

- **"Data transparency":** Data sources used to train or test the model should be clearly explained.
- **"Algorithmic transparency":** Explanation of internal model structure and assumptions during the design of the system.
- **"Process transparency":** Development steps such as human interventions should be stated.
- **"Outcome transparency":** The procedure of result generation should be explained.

On the other hand, the **Explainability** of an AI system refers to describing the steps or processes in the system that have been executed for a specific output to be produced [9]. XAI is a set of methods that aim to enhance the transparency and interpretability of AI models to enable healthcare experts to understand the reasoning behind AI model decisions and, therefore, use them more confidently [1].

### 5.3.2 XAI Methodologies

XAI methodologies could be classified based on different features. Some of these features are interpretation type, scope, model's dependency, and its form [23]. Table 5.1 shows these features and their types. In this section, each type of method is briefly reviewed.

XAI methods classifications:

- **Interpretation type:** XAI methods are primarily categorized by the type of interpretation. These categories are known as intrinsic and post-hoc [23]. Intrinsic methods, which are also known as ante-hoc methods [22], are those in which the model structure itself is transparent. Some of the standard models, such as linear regression or decision trees, have simple structures and can be interpreted easily [2, 8]. Post-hoc methods involve generating interpretations after a complex model has been trained, and they work separately from the main "black-box" model [8, 23]. In these methods, the original model is analyzed using another external model to describe how the outputs are produced [23].

**TABLE 5.1**
**XAI Features and Their Types**

| Feature | Types |
|---|---|
| **Interpretation type** | Intrinsic, Post-hoc |
| **Scope** | Local, Global |
| **Model's dependency** | Model-specific, Model-agnostic |
| **Explanation form** | Feature-based, Example-based, Textual |

- **Model's dependency:** Another way to group XAI methods is to group them by their dependency on the model's architecture. Model-specific methods refer to methods that need a specific structure within the target model. All intrinsic methods are also classified as model-specific methods. For example, Gradient-weighted Class Activation Mapping (Grad-CAM) works with CNN models [23]. Model-agnostic methods are those that could be applied to different black-box models without any structural requirement. Some of these methods are Local Interpretable Model-agnostic Explanations (LIME) and Shapley Additive Explanations (SHAP) [2], which will be discussed further in the chapter.
- **Scope:** Explanations of AI models' behavior could be classified based on whether the general logic or reasoning of the model is explained or a specific output of the model is the target of explanation. These are usually referred to as global and local explanations. Local explanations are specifically required in clinical settings to ensure that the model results are correct for each patient case [25].
- **Explanation form:** Explanations generated by XAI methods can come in different forms. These forms include feature-based, example-based, and textual [23]. Feature-based explanations involve producing visualizations, such as saliency maps overlaying the original input, that show how much the different input variables or regions influenced the final result. Textual explanations are natural language descriptions generated to explain the model's decision [23]. Example-based explanations provide a few examples similar to the case that is being investigated to support the decision of the model [23, 26].

  AI models used in medical cases are mostly based on deep learning techniques to achieve a decent accuracy, but as mentioned earlier, this means the models are also more complex and harder to interpret [9]. As a result, XAI methods in this field are usually classified as post-hoc techniques in terms of interpretation due to the model's black-box nature [8]. Two of the commonly used post-hoc techniques in medicine are called SHAP and LIME [9]. These methods are also model agnostic. This means they can be applied to various deep learning models to generate explanations regardless of the internal model structure [2].

  The main function of these methods is called feature attribution or feature contribution. This process involves giving a value to each feature of the input that shows how influential they were in creating the output [2]. This helps clinicians to understand the reasons behind the decisions made by AI models.
- **Shapley Additive Explanations (SHAP):** SHAP is one of the most frequently used methods in the field of XAI [9]. Founded on game theory, it helps us interpret model outputs by providing a consistent approach to estimate the importance of each input feature for the model output [11, 25]. A simple example of using SHAP is predicting the probability of a disease based on patient characteristics such as age, weight, and medical history.

  For a single prediction, SHAP decomposes the model output into attribution units that represent the contribution of the input features to the output. SHAP can be used for local and global interpretability. It can calculate feature attributions across the entire dataset to show the overall feature importance, and it can calculate them for a single sample to explain a specific output [11].

SHAP has been widely used in disease prediction and detection. Some of the examples are early Parkinson's disease detection, supporting hepatitis detection, acute kidney injury prediction, heart attack prediction, preterm birth prediction, and detecting important factors of breast cancer survival. It could also be used to provide personalized treatment plans for patients based on their medical history and characteristics of diseases such as prostate cancer [9]. A study developed an XAI clinical decision support system named CORONET, which generates a score that helps clinicians decide if a patient with COVID-19 illness needs to be admitted or discharged, especially if they have cancer [21].

Using SHAP comes with limitations and challenges. Calculating SHAP values can be a computationally heavy process, and it needs a lot of time. Although methods like deep SHAP can help accelerate this process in neural-network-based models [23]. The number of samples can affect the stability of SHAP as well [23]. Methods based on SHAP can also be sensitive to the baseline chosen for calculating SHAP values [11].

- **Local Interpretable Model-agnostic Explanations (LIME):**

  Another widely adopted XAI method is LIME, which is an acronym for local interpretable model-agnostic explanations. As the name indicates, this method provides explanations locally for each output and can be applied to various ML models [23].

The idea behind the mechanism of LIME is that the behavior of black-box models, while complex and unpredictable globally, can be replicated locally by simpler models that are interpretable [20, 23]. For a single sample, this process starts by perturbing the sample to produce new synthetic samples that are slightly different from the original one. Perturbations are done by randomly changing the sample features. For instance, in text datasets, this could be done by removing or adding words, while in image datasets, this is done through overwriting parts of the images with random data. These new samples are then weighted based on their distance from the original one. Closer samples get a higher weight. Finally, a sparse surrogate model is trained on these weighted perturbed samples. Figure 5.2 shows a simple visualization of the LIME method. This

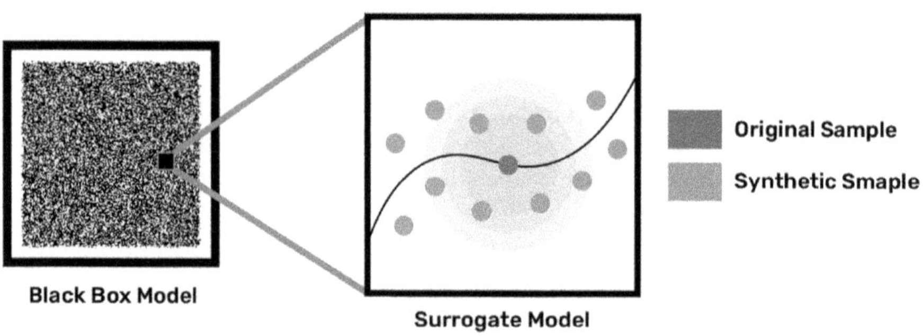


FIGURE 5.2 A simple visualization of the LIME method.

model can be interpreted easily and helps us understand how different features affect the model output in the neighborhood of the original sample [23].

LIME is one of the most important XAI methods in healthcare because it offers explanations for each patient independently, which helps doctors evaluate the AI output for a particular patient before putting it to use [2].

Applications of LIME are wide-ranging. It has improved AI models' interpretability across different illness diagnoses. This includes explaining the AI model's reasoning behind the detection of different cancers, such as colorectal cancer, breast cancer, and prostate cancer [9]. It has also been used to develop interpretable models to diagnose cardiovascular problems like heart arrhythmia [20] and acute myocardial infarction [27]. Other diagnosis applications include producing explanations for COVID-19, hepatitis, and diabetes diagnoses using AI models [9, 27].

Despite the widespread use of LIME in the XAI field, some disadvantages need to be addressed. LIME can produce inconsistent results across different datasets [9]. Results generated by LIME have low repeatability, which makes it harder for clinicians to rely on it [23]. There is a chance that LIME omits critical features while producing outputs as well [27]. And finally, LIME can be computationally expensive depending on how large the dataset is [9].

- **Class Activation Mapping (CAM) and Gradient-weighted Class Activation (Grad-CAM)**

CAM and its advanced version, Grad-CAM, are major XAI techniques specialized in generating explanations for image-based deep learning models like CNNs [11, 23].

These methods' main function is called saliency mapping, which tries to reveal parts in the input (usually an image) that are most influential in the model output [11].

CAM calculates a weighted sum of the feature maps of the last convolution layer, where the weights are obtained from the average pooling layer that replaces the model's fully connected layer [23] to create a heat map or saliency map that is overlaid on the input image to show which parts were more important to the model while making a decision [11]. However, Grad-CAM calculates "partial derivatives of the model outputs with respect to the pixel intensities found during the back-propagation step" for this procedure [11]. While CAM relies on global average pooling to get the necessary weights, Grad-CAM uses gradients to compute the weights. This allows Grad-CAM to be used with any CNN [23].

CAM and Grad-CAM have been widely used in healthcare, especially to help clinicians interpret complex CNN models' outputs when medical images are analyzed. They have been used to explain the COVID-19 diagnosis from CT and X-ray images [23]. They have also assisted clinicians in diagnosing lung diseases such as tuberculosis and pneumonia or detecting lung abnormalities [9, 23].

While Grad-CAM has addressed some of the CAM limitations, such as being limited to specific types of CNNs or the need to change the model structure for CAM to work [11], there are some challenges remaining to be addressed. Saliency mapping methods' errors can be misleading for clinicians when they are searching for reasons behind AI predictions, which might have serious consequences in the field of medicine [22]. These methods have also been reported to have insufficient accuracy in some medical activities and cannot be used reliably [11].

In addition to these methods that have been widely used in the field of XAI, there are other methods worth noting. Partial dependence plots (PDP) can help us better understand how AI models perform by visually displaying the relationship between target variables and input variables [27]. The permutation feature importance (PFI) method determines the importance of features by measuring the change in model performance after shuffling the value of a feature [20]. Rule-based methods like LORE can build local explanations by creating a synthetic neighborhood around an instance. These explanations include decision rules and counterfactual scenarios. Methods like LORE that provide counterfactual explanations help to examine the model's decision-making process by examining how much of a change in input is required to change the output [25]. This approach can be helpful in mitigating biases [13].

## 5.4 TRANSPARENCY IN ETHICS

Many methods have been proposed to understand how AI models make decisions. But these technical methods alone cannot win the trust of doctors, patients, and regulators in these models. To do this, we need to look at the ethical issues surrounding the use of AI in healthcare [2, 16].

### 5.4.1 Fairness and Bias

The safe use of AI in medicine requires us to consider various ethical issues surrounding it. One of the important issues is the fairness of AI. These models should be able to provide solutions and suggestions that are beneficial to all people and prevent the exacerbation of existing differences. Gender, age, race, and other such characteristics should not have an impact on the accuracy of the model's results. As a result, it is necessary to provide solutions to eliminate possible biases [18].

In order to eliminate biases, it is best to first see what causes bias in an AI model and what the sources of these biases are. In general, bias in a model can be divided into three categories [18]:

- **Data bias:** One of the most common types of bias is data bias. Data bias refers to the fact that the data used to train a model may not be representative of all patients. Many medical AI models are trained using datasets that are predominantly representative of people of a particular race or region. Even if representativeness is taken into account in the preparation of the datasets, there may not be enough data for many minorities. This could be due to their lack of access to healthcare facilities or the lack of electronic medical records [13, 18]. One common problem with this type of bias is in identifying common skin conditions. Many AI models trained on data that is mostly from lighter-skinned patients have trouble identifying the condition in darker-skinned patients [1].
- **Development bias:** This type of bias can occur due to the structure or optimization process of the model [1]. If a model is only considered for accuracy

and does not take into account considerations related to the fairness of the model, its performance may not be consistent across different social groups [28]. It is even possible that the model may achieve causal relationships that are not true by using identity features in the output generation process [11].
- **Interaction bias:** Interaction bias can arise from poor communication between the user and the system. If the physician is unaware of the model's weaknesses in identifying disease in minorities, overconfidence in the system can lead to misdiagnosis [18].

The importance of transparency in this context is that biases in an AI model become apparent if we can see and analyze its decision-making process, and if possible biases are observed, make the necessary changes to address them [1].

To ensure that models are fair, we need to constantly check them through tools and frameworks that are designed to assess AI models for fairness. These tools should check the accuracy of the models across different demographic groups [2]. For example, the FairLens tool is designed for this purpose. It first groups all the patient data based on characteristics such as age, gender, and race. It then examines the model's accuracy in diagnosing each of these groups. Finally, by comparing the model's accuracy in diagnosing the disease in each group, biases in the model can be detected [25].

In addition to these tools, mandatory documentation of model development and performance plays an important role in controlling the risk of using these models. This documentation should include information about the data used for training and testing, the coverage of different demographic groups, and the model's performance in diagnosing diseases in these groups. This information helps patients and physicians understand and assess the potential risks of using the model [7, 15].

AI biases in medicine can manifest in many ways. For example, the racial differences in patients are one of the most common factors that introduce bias in AI models. Models developed for skin diseases are usually trained on datasets that are predominantly of lighter-skinned individuals and do not perform well on darker-skinned individuals [2]. One study of 14 public skin image datasets found that 11 datasets did not adequately account for race and contained few images of darker-skinned individuals [11]. In radiology, studies of the performance of models trained on public chest X-ray datasets have shown that they are less accurate in detecting problems in underserved female, Black, and Hispanic populations [11]. Models that predict medical costs also tend to underestimate costs for Black people because there is less data on these people due to their lack of access to the medical system historically [29]. In addition to racial differences, gender differences are also a factor in biasing medical AI models. For example, cardiovascular disease diagnosis models tend to perform worse on women because women are underrepresented in cardiac research [30].

There are different methods that can be used to eliminate bias in AI models. The important point is that controlling bias in these models is not limited to the design and implementation time but should be considered throughout the entire life cycle of the model [30]. Ensuring that the dataset is diverse and representative is a key strategy for eliminating bias. One way to do this is to collaborate globally to produce diverse datasets [9]. When sufficient data from all patient groups are not available, oversampling techniques such as SMOTE or ADASYN can be used to balance the data [9, 19]. In addition to these methods, one study has proposed a method called AEquity that can identify biases in the data and identify their types. With the help of this method, it is possible to determine whether a particular bias is simply due to a lack of data and can be resolved by oversampling or whether the complexity of the data is high and more data is required [29]. In addition to a representative dataset, AI model algorithms need to be bias-aware. This can be achieved by using techniques such as re-weighting training data, adversarial training, and differential model tuning, or, where possible, using models such as decision trees or random forests, which are inherently interpretable and more resistant to bias [2, 24]. Finally, regular and periodic testing is necessary to verify the fairness of the model [10].

By applying these methods and strategies to eliminate biases in artificial intelligence models in medicine, we can take a step closer to safer use of these systems and gain the trust of stakeholders.

### 5.4.2 Accountability and Liability

One of the most important principles of safe use of AI is accountability. Accountability in the use of AI for treatment means being obliged to justify and explain decisions based on the model's suggestions [24]. Given the rapid development of AI in this field, the status of many ethical issues, such as accountability, is unclear [3]. The lack of a clear framework for determining the responsibility of different individuals has currently led to doctors being unfairly held responsible for the results of AI models that even go beyond their knowledge [31].

Given the complexity of distributing responsibility in situations where artificial intelligence is used, we need a unified structure to determine the responsibilities of all entities.

In the case of clinicians, while participants in a survey of clinicians believed that the ultimate responsibility for implementing AI suggestions in the treatment process lies with the doctor, [12] the extent of this responsibility is unclear, and an unfair amount of responsibility for AI errors falls on the doctors [31].

Some developers believe that the AI systems they design are merely recommender systems and cannot be used fully automatically. They also include features such as log monitoring to reduce the risk of errors. However, some experts believe that when the decision-making logic of the models is not clear, developers and related institutions also have a share of responsibility for the results of these models. Currently, determining the legal responsibility for the error of an AI model and compensating for it remains a big challenge [12].

Regulatory agencies now need a reliable framework to monitor the activity of AI models and ensure they comply with the law, but the rapid advancement of AI has outpaced these institutions, creating uncertainties in areas such as liability [2]. Healthcare institutions should require developers and providers of AI in healthcare services to follow clear protocols to ensure the safe use of these tools and to be transparent about how they operate. They should also take steps to increase public education about the safe use of AI [31].

A mechanism that can help with the responsible use of AI is human-in-the-loop (HITL). In such a system, the constant presence and supervision of an expert over the performance of the AI is required. HITL makes the responsibility for implementing AI decisions ultimately the responsibility of an expert. However, developers are also required to configure the system in such a way that the doctor can see the history of the system's outputs, run quality tests, and identify and correct errors or biases in the system [2, 12, 15].

Finally, such a system can, with the help of human supervision and traceability, largely remove ambiguities in liability for AI errors [12].

### 5.4.3 Patients and Clinicians' Trust

One of the most important factors for the ethical and effective use of AI in medicine is the trust of doctors and patients. Transparency in AI-based tools in health plays an important role in building trust [1].

For doctors and healthcare professionals, gaining trust is achieved by using transparency in explaining the decision-making logic of these systems. As a result, the use of XAI techniques can enhance doctors' trust in AI, but the important thing is that these explanations are relevant and understandable to doctors, because vague and complicated explanations can have the opposite effect and make doctors' trust in AI less than before [1, 19, 26].

Patients' trust in artificial intelligence and the quality of their treatment also depend on transparency in the treatment process. Providing understandable and clear explanations to patients helps them feel involved and informed and ensures their autonomy in the treatment process [1, 19].

On the other hand, the opacity of AI tools destroys stakeholders' trust. When doctors cannot be sure that the output of AI systems is correct, their trust is undermined [1]. Also, the misuse of these tools or the production of wrong results can damage people's trust. For example, generative AI can suffer from hallucination, which means the production of fake information, and generally occurs in situations where the model does not have enough information [32, 33]. The presence of bias in these systems also prevents people from trusting, especially minority patients [12].

The important point about trust is that the goal is not simply to increase stakeholder trust. Rather, it is to reach an appropriate level of trust that is consistent with the limitations and accuracy of the AI models' algorithms. Just as doctors' lack of trust in AI models can prevent their use, excessive and unquestioning trust in these models is risky, and doctors must always be in control of decisions [26].

## 5.5 THE ROLE OF OVERSIGHT AND GOVERNANCE IN TRANSPARENCY

The rapid advancement of artificial intelligence in the medicine field and its integration into patient care have created an urgent need for robust regulations and oversight by relevant organizations. The lack of regulations related to the use of AI in sensitive areas such as medicine is a major barrier to the responsible and safe deployment of these models [9, 34]. This section reviews current AI oversight regulations, as well as the frameworks needed to document and monitor AI models.

Legal oversight and clear ethical frameworks are a must for the safe and trustworthy use of AI in medicine. Such laws and frameworks should clearly define the conditions for the responsible, ethical, and transparent use of AI [2]. Several key points should be considered when establishing legal oversight:

First, transparency in AI-based systems is essential to ensure legal compliance and accountability. So, transparency of AI models is not just an advantage but a requirement for their use [24].

Second, current models are generally evaluated by static metrics at the time of initial validation and commissioning. This approach is fundamentally flawed for AI models, especially LLMs and other machine learning models that change and adapt over time. Thus, there is a need for methods that can monitor AI performance periodically or in real time throughout its lifetime [2].

Third, the current legal frameworks for the use of AI vary and are inconsistent worldwide, making it challenging for AI developers and service providers to comply with all legal frameworks. As a result, there is a need for international cooperation among global regulatory bodies to adopt a coherent and global framework for the safe use of AI [2].

### 5.5.1 Regulatory and Documentation Frameworks

Current major legal frameworks for artificial intelligence oversight are the EU AI Act and the US FDA's Software as a Medical Device framework, which we will explore below. These frameworks are designed to address concerns related to transparency, accountability, bias, and privacy [2, 7].

#### 5.5.1.1 The EU AI Act

The European Union has attempted to create a coherent framework for ensuring the safety of AI-based systems by creating the AI Act. The law has a human-first, risk-based structure that currently classifies all medical AI tools as high-risk tools [15]. This classification forces developers to carry out various assessments to check the safety and quality of the system [15]. The Act also requires AI models to undergo rigorous testing to check for bias and data governance. Despite the strict rules imposed by the framework, there are still uncertainties in various areas. For example, there has been no action taken on changing the risk classification of these tools after initial approval. This issue is problematic if a tool is approved with a "low risk" category and later falls into the "high risk" category due to changes in the logic of the machine learning models. Also, given that the law is specifically based on human rights, it has not taken action on the environmental impacts of AI [2].

#### 5.5.1.2 The US FDA's Software as a Medical Device (SaMD) Framework

In the United States, the Food and Drug Administration is responsible for overseeing AI-based medical devices [10]. The Administration is constantly regulating such systems, requiring high-risk devices to have pre-use assessments and quality control and performance monitoring [19]. In 2021, the FDA's Center for Devices and Radiological Health published an action plan that encourages the movement of AI-based devices in medicine toward a human-centered and transparent approach, which shows how the main focus has shifted in recent years from raw performance to interpretability and transparency for medical AI devices [7]. In its Good Machine Learning Practices, the FDA emphasized the importance of eliminating bias and ensuring interpretability in building trust in AI devices [11]. One of the limitations of the FDA's approval method for AI medical devices is the use of static performance metrics, which are vulnerable to changes in AI in the real world. Also, tests performed on these devices are generally performed in the same and fixed conditions, which prevents the evaluation of the device's performance and its generalizability to unstable and different real-world conditions [2].

In addition to legal frameworks, other efforts have been made to create consensus frameworks for the safe and reliable use of AI in medicine. One of the efforts is the **FUTURE-AI** guidelines. This guideline is the result of the efforts of 117 experts from various disciplines in 50 countries. Inspired by the FAIR principles of data management, the guidelines are based on six principles. **Fairness** refers to the need for the model to perform equally among all patients regardless of their personal characteristics, which is possible by eliminating biases. **Universality** means that the desired performance of the model should not be limited to a specific place and should be adaptable to different treatment conditions. **Traceability** means creating facilities to monitor the performance of the system, perform quality tests, and create documentation to describe the model. **Usability** emphasizes the human aspects and accessibility of using AI. This principle is possible by creating mechanisms for easy human interaction with AI. **Robustness** refers to the importance of maintaining the accuracy and performance of the system when facing variations in data, and finally, **Explainability** refers to producing simple and comprehensible explanations for the outputs produced by the system [15].

Another way to bring transparency to AI-based tools in medicine is to create documentation that describes in detail how the model works and the data used to train it. This documentation helps doctors, patients, and regulators assess the model's safety, fairness, and reliability and be aware of its limitations [2].

Examples of this type of documentation are Google Model Cards and IBM's AI Fact Sheets. These documents are very similar to nutrition labels. While nutrition labels provide basic information about a food product, these documents provide information about a model, including hyperparameters, a summary of the model's performance tests, potential biases, limitations, and information about the training and testing data, all clearly and transparently presented to everyone [15].

### 5.5.2 Protecting Patient Information and Privacy

One of the most important concerns in the use of artificial intelligence in medicine is the protection of patient information. In a situation where these systems operate on the basis of data, and the more data they receive, the better they perform, the more complex it is to manage and protect this volume of data. In fact, protecting patient information and preventing unauthorized access or misuse of this information is as important as ensuring that artificial intelligence equipment in medicine is safe and ensuring the physical health of patients. As a result, just as patients have the right to be informed about how these systems work and the risks, they should also be informed and consent to how these systems use their information [3].

The use of patient data in AI models creates the need to create legal frameworks regarding the privacy and protection of patient data used by these models. While similar frameworks such as the General Data Protection Regulation (GDPR) and Health Insurance Portability and Accountability Act (HIPAA) exist, adapting them to the specific circumstances of AI has presented challenges [2, 4, 35].

#### 5.5.2.1 General Data Protection Regulation (GDPR)

The GDPR, which was established in the European Union in 2018, enacted laws on privacy and data protection that specifically give European residents rights regarding their personal information [1]. These rights require systems such as AI-based devices in medicine to be transparent and obtain consent in the use and storage of patient data [2]. The regulation also requires developers of AI models to explain the decision-making process of the AI model's algorithm [20].

Given the specific characteristics of AI, there are conflicts between the GDPR and the way AI-based devices operate that could currently make the widespread use of AI models in medicine problematic. While the GDPR assumes that an entity is responsible for the protection of individuals' data, in modern AI structures such as blockchain-based systems, data is stored in a decentralized manner. The rules also state that each person's data can be deleted or changed at the request of the individual. For example, in the case of search engines, each person can request to be removed from search results, but in the case of AI models, the information may be processed in such a way that it cannot be deleted or changed after the model has been trained. Finally, the GDPR rules say that any individual can access information about how their data is used by automated systems, but in the case of AI, this is complicated, and the extent of this access is not specified by the GDPR [1, 3, 24].

#### 5.5.2.2 Health Insurance Portability and Accountability Act (HIPAA)

In the United States, HIPAA is designed to protect citizens' health information. According to this law, if health care providers want to use a patient's private health information in any context other than treatment, payment, and other health services, they must inform the person and obtain consent. To do this, the type of use of the patient's information and its purpose must be clearly explained to the person. Patients should also have the right to access their health information and correct it if necessary. This law reserves the right for any person to request a report on the use of health data by various entities [1].

While these rules are in line with transparency in AI-based healthcare, they pose challenges for the development of these models. Compliance with these rules by models requires precise and heavy processes, given their complex structure. Also, the existence of different laws in different parts of the world creates many challenges for models that are trying to train using international data and avoid biases [2].

One way to solve the challenges related to protecting personal health data is to implement privacy-preserving techniques. These techniques can be effective in solving problems related to unauthorized access or data leakage, especially in the case of artificial intelligence models that work with large volumes of data [3, 10].

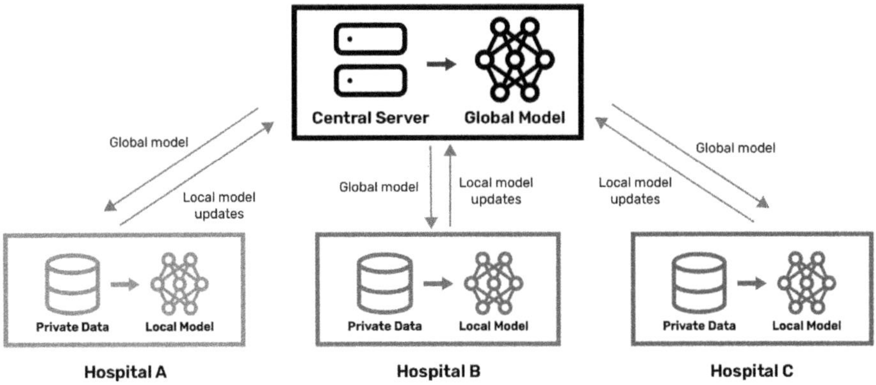


**FIGURE 5.3** A simple workflow showing how federated learning operates.

Examples of these techniques include federated learning. In federated learning, artificial intelligence models can be trained jointly by several institutions without the need to transfer private patient data to each other. In fact, each hospital or institution trains a local model with its own local data, and only the trained model parameters or features are shared between these institutions through a central server that trains a global model using the institution's local model updates and then shares it with the participants. Figure 5.3 shows a simple workflow of federated learning. This technique can be significantly effective in solving patient privacy problems or international collaboration challenges [3, 36].

In order to further improve privacy in this method, other methods such as differential privacy are used. This method makes it significantly difficult and challenging to discover private data of individuals by adding noise to the data or model output [3].

By using these technologies and complying with patient privacy laws, responsibility can be promoted in protecting patient data and using their data, and as a result, patients' trust in artificial intelligence devices in medicine will increase.

## 5.6 CONCLUSION

Using artificial intelligence in the treatment process has created new opportunities to improve treatment outcomes and use more accurate tools in health. However, to consolidate these opportunities, it is necessary to reduce the risks of using these tools by creating transparency and resolving the ethical challenges surrounding the use of artificial intelligence models. As discussed in this chapter, transparency is one of the main features of artificial intelligence that can be used safely and reliably in medicine. Therefore, transparency is not only a desirable feature in artificial intelligence models, but its existence is also essential to meet the needs of stakeholders and gain their trust. It was examined that one of the most important reasons for the need for transparency in artificial intelligence models is the inherent opacity of these models and the hiddenness of their decision-making logic. So far, various methods have been proposed under the title of XAI to explain the decision-making process of machine learning models, and a few of the most widely used ones were reviewed. Despite the value of the explanations generated by these methods for better understanding the model outputs, these explanations alone are not sufficient to gain the trust of doctors and patients in the medical field because they do not adequately match clinical situations and can be complex and technical for people.

We have also seen how ethical issues, such as the fairness of models, can be challenging. The presence of bias in AI tools weakens the accuracy of the model in identifying various diseases in minorities and reduces the trust of patients in these models. Eliminating biases in models requires that transparency be observed in the data used and in the model algorithm so that they can be identified. Transparency in AI models can also help establish trust in patients and doctors, but another important point is that doctors need to know how reliable such tools are and be aware of the possible risks to avoid blind decision-making.

Another reason why a black box model is not suitable for use in medicine is the ambiguity of liability in the event of a medical error. To solve this problem, it is necessary to clearly define the responsibilities of each relevant entity and to closely monitor their accountability. Doctors are ultimately responsible for treatment decisions, but they need interpretable tools to make the right decisions, and developers are responsible for creating these tools.

In addition, in order to protect the rights of all parties in the use of AI in the treatment process, we need coherent laws that are compatible with the complex structure of AI. Although current laws protect patient rights to some extent, we need a global legal structure that is adjusted according to the characteristics and limitations of AI, and its coherence will facilitate international legal cooperation for the development of AI. Another aspect of transparency in AI is that developers document information about their models, including the data used, the accuracy of the model, and its risks, in a clear and understandable way so that users can better understand the model and prevent misuse.

There are still challenges in protecting user data. Existing privacy laws complicate data processing for models, and implementing privacy-enhancing methods can address some of these issues. Finally, as mentioned, the widespread use of AI in medicine requires transparency in several aspects that lead to trust, safety, and accountability.

## REFERENCES

1. Nasir S, Khan RA, Bai S. Ethical Framework for Harnessing the Power of AI in Healthcare and Beyond. IEEE Access. 2024;12:31014–35. https://doi.org/10.1109/ACCESS.2024.3369912
2. Goktas P, Grzybowski A. Shaping the Future of Healthcare: Ethical Clinical Challenges and Pathways to Trustworthy AI. J Clin Med. 2025;14:1605. https://doi.org/10.3390/jcm14051605
3. Williamson SM, Prybutok V. Balancing Privacy and Progress: A Review of Privacy Challenges, Systemic Oversight, and Patient Perceptions in AI-Driven Healthcare. Appl Sci. Multidisciplinary Digital Publishing Institute. 2024;14:675. https://doi.org/10.3390/app14020675
4. Faiyazuddin M, Rahman SJQ, Anand G, Siddiqui RK, Mehta R, Khatib MN, et al. The Impact of Artificial Intelligence on Healthcare: A Comprehensive Review of Advancements in Diagnostics, Treatment, and Operational Efficiency. Health Sci Rep. 2025;8:e70312. https://doi.org/10.1002/hsr2.70312

5. Alizadehsani R, Oyelere SS, Hussain S, Jagatheesaperumal SK, Calixto RR, Rahouti M, et al. Explainable Artificial Intelligence for Drug Discovery and Development: A Comprehensive Survey. IEEE Access. 2024;12:35796–812. https://doi.org/10.1109/ACCESS.2024.3373195
6. Farhadi A, Zamanifar A, Faezipour M. Application of Generative AI in Drug Discovery. In: Zamanifar A, Faezipour M, editors. Appl Gener AI Healthc Syst [Internet]. Cham: Springer Nature Switzerland; 2025 [cited 2025 Dec 8]. p. 155–74. https://doi.org/10.1007/978-3-031-82963-5_6
7. Shick AA, Webber CM, Kiarashi N, Weinberg JP, Deoras A, Petrick N, et al. Transparency of Artificial Intelligence/Machine Learning-Enabled Medical Devices. Npj Digit Med. Nature Publishing Group; 2024;7:21. https://doi.org/10.1038/s41746-023-00992-8
8. Joyce DW, Kormilitzin A, Smith KA, Cipriani A. Explainable Artificial Intelligence for Mental Health through Transparency and Interpretability for Understandability. Npj Digit Med. Nature Publishing Group; 2023;6:6. https://doi.org/10.1038/s41746-023-00751-9
9. Alkhanbouli R, Matar Abdulla Almadhaani H, Alhosani F, Simsekler MCE. The Role of Explainable Artificial Intelligence in Disease Prediction: A Systematic Literature Review and Future Research Directions. BMC Med Inform Decis Mak. 2025;25:110. https://doi.org/10.1186/s12911-025-02944-6
10. Varnosfaderani SM, Forouzanfar M. The Role of AI in Hospitals and Clinics: Transforming Healthcare in the 21st Century. Bioengineering [Internet]. 2024; 11:268830921. https://api.semanticscholar.org/CorpusId
11. Chen RJ, Wang JJ, Williamson DFK, Chen TY, Lipkova J, Lu MY et al. Algorithmic Fairness in Artificial Intelligence for Medicine and Healthcare. Nat Biomed Eng. 2023;7:719–42. https://doi.org/10.1038/s41551-023-01056-8
12. Nouis SC, Uren V, Jariwala S. Evaluating Accountability, Transparency, and Bias in AI-Assisted Healthcare Decision-Making: A Qualitative Study of Healthcare Professionals' Perspectives in the UK. BMC Med Ethics. 2025;26:89. https://doi.org/10.1186/s12910-025-01243-z
13. Haider SA, Borna S, Gomez-Cabello CA, Pressman SM, Haider CR, Forte AJ. The Algorithmic Divide: A Systematic Review on AI-Driven Racial Disparities in Healthcare. J Racial Ethn Health Disparities [Internet]. 2024. [cited 2025 Oct 30]; https://doi.org/10.1007/s40615-024-02237-0
14. Stroud AM, Minteer SA, Zhu X, Ridgeway JL, Miller JE, Barry BA. Patient Information Needs for Transparent and Trustworthy Cardiovascular Artificial Intelligence: A Qualitative Study. PLOS Digit Health [Internet]. 2025;4:277960320. https://api.semanticscholar.org/CorpusId
15. Lekadir K, Frangi AF, Porras AR, Glocker B, Cintas C, Langlotz CP, et al. FUTURE-AI: International Consensus Guideline for Trustworthy and Deployable Artificial Intelligence in Healthcare. BMJ. 2025;e081554. https://doi.org/10.1136/bmj-2024-081554
16. Bienefeld N, Boss JM, Lüthy R, Brodbeck D, Azzati J, Blaser M, et al. Solving the Explainable AI Conundrum by Bridging Clinicians' Needs and Developers' Goals. Npj Digit Med. Nature Publishing Group; 2023;6:94. https://doi.org/10.1038/s41746-023-00837-4
17. El, Arab RA, Al Moosa OA, Abuadas FH, Somerville J. The Role of AI in Nursing Education and Practice: Umbrella Review. J Med Internet Res. 2025;27:e69881. https://doi.org/10.2196/69881
18. Anderson JW, Visweswaran S. Algorithmic Individual Fairness and Healthcare: A Scoping Review. JAMIA Open. 2024;8:ooae149. https://doi.org/10.1093/jamiaopen/ooae149
19. Weiner EB, Dankwa-Mullan I, Nelson WA, Hassanpour S. Ethical Challenges and Evolving Strategies in the Integration of Artificial Intelligence into Clinical Practice. PLOS Digit Health. 2025;4:e0000810. https://doi.org/10.1371/journal.pdig.0000810

20. Jung J, Lee H, Jung H, Kim H. Essential Properties and Explanation Effectiveness of Explainable Artificial Intelligence in Healthcare: A Systematic Review. Heliyon. 2023;9:e16110. https://doi.org/10.1016/j.heliyon.2023.e16110
21. Wysocki O, Davies JK, Vigo M, Armstrong AC, Landers D, Lee R et al. Assessing the Communication Gap between AI Models and Healthcare Professionals: Explainability, Utility and Trust in AI-Driven Clinical Decision-Making. Artif Intell. 2023;316:103839. https://doi.org/10.1016/j.artint.2022.103839
22. Wabro A, Herrmann M, Winkler EC. When Time Is of the Essence: Ethical Reconsideration of XAI in Time-Sensitive Environments. J Med Ethics. Institute of Medical Ethics. 2025;51:516–20. https://doi.org/10.1136/jme-2024-110046
23. Chaddad A, Peng J, Xu J, Bouridane A. Survey of Explainable AI Techniques in Healthcare. Sensors. Multidisciplinary Digital Publishing Institute. 2023;23:634. https://doi.org/10.3390/s23020634
24. Radanliev P. Privacy, Ethics, Transparency, and Accountability in AI Systems for Wearable Devices. Front Digit Health [Internet]. Frontiers; 2025 [cited 2025 Oct 30];7. https://doi.org/10.3389/fdgth.2025.1431246
25. Metta C, Beretta A, Pellungrini R, Rinzivillo S, Giannotti F. Towards Transparent Healthcare: Advancing Local Explanation Methods in Explainable Artificial Intelligence. Bioengineering [Internet]. 2024;11. https://api.semanticscholar.org/CorpusId:269124762
26. Rosenbacke R, Melhus Å, McKee M, Stuckler D. How Explainable Artificial Intelligence Can Increase or Decrease Clinicians' Trust in AI Applications in Health Care: Systematic Review. JMIR AI. 2024;3:e53207. https://doi.org/10.2196/53207
27. Hettikankanamage N, Shafiabady N, Chatteur F, Wu RMX, Ud Din F, Zhou J. eXplainable Artificial Intelligence (XAI): A Systematic Review for Unveiling the Black Box Models and Their Relevance to Biomedical Imaging and Sensing. Sensors. 2025;25:6649. https://doi.org/10.3390/s25216649
28. Joseph J. Algorithmic Bias in Public Health AI: A Silent Threat to Equity in Low-Resource Settings. Front Public Health [Internet]. Frontiers; 2025 [cited 2025 Oct 25]; 13. https://doi.org/10.3389/fpubh.2025.1643180
29. Gulamali F, Sawant AS, Liharska L, Horowitz C, Chan L, Hofer I. Detecting, Characterizing, and Mitigating Implicit and Explicit Racial Biases in Health Care Datasets with Subgroup Learnability: Algorithm Development and Validation Study. J Med Internet Res. 2025;27:e71757–e71757. https://doi.org/10.2196/71757
30. Chan SCC, Neves AL, Majeed A, Faisal A. Bridging the Equity Gap towards Inclusive Artificial Intelligence in Healthcare Diagnostics. BMJ. British Medical Journal Publishing Group. 2024;384:q490. https://doi.org/10.1136/bmj.q490
31. Comeau DS, Bitterman DS, Celi L. Preventing Unrestricted and Unmonitored AI Experimentation in Healthcare through Transparency and Accountability. NPJ Digit Med [Internet]. 2025;8. https://www.ncbi.nlm.nih.gov/pubmed/39827300
32. Gorelik AJ, Li M, Hahne J, Wang J, Ren Y, Yang L et al. Ethics of AI in Healthcare: a Scoping Review Demonstrating Applicability of a Foundational Framework. Front Digit Health. [Internet]. Frontiers; 2025 [cited 2025 Oct 25];7. https://doi.org/10.3389/fdgth.2025.1662642
33. Taheri A, Farhadi A, Zamanifar A. Application of GenAI in Clinical Administration Support. In: Zamanifar A, Faezipour M, editors. Appl Gener AI Healthc Syst [Internet]. Cham: Springer Nature Switzerland; 2025 [cited 2025 Dec 8]. p. 91–117. https://doi.org/10.1007/978-3-031-82963-5_4
34. Rashidieranjbar F, Farhadi A, Zamanifar A. Revolutionizing Healthcare with Generative Artificial Intelligence Technologies. In: Vajjhala NR, Roy SS, Taşcı B, Hoque Chowdhury ME, editors. Gener Artif Intell AI Approaches Ind Appl [Internet]. Cham: Springer Nature Switzerland; 2025 [cited 2025 Dec 8]. p. 189–221. https://doi.org/10.1007/978-3-031-76710-4_10

35. Farhadi A, Taheri A. Application of GenAI in Synthetic Data Generation in the Healthcare System. In: Zamanifar A, Faezipour M, editors. Appl Gener AI Healthc Syst [Internet]. Cham: Springer Nature Switzerland; 2025 [cited 2025 Dec 8]. p. 67–89. https://doi.org/10.1007/978-3-031-82963-5_3
36. Rahman A, Debnath T, Kundu D, Khan MSI, Aishi AA, Sazzad S et al. Machine Learning and Deep Learning-Based Approach in Smart Healthcare: Recent Advances, Applications, Challenges and Opportunities. AIMS Public Health. 2024;11:58–109. https://doi.org/10.3934/publichealth.2024004

# 6 Detection and Prevention of AI Failures and Anomalies

*Alireza Taheri, Azadeh Zamanifar, and Amirfarhad Farhadi*

## 6.1 INTRODUCTION

The shift of artificial intelligence (AI) research from theoretical toward pervasive, transformative applications in various spheres, including healthcare utilizing generative technologies [1] and applied in complex fields like immunogenetics [2], finance, transportation, and industrial automation, has greatly increased the demand for strong means of failure and anomaly detection and prevention mechanisms [3]. Organizations in different fields are increasingly incorporating complex AI models into core operational infrastructure to catalyze innovation and improve decision-making. Applications vary across medical diagnosis, including AI for hard-to-treat and unknown-origin cancers [4], complex autonomous navigation systems, and others. For example, autonomous dental treatment planning utilizes deep learning for object detection [5]. From simple to very complicated financial forecasts [6], they all rely on AI. Despite the impressive performance attained in highly controlled settings, the actual deployment of these systems into the unpredictable real world faces severe challenges in terms of reliability and safety. The discrepancy between idealized performance and operational reality underscores the urgent need for comprehensive strategies to detect and mitigate AI failures and anomalies.

The inherent nondeterministic nature of many AI or machine learning (ML) workloads makes their effective monitoring and accountability hard to achieve. Unlike traditional, deterministic software, AI systems create results via inherently stochastic processes, probabilistic inference, and adaptive algorithms. Even given identical inputs, results are unreliable [7]. Failures emanate from various vectors, which are normally grouped into three categories: data shift, model drift, and adversarial attacks. Primary causes of abnormalities and degradation in performance have to do with data distribution shifts, characterized by time-spaced changes in statistical properties of data, which are generally defined as concept drift [8]. These shifts may emanate across different environments (spatial variation) or insidiously over time (temporal variation), a phenomenon sometimes better described as AI aging. Besides this, in distributed environments such as federated learning, concept drift raises other challenges. Drifts can occur in space and time staggered across multiple clients. This calls for multimodel solutions rather than a single global model for effective adaptation.

 DOI: 10.1201/9781003743422-6

Beyond natural degradation, AI systems are vulnerable to intentional threats. Adversarial attacks are subtle, often imperceptible manipulations of the input data aimed at deceiving the model into incorrect predictions [9]. These attacks compromise the integrity of the AI supply chain at various touch points; the supply-side attack tampers with data poisoning at the time of training, while the demand-side attack introduces adversarial perturbation during runtime. Furthermore, complex models such as deep neural networks (DNNs) often act as black boxes, which inhibit human understanding of internal decision-making processes [10]. This is another reason for the difficulty in predicting unknowns, emergent behaviors, or out-of-distribution (OOD) data points that are far away from the training distribution of the model and may cause sudden and severe failures. Since AI systems are increasingly applied in safety-critical areas such as autonomous vehicle control and clinical decision support, undetected errors or degraded performance can lead to serious consequences, including misdiagnosis, accidents, and financial losses [3, 11].

Against the multidimensional vulnerabilities presented by this class of applications, AI failure detection and anomaly prevention are crucial to maintaining reliability and safety. A good strategy begins with well-practiced monitoring that will need to expand beyond traditional infrastructure metrics, such as CPU usage, to include domain-specific measures, such as feature drift assessments, prediction confidence, and model accuracy [7]. Detection systems can use several techniques to gather and monitor real-time system data, including logs and system performance metrics: for known faults, supervised learning models are trained on historical failure data, while for detecting new anomalies, unsupervised methods apply, such as clustering or autoencoders. Interpretation of complex system logs and fault prediction can also be possible with large language models (LLMs) and transformers using semantic analysis. This advanced monitoring, often coined as observability, is basically essential to infer the internal state of nondeterministic systems from their external outputs.

Detection needs to be closely coupled with the prevention strategy, which in most cases involves automated alerts that shall promptly notify stakeholders on the detection of an anomaly. Prevention strategies include periodic model maintenance with more current data to avoid model degradation, as well as a fallback mechanism to keep systems up during recovery. Advanced systems will have self-healing AI that combines the process of detection with autonomous recovery activities, like dynamic replacements of compromised containers, to enable real-time mitigation of faults without human intervention [12]. It is very important to know the root cause of degradation in order to drive an intervention that is targeted and diagnosis-driven and not a generic correction. This necessitates embedding explainability techniques into monitoring frameworks, enabling engineers to interpret flagged anomalies and bolstering overall system accountability. Lastly, ensuring operational safety demands ongoing robustness analysis. This evaluative process monitors decisions over time to verify that the system can withstand environmental noise and adversarial perturbations without compromising performance [13]. Figure 6.1 depicts the hierarchy of a sample diagnostic granularity, moving from superficial symptom detection to deep causal understanding. While basic monitoring and detection flag anomalies and failures, more sophisticated analysis is required to identify the reason via feature-level

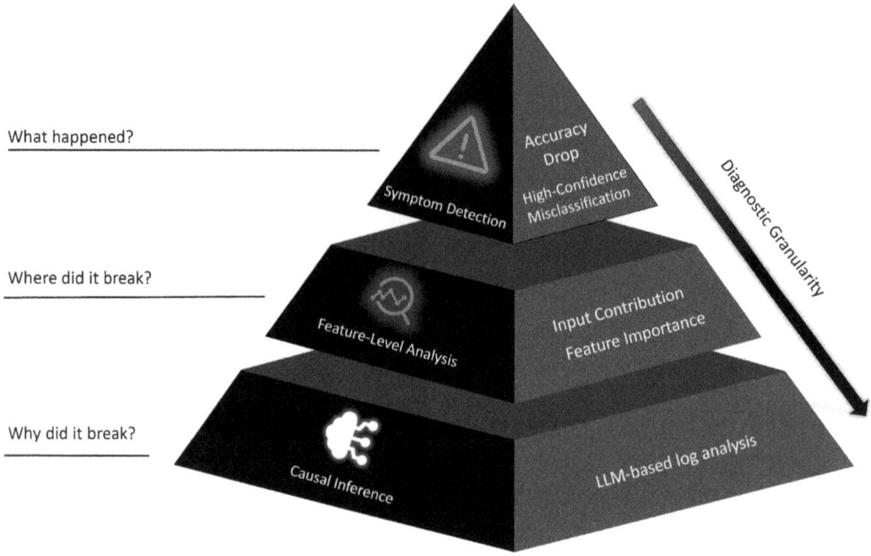


**FIGURE 6.1** Hierarchical framework for the detection and diagnosis of AI failures and system anomalies.

analysis. The base of the pyramid represents the most advanced diagnostic tier, utilizing LLM-based log analysis and causal inference to answer the fundamental question of the detected anomaly. These concepts will be discussed later in this chapter.

The remainder of this chapter is structured to provide a comprehensive trajectory from the identification of AI vulnerabilities to the implementation of resilient, self-healing architectures. Section 6.2 establishes a theoretical taxonomy of AI failures, focusing specifically on the mechanics of data distribution shifts, including covariate, label, and concept drift. Section 6.3 transitions from theory to observability, detailing proactive detection strategies that utilize prediction confidence metrics and feature-drift monitoring. In Section 6.4, we explore the black-box diagnostic challenge. Section 6.5 discusses mitigation and recovery, outlining the transition from manual model retraining to the deployment of autonomous, self-healing agents. Finally, Section 6.8 concludes the chapter.

## 6.2 TYPES OF AI FAILURES

The effective integration of AI systems into operational applications is constantly undermined by various types of failures and anomalies that hamper reliability and predictivity. Contrary to traditional software applications, AI and ML applications tend to perform stochastic processing due to stochastic processing and adaptive algorithms, thus hindering the monitoring and troubleshooting process [11]. The presence of varying levels of predictability forces a study of the types of potential failures expected to occur within the operational life cycle of the AI system. The potential sources include changes occurring in input data properties as well as manually stimulated malicious attacks or even the stochastic nature within the model [8]. The identification and classification of potential sources within this context represent the first line of defense for developing effective tools for detecting and preventing threats within the context of degraded system integrity. The following classification of potential types of failures and anomalies within AI systems reveals a comprehensive view into the significant sources that tend to impinge upon the performance levels of operational AI systems.

### 6.2.1 Data-Driven Failures

Data form the basis of any AI system, making data anomalies and inconsistencies a major attack vector against AI models. Data failures may result in a system exhibiting a subtle change in a distribution, which might affect generalization, to a noticeable point, which causes hard failures in AI systems.

The most common data-related risk is data distribution shift, whereby the data characteristics observed during deployment in the target distribution are different from the ones during training in the source distribution [14]. ML systems are designed with the assumption that training and testing data are samples from the same data source, which is common in most real-world environments with changing characteristics. This common problem results in model deterioration or model drift, causing ineffective model performance over time. The data sources related to data distribution shift can shift in the following data-distribution forms:

- Covariate Shift: This is the phenomenon where the marginal distribution of the features varies while the relation between the features and the targets stays the same in the source as well as the target domains. For instance, when the training model of the elderly is applied to the younger population with the reasoning of the medical logic intact, the model may produce inaccurate predictions because the input data distribution has changed, even though the underlying conditional probability remains constant.
- Label Shift: This type of failure happens when there is a change in the marginal distribution of the labels but the conditional input distribution is held constant. It happens when there is a change from a disease-off-season model to disease-outbreak scenarios, where the disease is much more prevalent. This type of change is also known by the name prior probability shift [8].
- Concept Shift: This is a change in the mapping from input features to target labels, where there is a change in the conditional distribution probability. This change has a direct effect on the target concept, where there is a need to change the decision boundary. The reasons for a concept shift could be changes in various factors, for instance, clinical practice updates or changes in user patterns [15].

Apart from the categories based on the source of the probabilistic change, the distribution shift can also be classified on the basis of the pattern according to which the distribution shift changes over time. This pattern is commonly termed *concept drift*. There are various patterns based on which the distribution shift changes over time.

These patterns involve sudden drift (sharp transition from one concept to another), which can happen anywhere, anytime. However, it has been considered under the category of the absence of determinism due to its sharp nature. Gradual drift is another pattern based on which the distribution shift changes over time. This pattern refers to the smooth transition from one concept to another. This can happen anywhere, and hence, it falls under the absence of determinism. There is another pattern based on which the distribution shift changes over time [16].

In addition to the shifts that impact the entire data distribution as a whole, data anomalies can be understood as isolated instance-level anomalies in the data input that are far beyond the region of data distribution in the training data, which belongs to OOD data detection. OOD inputs are those data examples a model fails or chooses not to generalize to [17]. Data anomalies differ fundamentally from data shifts: while shifts typically cause progressive performance degradation, anomalies represent abrupt, catastrophic triggers that result in hard failures of deep learning algorithms. These hard failures occur when a system encounters sudden, extreme irregularities, such as excessively noisy inputs or the absence of domain-critical features that immediately compromise the model's operational integrity. Anomalies in the data are identified as a key challenge in model trustworthiness.

AI models, specifically deep learning models, are highly vulnerable to attacks that involve minor, even insignificant, modifications of input data for the purpose of misleading models into producing erroneous outputs. We consider part of adversarial attacks as part of failures and anomalies that can happen to an AI model. Adversarial attacks can be considered major threats, particularly for safety-sensitive areas such as autonomous vehicles or health informatics, since errors can cause deaths [18]. The types of adversarial attacks, depending on the knowledge and objectives of the attackers, include the following:

- White Box Attacks: The attacker has complete knowledge of the architecture and parameters of the target machine, as well as complete knowledge of how it works (e.g., the gradients of the loss function), enabling them to craft very effective attacks [19].
- Black-Box Attacks: The attacker has limited information and can query the attacked model for predictions or confidence values [18].
- Targeted Attacks: The aim is to compel the model to incorrectly categorize the input as a predefined class.
- Non-Targeted Attacks: The aim is simple, which is to deceive the model into misclassifying the input data away from its original class but not caring about the resulting class [19].

Aside from the runtime modification of input, the AI supply chain is vulnerable throughout its entire life cycle, from the acquisition of data to the deployment and maintenance of the AI model. The key areas in the AI supply chain are:

- Data Poisoning: Data poisoning attacks refer to actions whereby an attacker injects harmful, corrupted, and deceptive information into the training set to result in erroneous model behavior and biased prediction outputs. Data poisoning attack is considered a supply-side attack that affects the integrity of the model construction [9, 11].

- Model Theft and IP Leakage: The attacker could use model extraction attacks to clone valuable AI functionality and/or model inversion attacks to infer valuable information related to the original training data, resulting in intellectual property theft and data privacy violations.
- Adversarial Input Manipulation: Attacks using adversarial perturbations may be performed in terms of deployment to affect real-time decision-making.

### 6.2.2 Model-Driven and Operational Failures

Failures of models are not solely due to data problems or malicious attacks; they might also result from the very nature of the models or the context in which they exist, especially regarding their complexities and lack of transparency. Complex models, such as deep learning models, are typically opaque black boxes, and their internal processes, resulting in decision-making, cannot be understood by humans. This problem of complexity leads to unmonitorability, implying the impracticality of effectively monitoring the sophisticated AI system to forecast some capabilities or unsafe outcomes in advance, before they happen. This becomes difficult, as complex properties emerge from the interactions of components not explicitly designed or foreseen by the designers themselves [10].

The temporal variability of AI algorithms, including highly complex ones like LLMs, and the resulting staleness of knowledge occur because the model is not regularly updated. As a result, there is a mismatch in the internal model representations and the actual conditions in the world, resulting in misclassifications or the production of confident but inaccurate responses, referred to as hallucinations [8]. This form of model degradation refers to the phenomenon where the predicted probabilities of the model are no longer consistent with the observed outcomes. Although the model performs discriminately well even with accurate classification of observed outcomes, calibration drift makes the predicted risk scores less interpretable in the context of risk stratification in the safety-critical domain of healthcare risk prediction.

While the AI model is being updated for keeping up with relevance (plasticity), there are chances of forgetting the previously learned knowledge. This is known by the name stability and plasticity dilemma because if plasticity increases, stability decreases, and vice versa [8]. In a more complex setup like a multi-autonomous agent system or industrial setup, the sensors and hardware that the AI models depend upon can fail. For instance, a failure in a component, like a damaged LiDAR sensor in an autonomous vehicle, can cause the model to receive abnormal input, resulting in the model failing or acting abnormally [11, 20]. Autonomous agents function in a dynamic environment and should act normally despite being exposed to abnormal inputs [13].

Accountability also extends to human decisions made during the design and development phases, rather than just those occurring during real-time operation. In safety-critical fields such as healthcare, flaws in oversight, design, and testing create latent risks. For example, failing to adhere to industry standards or neglecting to test common operational scenarios creates a responsibility gap. This gap obscures liability, making it difficult to determine who is at fault when the system eventually fails [11].

## 6.3 DETECTION STRATEGIES

The task of ensuring the reliability and safety of AI systems functioning in real-world, ever-changing, and varied environments demands the adoption of efficient and watchful approaches for the detection of failures in AI systems. Unlike traditional software programs, the nondeterministic nature of AI/ML tasks indicates the possibility of system failure and events of anomaly occurring due to reasons of unseen changes in data, deterioration of models, or attacks from malicious sources, often initially with latent or hidden symptoms resulting in catastrophically disastrous outcomes [21]. As a consequence, for efficient AI failure detection, we have to depart from traditional approaches for AI system failure, thereby enabling continuous real-time acquisition and observation of system data, such as system logs, sensors, or performance metrics, to observe initial signs of failure of AI systems or models. The approaches for anomaly or failure detection in AI models can be generally classified depending on the nature of the sources of information used, namely statistical and other expert approaches for data, or methods of observing their performance or outputs, and AI models themselves [7].

### 6.3.1 Methods of Monitoring Data and Distribution

The reliability of an AI model depends directly upon how consistent its input data is; hence, the monitoring of changes and shifts within the input data distributions forms the nucleus of methodical techniques for detecting drifts. Data observation and monitoring are centered upon discovering changes within the distributions of the input space that might eventually result in inferior model performance. Sophisticated techniques within statistics and ML are required for monitoring and discovering changes that are important yet infinitesimally small in nature [8].

The detection systems aim to keep observing the deviations between the current distribution of the data and the reference distribution on a constant basis, often raising an alarm whenever the indicated deviation value goes beyond a certain predefined margin. The prominent approaches include statistical approaches founded on the concept of distance measurement, aiming to assess the deviation between the distributions of the features. The maximum mean discrepancy (MMD) function, for instance, tries to estimate the difference in the embeddings with the highest values in the two probability distributions in the feature space. The Wasserstein distance, or Earth Mover's distance function, will assess the minimum cost that is required to transport the probability distribution from one to the other, attempting to reflect the total amount of effort that is necessarily involved in the process. Other approaches include the use of information theory-related measurements, like Kullback-Leibler divergence and Jensen-Shannon divergence, aiming to assess the deviation between a certain probability distribution and the predefined distribution. To detect the process in the streaming data, the CUSUM statistical approaches work effectively in observing the incremental deviations with respect to the predefined base value. Finally, the categorical data approaches aim to compare the categories' values in the two datasets using simple hypothesis testing approaches like the Chi-Square test statistic [8].

### 6.3.2 Model Performance and Output Monitoring

Model monitoring is the observation of the internal state and functioning of the AI system regarding the model's possible and sometimes necessary change due to the change in the data. This type of model is then bifurcated into supervised and unsupervised models on the basis of whether the model uses the ground truth or not [22].

Performance-based methods require the presence of ground truth in order to compute the standard performance metrics, including accuracy, F1 score, and Area Under the Receiver Operating Characteristic Curve (AUROC) on the time series of performances. The degradation of the model is determined by the time the above metrics go below a certain threshold set by the validation set. It is a very straightforward method of model degradation, and the model's condition is very transparent, which is especially valuable for model checking on occasions or retrospective checking. Techniques include error rates above a certain threshold, and the model sends out notifications when it crosses the threshold [23].

Model output-based methods provide a label-free, scalable solution that is essential in situations involving delayed or no access to ground-truth labels. Model output-based methods monitor changes in the model predictions, considering them indicators of model behavior changes. This can involve the application of distance-based output monitoring, wherein the distribution of the softmax output feature vector is compared for the current and reference data based on statistical distances such as MMD metrics. In other approaches, score-based output monitoring monitors scalar measures that can be calculated based on model outputs, including maximum softmax probability (MSP), entropy, or energy scores calculated from logits, for changes in confidence or uncertainty levels. There also exist auxiliary model-based methods that rely on an additional model like a discriminative model or a conditional generative model [24] that measures the reliability of a prediction or the likelihood of the input based on the predicted label, offering a measure of the reliability or trustworthiness of the primary model's predictions.

A particular and problematic type of degradation is calibration drift, which is applied when predicted probabilities do not correspond to actual outcomes while maintaining calibration of their discriminative capability. Identification relies on dynamic calibration curves learned from true labels or, for calibration assessment without labels, regression of calibration to characterize the calibration conditions of cohorts [8].

### 6.3.3 Anomaly and Fault-Specific Detection Techniques

This includes techniques designed specifically for recognizing either immediate or specialized indications of failure, specifically targeting sudden and specific deviation instances of system failure.

OOD detection is a technique used to detect instance-level peculiarities or inputs that differ substantially from the training distribution, often utilized as warning signs for impending failures of models [25]. Such points, as opposed to gradual distribution shifts, are likely to cause dramatic failures, often termed hard failures. OOD detection is a vital technique used to discover high-risk examples before a large distribution shift has happened. In addition to being dependent on traditional confidence information such as MSP, there has been a focus on energy and density methods to provide a more efficient insight into the geometric structure of the data or contrastive learning to increase separability in the representation space [26].

ML for fault diagnosis deals with the application of ML models to the data collected from system monitoring to predict or identify potential faults. The identification process can make use of a combination of models: Supervised learning models are trained with past data from potential system failures and are very effective at identifying known system faults with high accuracy. On the other hand, unsupervised learning models like cluster models and autoencoders are used specifically for identifying unknown system faults with no predefined labels based on past system data observations [27]. The application of hybrid models of AI makes use of both supervised and unsupervised models to identify a wider spectrum of system faults with high accuracy.

### 6.3.4 Advanced Log Analysis and Behavioral Observability

With the increasing sophistication of AI systems, there is nuanced, non-numeric data in the form of logs and traces that is crucial for diagnosis. Sophisticated methods utilize language models and complex system knowledge for the analysis of this data. Semantic Analysis using LLMs refers to using advanced modeling capabilities and transformers for semantic analysis of system log data to predict system failures based on patterns. For instance, LLMs can analyze text data that might point to underlying issues or develop system behavior that would otherwise go unnoticed through mere keyword search analysis [28].

Observability and distributed tracing involve methods that aim at estimating the inner working of nondeterministic systems based on external outputs, which goes beyond the realm of the traditional concept of monitoring [7, 29]. This requires the consolidation of diverse information sets such as domain-centric metrics, feature drift scores, prediction trust scores, and explainability datasets. Cross-service observability traces interactions among diverse system components, including data flows, feature repositories, API systems, and more. Facilitating distributed tracing and version management (lineage tracing) is imperative for ensuring end-to-end traceability in ML-based applications once a discrepancy is observed [30]. Table 6.1 summarized failure detection strateies.

**TABLE 6.1**
**Summary of AI Failure Detection Strategies: Methods, Categories, and Principles**

| Category | Specific Technique/ Method | Description |
|---|---|---|
| Foundational Monitoring and Observability | Real-Time Data Collection | Continuous collection of real-time data, including system logs, sensor inputs, and performance metrics, to identify early signs of malfunction. |
| | Observability Framework | Method for inferring the internal state of nondeterministic systems from their external outputs, integrating metrics like feature drift and prediction reliability. |
| | Explainability Integration | Utilizing techniques to help engineers understand the root cause of failures by revealing why an AI system flagged certain anomalies, thereby enhancing accountability. |
| Data and Distribution Monitoring | Distance-Based Metrics (MMD, Wasserstein, KL/JS Divergence) | Statistical comparison of the current data distribution against a reference distribution to quantify distributional discrepancy. |
| | Sequential Statistical Methods (CUSUM) | Tracks incremental deviations from an expected baseline over streaming data, useful for detecting gradual or temporal concept drift. |
| | Hypothesis Testing (Chi-Square Test) | Compares the frequency of categories between datasets to detect shifts in structured or categorical input data. |
| | Supervised ML for Data Shift Detection (Domain Classifier) | Trains a model to classify whether an input belongs to the source or target distribution; a high classification score signals a clear distributional difference. |
| | Unsupervised ML for Data Shift Detection (Autoencoders) | Detects shifts when the reconstruction error of the model significantly increases upon receiving new input data, suggesting inability to reconstruct OOD inputs. |
| Model Performance and Output Monitoring | Performance-Based Metrics (Accuracy, AUROC, F1 Score) | Tracks metrics against a predefined degradation threshold, relying on available ground-truth labels for retrospective performance assessment. |
| | Score-Based Output Monitoring (MSP, Entropy, Energy Scores) | Monitors scalar statistics derived from model predictions to detect behavioral shifts when ground-truth labels are unavailable or delayed. |
| | Calibration Drift Detection | Tracks whether predicted probabilities align with actual outcomes over time, crucial for identifying degradation in risk assessment systems even if classification accuracy remains stable. |

*(Continued)*

**TABLE 6.1** *(Continued)*
**Summary of AI Failure Detection Strategies: Methods, Categories, and Principles**

| Category | Specific Technique/ Method | Description |
|---|---|---|
| Anomaly and Fault-Specific Detection | Out-of-Distribution (OOD) Detection | Identifies individual inputs that lie far outside the training distribution, using confidence signals or density/energy-based methods to flag high-risk cases. |
| | Supervised Learning for Fault Diagnosis | Uses models trained on past failure data to recognize known and recurring types of faults with high accuracy. |
| | Unsupervised Learning for Fault Diagnosis | Uses clustering or autoencoders on system monitoring data to detect novel or previously unseen anomalies that lack prior fault labels. |
| | Semantic Analysis using LLMs/Transformers | Leverages the semantic analysis and pattern recognition capabilities of sophisticated models to interpret complex system logs and predict impending faults. |

## 6.4 DIAGNOSIS

However, the movement from being able to observe the existence of the anomaly in the AI system to knowing its cause is implemented via diagnosis and root cause analysis (RCA) techniques [8, 31]. In the life cycles of AI systems, particularly in AI systems that run in a nondeterministic fashion in a complex real-world scenario, being able to indicate a possible failure in performance is not adequate; rather, knowing the root cause is essential in ensuring that there are specific and timely interventions in place in order to guarantee overall system safety and trustworthiness. The RCA stage can be considered as the urgently needed middle ground of the overall detection-diagnosis-correction (DDC) loop in being able to favor stakeholders from having to administer generic corrections instead of starting precision-tracking correction actions [12, 32]. This particular stage in the DDC primarily demands very advanced analysis capabilities and knowledge beyond mere system output data points. As illustrated in Figure 6.2, the RCA stage serves as the urgently needed middle ground of the overall DDC loop. This framework prevents stakeholders from administering generic corrections by favoring precision-tracking actions based on advanced analysis and knowledge beyond system outputs.

In model degradation diagnosis, a fundamental issue lies in identifying data distribution shifts that contribute to the performance degradation. Data shifts have been considered the primary contributor to anomalies and thus have to be properly diagnosed [33]. In this case, shifts can either be a result of changes in the data characteristics known as covariate shifts, changes in the label known as label shifts, or changes in the underlying targets known as concept shifts. Each distinct type calls

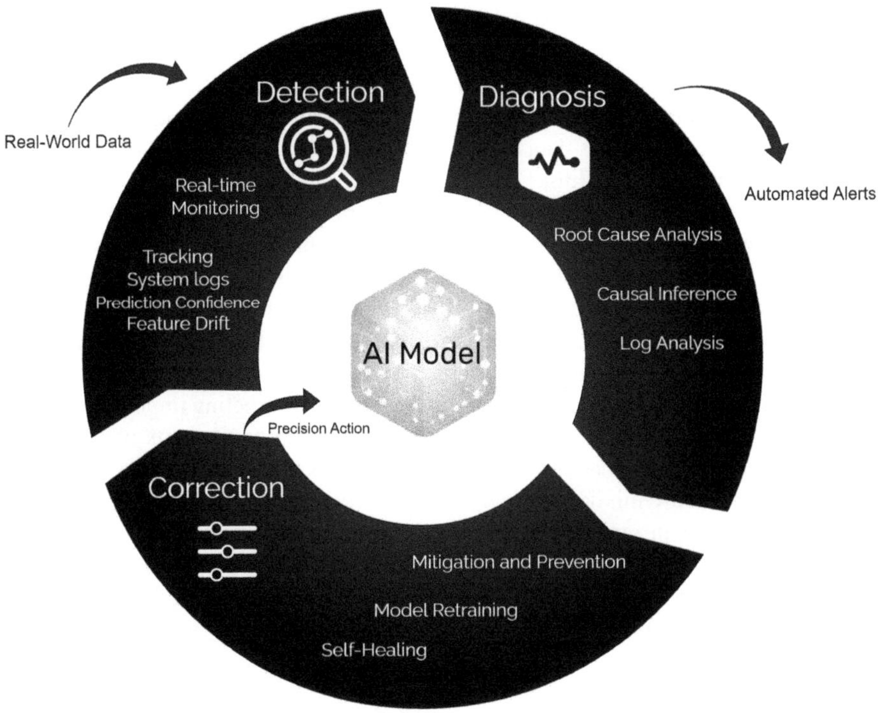


**FIGURE 6.2** The detection-diagnosis-correction (DDC) loop: A conceptual framework for transitioning from anomaly observation to precision-tracking interventions.

for a distinct diagnosis and correction process. For example, in covariate shifts, there is a change in the input attributes only, and the relationship between the attributes and the targets is unaltered. In this scenario, model correction will require domain adaptation (DA) with a focus on aligning the attributes. Secondly, a label shift where the probability distributions change will require output reweighting or calibration correction [34]. Finally, in case of a concept drift where there is a total change in the relationship between attributes and targets, a model reset will thus require redrawing the entire boundary for correct model prediction [14]. The distinction between each form is imperative because failing to diagnose the real nature of a simple drift could make correction very expensive and laborious, while overlooking a concept drift could make model failures catastrophic [35].

Diagnosis requires extensive work with system logs and various other real-time measures of system performance to identify potential failures. Sometimes, simple system data cannot, by itself, determine cause and effect. Causal inference-based methods offer a way to trace model failures upstream based on system data and policy change to better identify the relationship between system output and input parameters by measuring correlations between various system elements [27]. This requires the application of explainable methods and techniques, which are very important within system explanations to provide a better "*why*" related to system errors and improve system accountability. This process attempts to improve AI system diagnostic efficiency by analyzing various graphs and models involved within causality to better point to actions within the data stream change to make system corrections. This process is further aided by system observability techniques to identify interactions between various data and system elements within cross-service observability and tracing methods [36].

Computational complexity and lack of monitorability in recent models of intelligence, such as DNNs and LLMs, often prevent human monitors from having complete awareness of the state processes within the models. To address this problem that can arise with the application of these advanced models, new techniques must incorporate the strength of AI itself. LLM-based diagnostic methods leverage the reasoning and semantic analytics strength provided by large language models for analysis purposes, focusing on complex system logs and predicting impending faults. Such models can quickly parse unstructured logs and large amounts of free-form information based on the pattern recognition capacities that human monitors lack. In environments that are mission-critical, such as healthcare applications, graph-based engines for RCA can rapidly and accurately point to the source of a discrepancy with the system by linking patterns associated with system flaws on the complex microservice relationships within a system. A time accuracy of milliseconds can be achieved through the application of these engines, making them imperative in the case of self-healing systems that require a certain degree of instant compliance recovery actions [37, 38].

RCA should also conduct an investigation of its own architecture characteristics, particularly in cases where errors in external data are not solely responsible for model failure. Model-centric analysis entails model assessment of its own internal behavior patterns for the employed neural network architecture. For example, advanced methods assess spectral characteristics of weight matrices for various layers of deep learning architectures. By using indicators based upon metrics related to both linear algebra norms and power laws, such methods can identify whether or not there might be issues of capacity loss, overparametrization, or inadequate training for any particular model. Such an analysis combines data-centric or causal inference approaches in model analysis for highly useful supplementary capacity in comprehensive RCA. By leveraging detection patterns for joint root cause determination, while weaving in explainability into process monitoring, model developers can provide for highly specific remedial treatment of exactly identified failure issues, focusing on accountability for model fidelity through precise remedial post-detection [3, 8, 39].

## 6.5 PREVENTION AND MITIGATION

The process of identifying the failures and anomalies in the functioning of an AI system must therefore be integrally linked with those of prevention and mitigation to ensure the integrity of the performance and trustworthiness of the system in the complex environment of real-world applications. Effective strategies in the process of mitigation include those that work toward the proactive preparation of the system to withstand risks that could make the system vulnerable in situations like shifts in the underlying data, the process of degradation with the age of the model, or even attacks that could compromise the integrity of the system. The process in these scenarios, therefore, is to work toward ensuring that the performance of the system is restored in the event of a degradation incident while making the system impervious to risks in the future. The process of prevention, in its alignment with the process of identifying failures, on the other hand, seeks to work toward ensuring the integrity of the performance of the system in the process of AI life cycle applications. The process of mitigation, on the other hand, is based on the concept of ensuring the continuity of the system in the process of identifying the failures in the application of the system.

### 6.5.1 Architectural and Design-Time Prevention

Prevention begins fundamentally with the design stage of the AI system and not with the deployment stage. Using model architectures and designing with defense mechanisms at the fundamental stages will greatly decrease vulnerability to natural attacks resulting in failures [9]. Given the fact that faults can be delivered through any part of the supply chain, from data sourcing to model deployment, a multilayered approach to safety that focuses on the AI supply chain is essential [9]. Prevention must cover various types of faults on the supply side of the chain, such as data issues on training datasets, as well as attacks on the demand side of the chain or from malicious input on a deployed model. Using blockchain-based data provenance solutions to securely track and prove the origin of the data, as well as ensuring that training datasets are tamper-proof and authentic, are essential in ensuring model safety. Leveraging blockchain and ANFIS can ensure optimal supply chain management [40, 41]. In decentralized ML frameworks, adopting a Zero Trust Architecture (ZTA) during deployment facilitates micro-segmentation and continuous authentication. By enforcing granular access controls at the model-segment level, ZTA prevents lateral movement during a security breach, ensuring that individual model components remain isolated and secure [9].

### 6.5.2 Proactive and Continuous Maintenance

The performance of AI will inevitably deteriorate as a result of changes in the data or the aging of models. Active maintenance means adjusting continuously to stay pertinent within the current environment, thereby preventing the deterioration from resulting in failure. Model updating and retraining AI models periodically by exposing them to fresh data helps mitigate the issues associated with model drift and degradation by maintaining the performance level on the new data distributions [42]. It may involve fine-tuning the model on a few samples or on large data sets [43]. However, it poses a problem of catastrophic forgetting, by which the incorporation of new information leads the system to unintentionally forget the previously learned tasks. Methods involving approaches like rehearsal or regularization techniques can be helpful while achieving the balance between plasticity and stability.

Domain Adaptation and Generalization to fill the potential performance difference caused by the data discrepancy between the training domain and the deployment domain, DA methods are used [3]. In the context of unsupervised domain adaptation (UDA), the aim is to match the hidden representations in the feature space across the two domains, utilizing the target domain's unlabeled data samples. This is highly effective in dealing with the issues due to covariate shifts, for instance, sensor changes in the imaging modality case, and more, caused due to the deployment domain's data difference from the training domain's data in the source domain [44]. The most effective method in practice is the model's adaptation to the deployment domain, directly utilizing the unlabeled input stream at the time of deployment in the context of test-time domain adaptation (TTDA).

### 6.5.3 Active Mitigation and Automated Recovery

When a failure or an anomaly has been successfully identified, there should be an automatic response to ensure business continuity and to act on that failure/anomaly. The initial stage of defense after the detection of potential issues is the automated notification of concerned individuals upon the detection of any anomalies and faults. At the same time, fallback options play significant roles within the context of ensuring uninterrupted operation and functioning of the AI module until the main AI module is repaired and rectified by diagnostic procedures for restoring normal AI operation and functioning.

The most sophisticated proactive countermeasure employs self-healing AI systems that integrate anomaly detection with autonomous recovery procedures. Such systems boast the transformation of fault recovery procedures from the typical reactive role of human operatives to intelligent, real-time automated recovery procedures [45]. The recovery agents in these systems frequently employ Reinforcement Learning (RL) to create dynamic policies that support adaptive autonomous decision-making procedures. The RL agent, trained on many failure instances, learns the best sequence of recovery steps, including the dynamic replacement of defective software containers with pre-scanned golden images or resource re-allocation, that optimizes system availability while ensuring the shortest recovery time [45, 46]. The autonomous recovery feature in these self-healing systems is essential in enabling zero-downtime availability in the mission-critical infrastructure of various systems [12, 47]. As shown in Figure 6.3, these systems create a closed-loop architecture where the monitoring layer triggers automated responses, such as model rollbacks, retraining, and safe mode, to maintain service continuity without human oversight.

Effective mitigation requires a shift from general repairs to guided interventions. A justification about why a given system has identified an anomaly or failure is required for developers to grasp the reason and provide a fitting response. Diagnosis-based intervention prevents inefficiencies from occurring during remediation and ensures targeted repairs are made, minimizing waste and any subsequent consequences. Additionally, in regulated fields such as finance and healthcare, recovery strategies also have to be compliance-conscious; this requires the inclusion of ethical constraints such as data locality rules within the reward function of the RL agent for maintaining legal compliance during autonomous behaviors [12]. Table 6.2 summarized AI prevention and mitigation strategies.

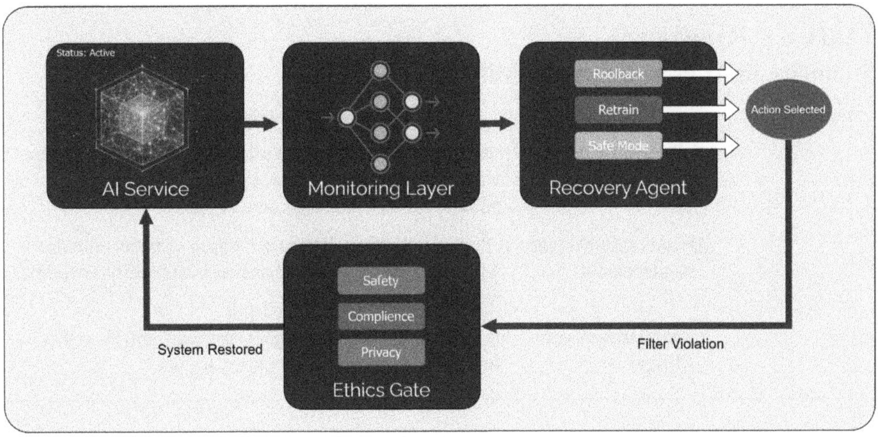


**FIGURE 6.3** Architecture of an autonomous self-healing AI system.

## TABLE 6.2
## Summary of AI Prevention and Mitigation Strategies

| Category | Strategy | Description |
|---|---|---|
| **Architectural and Design-Time Prevention** | **Multilayered Supply Chain Safety** | Implementing safety measures from data sourcing to deployment to protect both the supply side (training data) and demand side (deployed models). |
| | **Blockchain Data Provenance** | Utilizing blockchain to securely track data origins and ensure training datasets are authentic and tamper-proof. |
| | **Zero Trust Architecture (ZTA)** | Adopting micro-segmentation and continuous authentication to isolate model components and prevent lateral movement during security breaches. |
| | **Inherently Robust Architectures** | Choosing model designs that demonstrate natural resistance to perturbations compared to more vulnerable models. |
| **Proactive and Continuous Maintenance** | **Periodic Retraining and Updating** | Continuously exposing models to fresh data to mitigate aging and drift, ensuring performance remains relevant to current environments. |
| | **Regularization and Rehearsal** | Using specific training techniques to balance stability and plasticity, preventing the catastrophic forgetting of old knowledge during updates. |
| | **Domain Adaptation** | Aligning hidden representations between training and deployment domains using unlabeled data to handle covariate shifts and data discrepancies. |
| **Active Mitigation and Automated Recovery** | **Automated Alerts and Fallbacks** | Ensuring business continuity by immediately notifying stakeholders of anomalies and switching to redundant modules during repair. |

*(Continued)*

**TABLE 6.2** *(Continued)*
**Summary of AI Prevention and Mitigation Strategies**

| Category | Strategy | Description |
|---|---|---|
| | **Self-Healing AI** | Integrating detection with autonomous recovery procedures where Reinforcement Learning agents learn optimal policies for real-time fault correction. |
| | **Dynamic Container Replacement** | Automatically swapping compromised software containers with pre-scanned golden images to enable zero-downtime recovery. |
| | **Compliance-Aware Mitigation** | Incorporating ethical and legal constraints into the reward functions of autonomous recovery agents. |

## 6.6 CASE STUDIES

The implementation of AI in healthcare presents a critical landscape for analyzing failures and anomalies. Applications range from generative AI for clinical administration [48, 49] and synthetic data generation [50] to highly specialized use cases like precision chronotherapy for neurodegenerative disorders [51]. In these high-stakes environments, predictive errors can lead to catastrophic clinical repercussions, such as misdiagnosis or erroneous treatment protocols [8]. Despite AI models being highly efficient when tested in clinical data setups [52], their practical application in real-world medical situations reveals potential weaknesses due to data dynamics, structural paradigms, and the nature of the highly intricate models such as LLMs [3, 53]. Analyzing real-life situations of AI model degradation and carefully planned experimental analysis to determine the robustness of models remains highly informative to develop trustworthy, reliable, and safe AI systems for medical practices. The following case studies describe crucial challenges involved in utilizing AI models for different tasks and the prevention methods to ensure model integrity and safeguard healthcare services.

A case study evaluating ML models applied for the prediction of Acute Kidney Injury risk observed model accuracy over a period of nine years. The results identified a highly dangerous form of model accuracy loss referred to as calibration drift. Calibration drift refers to a situation or scenario whereby the model's predictive probabilities are no longer related in a precise manner to the actual observed event occurrences, while at the same time the model's predictive classes are properly distinguished. In this particular study, there was no degradation in the discriminatory accuracy of the models for nine years, but the calibration of their predictive outputs was severely degraded. The degradation was mainly due to event rate distributions and relationships between predictors and outcomes. The calibration mismatch between predictive outputs affects the healthcare relevance of the models and could potentially mislead important tasks such as patient triaging and stratification for care based on their predictive outputs of disease risk and severity. This underscores the critical need to monitor model outputs for confidence and calibration drifts, as degradation in these areas directly compromises patient safety. Implementing proactive healthcare corrections requires specialized techniques, such as dynamic calibration curves and regression models for feature-level cohort estimation. These methods are essential for maintaining model reliability, particularly in clinical settings where ground-truth labels are often delayed [8].

As highly complex AI architectures, LLMs, especially GPT-4, begin to be applied in medical environments, including psychological interventions and therapies [54], some particular problems could result in terms of stability and reliability [10]. Although very advanced in performance, LLMs have shown some unexpected behavior in medical environments in terms of performance decrease over short periods of time. The evaluation of the GPT-4 model was carried out on the American College of Radiology In-training Examination. To check the consistency of the model over time, the study required the model to answer the questions several months later. The study established that GPT-4 changed its response 25.5% of the time, showing high levels of temporal variability. This level of degradation was also exhibited by the GPT-4 model when assessing radiology question answering and interpretation capabilities. This degradation is evidence of the general problem that GPT models have been known to experience in other evaluations related to the degradation of the model's ability to follow user instructions over time [55]. The emphasis of this LLM degradation experiment is that even very complex models are not exempt from problems that generally relate to internal optimization resolutions concerning speeds and efficiency that affect accuracy or staleness of knowledge updates. These results confirm again that any kind of AI tool needs to always be continuously monitored concerning its performance, no matter what level of complexity it possesses.

A specific study was conducted for the robustness of the models used in computational pathology, wherein CNNs are commonly used. It was observed that CNN models are highly vulnerable to attacks for realistic pathology classifications, such as subtyping RCC or gastric cancer [3, 18]. In striking contrast, vision transformers, which perform equally well at baseline, showed several orders of magnitude more robustness to the same set of adversarial attacks. This empirical evidence suggests that architectural choice is a significant prevention strategy. Large-scale deployment of AI models in computational pathology should be implemented using inherently robust models for protection against input perturbation.

One simulation study investigated the impact caused by event-driven data shifts, such as that brought on by the COVID-19 pandemic, on models deployed for clinical sepsis prediction [56]. Results underlined that data shifts greatly affect model performance and that monitoring and intervention are continuous processes. This challenge in the real world was explicitly acknowledged when a major hospital deactivated its sepsis-alerting model after demographic shifts triggered spurious alerts during the COVID-19 pandemic. A sepsis model, trained on previous patient populations and conditions, was unable to generalize properly upon exposure to the new cohort and pathology presented by the pandemic. This was a failure due to data shift. A primary takeaway is that AI monitoring must prioritize the early detection of performance-degrading data shifts. This proactive approach ensures timely interventions, such as model retraining and maintenance, which are essential for sustaining accuracy and relevance within dynamic clinical environments.

## 6.7 CHALLENGES AND CONSIDERATIONS

The application of AI systems in real-life operational scenarios, especially in the sensitive sectors such as medicine, brings forth an unprecedented challenge with a spectrum of essential considerations that need to be systematically focused on the safety and integrity of the system. Though advanced detection and preventive strategies work toward the reduction of failures and anomalies, the complex patterns and the nondeterministic properties of these algorithms, along with the dynamic environment in operational scenarios, bring forth irremovable risks that cannot easily be remedied. The aforementioned tasks include the strategic technical challenge of missing values to the broader complexities of ethics and regulative policies in relation to bias, privacy, and accountability of the system performance in clinical applications. The acknowledgment of these imperfections is not just an intellectual pursuit in the development of these AI systems to focus on the long-term integrity and credibility in their usage in the like of clinical decision support systems.

### 6.7.1 Missing or Delayed Ground-Truth Labels

A significant challenge in the evaluation cycle of AI safety programs is the latency or absence of ground-truth labeling, particularly in medical and high-velocity domains [22]. While continuous ground truth is the gold standard for validating predictive accuracy and detecting model degradation, it is often prohibitively expensive, delayed, or even impossible to obtain in real-time [8]. This creates a critical bottleneck: effective surveillance requires immediate feedback, yet the clinical reality of delayed outcomes hinders the timely evaluation and correction of AI systems.

### 6.7.2 Explainability and Model Opacity

The critical factor in achieving success in the process of failure detection and correction in AI systems relates to explainability, which assists in understanding why AI systems identified a set of anomalies and why AI systems in general may fail. The lack of interpretability makes it difficult to diagnose and fix errors, hence causing a degradation of trust. It remains important to undertake RCA and make diagnoses to focus on corrective measures and not rely on generic methods for their application [8]. The inherent opacity of LLMs, compounded by their rapid evolution, results in significant unpredictability. This instability, which is characterized by performance variability over time, presents substantial challenges for effective monitoring and anomaly detection. Thus, their solutions require the application of methods and techniques from the field of XAI to make their monitors utilize SHAP and LIME methodologies to undertake dissections and detect potential biases in their models and processes [3, 7]. In addition to this complexity, highly advanced AI systems' complexity and size also present unmonitorability, which implies that it could be impossible to properly predict a capability or an undesirable effect in advance of its occurrence [10].

### 6.7.3 The Stability-Plasticity Dilemma

As AI models are updated to adapt to changing data environments, they begin to face a basic issue of stability versus plasticity, also known as the stability-plasticity dilemma. This basically includes equating system stability to retaining previously developed knowledge, which prevents any possibility of catastrophic forgetting, along with developing adaptability to learn new information, like updated medical guidelines. In medical environments, catastrophic forgetting of some rare diseases or particular subtypes of a disease, which is developed using past training data, might lead to critical knowledge gaps, resulting in potentially dangerous consequences. System updates to address this basic issue of adapting to new information might cause system variability in performance, introducing system behavior unpredictability [16].

### 6.7.4 Regulatory, Ethical, and Accountability Issues

With the growing integration of AI systems in strategic industries like healthcare for autonomous functioning, there is a need for a deep reflection on the ethical and governance implications of failures for AI systems. Failures and anomalies that emanate due to model drifts, data bias attacks, and adversarial attacks go beyond the performance metrics for a technology, portending future uncertainties for both compliance and human security. The growing use of AI systems in sensitive application areas calls for engineers to cross beyond the limitations of technology for ensuring the ethics associated with human security for appropriate functions and behaviors of AI systems upon failing or behaving in unexpected ways [10, 11].

### 6.7.5 Bias and Fairness

As AI systems tend to learn solely from training data, this automatically also tends to reflect and propagate any biases that exist in humans, leading to unjustified biased outputs when implemented. Thus, for instance, a medical AI-based risk evaluation system could work well on an aggregate basis but tend to fall short on a regular basis for particular ethnic or demographic sectors due to a lack or unrepresentation in training data sets. When AI systems fail or deviate from expected behavior, the consequences often fall disproportionately on specific societal groups. These failures exacerbate performance gaps, which are disparities in accuracy, robustness, and security that vary by social class. Ultimately, this results in a systemic inequality where certain sectors of society benefit from reliable AI while others remain vulnerable to malfunctions and tampering. The functionality and robustness testing for loss detection needs to be implemented in a manner that continuously tracks and watches for any manifestation of bias and inter-class differences for fairness and equity, and retention and replenishment for the continued public trust that needs to be nurtured for AI system integration and functionality, as well as on a related basis as mentioned accordingly [8, 57].

### 6.7.6 Data Privacy and Regulatory Compliance

Simply by achieving system observability, there are concerns regarding data privacy. This is because monitoring effectively requires continuous observation and recording of system input/output and intermediate values of features, which often can be highly sensitive in nature. Observability systems must therefore focus on compliance with privacy-preserving mechanisms like data anonymization, data aggregation, and differential privacy. However, implementing these privacy mechanisms introduces significant complexity and often degrades the precision of system metrics. This creates a trade-off between observability and compliance that can be difficult to navigate, as the noise required for privacy can mask the very anomalies the system is designed to detect. [7, 12, 58].

### 6.7.7 Scalability and Resource Intensity

The challenges posed by implementing sophisticated AI detection and prevention tools include scalability and resource intensity issues. The task of monitoring, computing drift metrics, or creating an explainability report (such as SHAP values) is computationally expensive. As discussed, such operations might affect system speeds in production tasks, which have low latency requirements for their execution [7, 29].

### 6.7.8 Tool Fragmentation in Observability

The observability landscape in AI is fragmented and tends to use different instruments to cater to infrastructure monitoring, data profiling, model registration, and drift analysis. This makes it very difficult for developers to gather and connect several different instruments effectively. As a result, they may end up facing issues regarding data coherence [7].

## 6.8 CONCLUSION

The pervasive integration of AI across critical societal sectors, from complex clinical decision-making to simpler administrative tasks in healthcare, fundamentally requires an active approach in managing system reliability and safety. This chapter reviews several multidimensional threats that compromise AI trustworthiness and advanced methodologies to ensure robustness throughout the life cycle of an AI system. The key challenge is rooted in the nondeterminism of the AI/ML workloads, which makes traditional, determinist monitoring inadequate and introduces additional vulnerability vectors, including model degradation, data shifts, adversarial attacks, and inherent model opacity.

In particular, the analysis of AI failures shows that performance degradation, or model drift, constitutes a continuous threat due to differences in the environment usually related to data, represented by covariate, label, or concept shifts. Besides these environmental dynamics, intentionally malicious manipulations, also referred to as adversarial attacks, pose extreme risks along the entire supply chain with potentially disastrous consequences in safety-critical systems. Extremely complex models behave as black boxes and therefore contribute to problems of unmonitorability, hindering root cause diagnosis in the case of emergent, unforeseen behaviors. The last shown case studies stress the need for stringent, continuous management of the health of an AI system.

The diversity of detection tools—from statistical distance measures, including MMD and Wasserstein distance, through ML-based classification to unsupervised anomaly detection—reflects the multilayered defense needed for discerning both the gradual soft failures and sudden hard failures. Diagnosis and RCA are critical steps in evolving detection into intelligent action. This context is critical for distinguishing whether a loss in performance stems from an external data shift, internal model calibration drift, or a targeted adversarial attack. This would call for diagnostic LLMs and shift-type disentanglement that enable symptomatic degradation to trace from its technical origin so that interventions would be diagnosis driven.

The prevention and mitigation strategies range from fundamental architectural decisions, such as the preference of intrinsically robust models over the vulnerable ones in high-stakes domains, to proactive model maintenance, which means continuously updating models with fresh data to counteract drift, or continuous deployment of advanced DA techniques. The other final frontier in mitigation is the implementation of self-healing AI systems. These intelligent, autonomous systems leverage RL to conduct the execution of recovery actions such as dynamically swapping out compromised services or utilizing compliant-aware policies to address faults within milliseconds to drastically minimize downtime and maximize operational resilience.

However, the road to universally robust AI is full of significant challenges and considerations. This includes, but is not limited to, the practical difficulty one encounters with missing or delayed ground-truth labels, mainly in clinical settings. Fundamentally, the so-called stability-plasticity dilemma points to a challenge in keeping the models updated for new knowledge without making them vulnerable to catastrophic forgetting of prior skills. Furthermore, the complexity of modern models creates a responsibility gap when human decisions in design and deployment result in systemic failures. This lack of transparency undermines trust, necessitating stringent regulatory oversight and the integration of explainability techniques to restore accountability. There is a need for human certification prior to deployment in safety-critical AI, which stands as a critical requirement for governance in order to keep human accountability central to autonomous systems.

What this means is that sustained AI trustworthiness is not a validation exercise but a dynamic, continuous commitment to the DDC cycle. The techniques discussed in this chapter offer the toolkit necessary for engineering resilient AI systems. To ensure that AI remains a safe and reliable force in modern digital ecosystems, we must move beyond maximizing performance and commit to robustness, accountability, and proactive failure management.

## REFERENCES


1. Rashidieranjbar, F., Farhadi, A., and Zamanifar, A., *Revolutionizing healthcare with generative artificial intelligence technologies*, in *Generative Artificial Intelligence (AI) Approaches for Industrial Applications*. 2025, Springer. p. 189–221.
2. Louia, S., et al., *Role of immunogenetics in the etiology, diagnosis, and treatment of diseases*. Kindle, 2025. **5**(1): p. 1–222.
3. Roy, P., *Enhancing real-world robustness in AI: Challenges and solutions*. Journal of Recent Trends in Computer Science and Engineering, 2024. **12**(1): p. 34–49.

4. Farrokhi, M., et al., *Artificial intelligence for hard-to-treat and unknown-origin cancers*. Kindle, 2025. **5**(1): p. 1–296.
5. Rashidi Ranjbar, F. and Zamanifar, A., *Autonomous dental treatment planning on panoramic x-ray using deep learning based object detection algorithm*. Multimedia Tools and Applications, 2024. **83**(14): p. 42999–43033.
6. Farhadi, A., et al., *A hybrid LSTM-GRU model for stock price prediction*. IEEE Access, 2025.
7. Subramanian, V.K., *Managing Observability for Non-Deterministic Workloads in AI and ML Systems*. International Journal of Engineering Technology Research & Management 2024. 8(6): p. 197–207.
8. Guan, H., Bates, D., and Zhou, L., *Keeping medical AI healthy and trustworthy: A review of detection and correction methods for system degradation*. IEEE Transactions on Bio-Medical Engineering, 2025. 71(5): p. 1483–1503.
9. Kezron, N., *Securing the AI supply chain: Mitigating vulnerabilities in AI model development and deployment*. World Journal of Advanced Research and Reviews, 2024. **22**(2): p. 2336–2346.
10. Yampolskiy, R.V., *On monitorability of AI*. AI and Ethics, 2025. **5**(1): p. 689–707.
11. Cummings, M.L., *Identifying AI hazards and responsibility gaps*. IEEE Access, 2025. 13: pp. 54338–54349.
12. Jha, N.N. and Manwani, P., *Self-healing payment systems via AI-driven anomaly recovery: A zero-downtime framework for secure and reliable transactions*. Technology (IJCET), 2025. **16**(2): p. 200–212.
13. Håkansson, A., Dündar, Y.C., and Hartung, R.L., *Towards robustness analysis for adaptive artificial intelligence in multi-autonomous agent systems*. Procedia Computer Science, 2023. **225**: p. 4657–4666.
14. Jothimurugesan, E., et al., *Federated learning under distributed concept drift*, in *International Conference on Artificial Intelligence and Statistics*. 2023. PMLR.
15. Lima, M., et al., *Learning under concept drift for regression—A systematic literature review*. IEEE Access, 2022. **10**: p. 45410–45429.
16. Bayram, F., Ahmed, B.S., and Kassler, A., *From concept drift to model degradation: An overview on performance-aware drift detectors*. Knowledge-Based Systems, 2022. **245**: p. 108632.
17. Yang, J., et al., *Openood: Benchmarking generalized out-of-distribution detection*. Advances in Neural Information Processing Systems, 2022. **35**: p. 32598–32611.
18. Ghaffari Laleh, N., et al., *Adversarial attacks and adversarial robustness in computational pathology*. Nature Communications, 2022. **13**(1): p. 5711.
19. Khedher, M.I., Jmila, H., and El Yacoubi, M., *On the formal evaluation of the robustness of neural networks and its pivotal relevance for AI-based safety-critical domains*. International Journal of Network Dynamics and Intelligence, 2023. **2**(4): p. 100018.
20. Zamanifar, A. and Nazemi, E., *EECASC: An energy efficient communication approach in smart cities*. Wireless Networks, 2020. **26**(2): p. 925–940.
21. Tocchetti, A., et al., *AI robustness: A human-centered perspective on technological challenges and opportunities*. ACM Computing Surveys, 2025. **57**(6): p. 1–38.
22. Mahida, A., *Integrating observability with DevOps practices in financial services technologies: A study on enhancing software development and operational resilience*. International Journal of Advanced Computer Science & Applications, 2024. **15**(7): p. 842–849
23. Vela, D., et al., *Temporal quality degradation in AI models*. Scientific Reports, 2022. **12**(1): p. 11654.
24. Mahalegi, H.S.M., et al., *Generative adversarial networks for heterogeneous unsupervised domain adaptation detection*, in *2024 IEEE 28th International Conference on Intelligent Engineering Systems (INES)*. 2024. IEEE.

25. Miyai, A., et al., *Generalized Out-of-Distribution Detection and Beyond in Vision Language Model Era: A Survey.* arXiv preprint arXiv:2407.21794, 2024.
26. Fang, Z., et al., *Is out-of-distribution detection learnable?* Advances in Neural Information Processing Systems, 2022. **35**: p. 37199–37213.
27. Mahida, A.M., *Machine learning for predictive observability—A study paper.* Journal of Artificial Intelligence & Cloud Computing, 2023. **2**(4): p. 1–3.
28. Xu, R. and Ding, K., *Large language models for anomaly and out-of-distribution detection: A survey*, in *Findings of the Association for Computational Linguistics: NAACL 2025.* 2025.
29. Manchana, R., *AI-powered observability: A journey from reactive to proactive, predictive, and automated.* International Journal of Scientific Research (IJSR), 2024. **13**: p. 1745–1755.
30. Sambamurthy, P., *Advancing Systems Observability through Artificial Intelligence: A Comprehensive Analysis.* ResearchGate, August, 2024.
31. Benson, T.A., *Rethinking Observability for AI Workloads on Multi-tenant Public Clouds.*
32. Moshkovich, D., et al., *Beyond Black-box Benchmarking: Observability, Analytics, and Optimization of Agentic Systems.* arXiv preprint arXiv:2503.06745, 2025.
33. Yang, J., et al., *Generalized out-of-distribution detection: A survey.* International Journal of Computer Vision, 2024. **132**(12): p. 5635–5662.
34. Cui, P. and Wang, J., *Out-of-distribution (OOD) detection based on deep learning: A review.* Electronics, 2022. **11**(21): p. 3500.
35. Hinder, F., et al., *Model-based explanations of concept drift.* Neurocomputing, 2023. **555**: p. 126640.
36. Lang, L., et al., *When your AIs deceive you: Challenges of partial observability in reinforcement learning from human feedback.* Advances in Neural Information Processing Systems, 2024. **37**: p. 93240–93299.
37. Sun, Y., et al., *Accurate and interpretable log-based fault diagnosis using large language models.* IEEE Transactions on Services Computing, 2025. 18(5): p. 2602–2615.
38. Ogunmolu, A.M., et al., *Autonomous artificial intelligence agents for fault detection and self-healing in smart manufacturing systems.* Journal of Energy Research and Reviews, 2025. **17**(8): p. 20–37.
39. Xiang, Q., et al., *Concept drift adaptation methods under the deep learning framework: A literature review.* Applied Sciences, 2023. **13**(11): p. 6515.
40. Farhadi, A., et al., *Leveraging Blockchain and ANFIS for Optimal Supply Chain Management.* arXiv preprint arXiv:2408.17161, 2024.
41. Lataran, P.N., et al., *Developing a BERT-enhanced blockchain model for health insurance fraud detection.* Journal of Information Systems Research and Practice, 2024. **2**(3): p. 56–61.
42. Fang, X., et al., *Your data is not perfect: Towards cross-domain out-of-distribution detection in class-imbalanced data.* Expert Systems with Applications, 2025. **267**: p. 126031.
43. Hong, Z., et al., *Out-of-Distribution Detection in Medical Image Analysis: A Survey.* arXiv preprint arXiv:2404.18279, 2024.
44. Farhadi, A., et al., *Unsupervised domain adaptation for image classification based on deep neural networks.* Intelligent Multimedia Processing and Communication Systems (IMPCS), 2023. **4**(1): p. 27–37.
45. Jangam, S.K., *Role of AI and ML in enhancing self-healing capabilities, including predictive analysis and automated recovery.* International Journal of Artificial Intelligence, Data Science, and Machine Learning, 2022. **3**(4): p. 47–56.
46. Shahl, H. and Patel, J., *Machine learning and self-healing capabilities combined in adaptive AI architectures.* International Research Journal of Engineering & Applied Sciences, 2023. **11**(1): p. 32–39.

47. Gadde, H., *Self-healing databases: AI techniques for automated system recovery.* International Journal of Advanced Engineering Technologies and Innovations, 2023. **1**(02): p. 517–549.
48. Zamanifar, A. and Faezipour, M., *Application of Generative AI in Healthcare Systems.* 2025, Springer.
49. Taheri, A., Farhadi, A., and Zamanifar, A., *Application of GenAI in Clinical Administration Support*, in *Application of Generative AI in Healthcare Systems.* 2025, Springer. p. 91–117.
50. Farhadi, A. and Taheri, A., *Application of GenAI in Synthetic Data Generation in the Healthcare System*, in *Application of Generative AI in Healthcare Systems.* 2025, Springer. p. 67–89.
51. Niloofar Taheri, N.T., Mosaddeghi-Heris, R., and Aghazadeh, H., *Precision Chronotherapy: AI and Personalized Treatment for Neurodegenerative Circadian Disorders.* 2025.
52. Taheri, A., et al., *Administrative efficiency: Providing healthcare operations*, in *Applications of Large Language Models (LLM) in Healthcare Systems.* 2025, Chapman and Hall/CRC. p. 33–64.
53. Tahavvori, A., et al., *Large language models and ChatGPT in medical sciences: Foundations, capabilities, and challenges.* Kindle, 2025. **5**(1): p. 1–222.
54. Naghib, A., Gharehchopogh, F.S., and Zamanifar, A., *The role of large language models in delivering artificial intelligence-based psychological interventions and therapies*, in *Applications of Large Language Models (LLM) in Healthcare Systems.* 2025, Chapman and Hall/CRC. p. 142–178.
55. Payne, D.L., et al., *Performance of GPT-4 on the American college of radiology in-training examination: Evaluating accuracy, model drift, and fine-tuning.* Academic Radiology, 2024. **31**(7): p. 3046–3054.
56. Finlayson, S.G., et al., *The clinician and dataset shift in artificial intelligence.* New England Journal of Medicine, 2021. **385**(3): p. 283–286.
57. Nama, P., Reddy, P., and Pattanayak, S.K., *Artificial intelligence for self-healing automation testing frameworks: Real-time fault prediction and recovery.* Artificial Intelligence, 2024. **64**(3S): p. 111–141.
58. Syed, A.A.M. and Anazagasty, E., *AI-driven infrastructure automation: Leveraging AI and ML for self-healing and auto-scaling cloud environments.* International Journal of Artificial Intelligence, Data Science, and Machine Learning, 2024. **5**(1): p. 32–43.

# 7 Patient Safety in AI-Driven Healthcare

*Amirfarhad Farhadi, Roya Noori,
Azadeh Zamanifar, Nasser Mozayani, and
Homayoun Safarpour Motealegh Mahaleg*

## 7.1 INTRODUCTION

Artificial intelligence (AI) is becoming more and more common in clinical practice, especially in areas where finding risk early is important for avoiding harm that could have been avoided. The last ten years have seen big improvements in algorithmic capability, but the link between AI and patient safety is based on much older ideas about how and why harm happens in healthcare. Traditional patient safety science, on the other hand, says that bad things happen because of complicated sociotechnical systems, not just one person's actions [1–4]. As health systems start to use AI tools in their daily work, this basic point of view is still very important. The goal of this introduction is to put AI in the context of well-known theories about patient safety, explain how AI came to be seen as a possible solution to ongoing safety problems, and make it clear why the two fields have become so closely linked. These themes are the starting point for the next sections, which look at AI's clinical uses, risks, governance needs, and long-term effects on safe care.

### 7.1.1 BASICS OF PATIENT SAFETY

The formal discipline of patient safety came about because there was proof that harm that could be avoided in healthcare is common, has many causes, and is often linked to problems with the system as a whole rather than just individual mistakes. According to important models like Reason's model of latent conditions and active failures [1, 4], clinical errors happen when multiple layers of protection fail. These new ideas changed the focus to designing systems, taking into account human factors, making communication more reliable, and learning from mistakes, which are all important parts of modern safety management. Patient safety reviews show that harm often happens when people, environmental stressors, and poorly designed tools or workflows interact in ways that are easy to predict [1–4]. Healthcare settings have features that make mistakes more likely, such as time limits, interruptions, complicated coordination, and too much information to process. Safety science stresses the need for interventions that help clinical cognition in the real world, such as making things less complicated, improving feedback loops, and making signal detection systems stronger [2, 3]. Digital health technologies were first used to make these strategies stronger. The goal of early electronic health records (EHRs) and decision-support tools was to reduce variability, improve documentation, and give

DOI: 10.1201/9781003743422-7

structured data to find new risks [5]. However, studies quickly showed that technologies that weren't properly integrated had unexpected effects, such as mismatched user interfaces, alert fatigue, and delays in entering orders [3, 5]. These challenges underscored a fundamental principle in safety science: technology can only improve safety when it is congruent with clinical workflows and underpinned by strong governance. Research on human factors consistently shows that tools that make cognitive load higher, confuse clinicians' judgment, or send poorly calibrated signals can unintentionally raise risk [2, 4]. AI brings this history into the clinical setting. The use of more advanced predictive models doesn't make safety less sociotechnical; in fact, it makes it more so. It is important to understand, talk about, raise, and act on AI predictions in the context of clinical work. This means that their safety impact depends on model performance as well as workflow design, clear communication, and clinician trust. When looking at AI's role in patient safety, these basic ideas—systems thinking, human factors, resilience, and learning—are the background. Even though people often think of AI as a technological advance, its effects on safety are still mostly sociotechnical because it works with and interacts with the complex systems that safety science has been studying for a long time.

### 7.1.2 The Rise of AI in Healthcare and Medicine

The growth of AI in healthcare happened at the same time as the growth of digital health infrastructure, especially the use of EHRs and the availability of large clinical datasets. Review articles show that the number of applications using machine learning (ML) and deep learning (DL) methods to solve clinical problems has grown at an exponential rate, from classifying diseases to predicting when a patient's condition will get worse [5, 6]. AI is becoming more common because it can help with earlier detection, better risk stratification, and spotting small changes in a patient's condition that might not be noticed otherwise. Several comprehensive reviews show that AI-based early-warning systems are often better than traditional rule-based ones in many areas where safety is very important [1, 5, 6]. ML models can find nonlinear connections between more than one clinical variable, such as lab results, vital signs, medications, comorbidities, and procedural information. This is not the same as strict scoring systems. This lets you change the risk level for each patient as their health changes. AI-based models for sepsis and deterioration, for instance, have shown that they can find clinical instability earlier by combining EHR data with continuous monitoring data [7–14]. These kinds of skills are completely in line with patient safety goals that have to do with stopping harm and getting care to people who need it right away. AI is also transforming how drug safety is monitored and ensured. Learning-based methods have done a better job of finding adverse drug events (ADEs) than older methods. They use structured EHR data, lab trends, and even unstructured free-text documentation through natural language processing (NLP) [15–19]. This has made people more interested in AI-enabled pharmacovigilance systems that can keep an eye on the safety of medications in a proactive way. AI models are doing much better than traditional algorithms in places where they had trouble. AI-based systems that predict falls in hospitalized patients have been shown to work better than traditional fall risk scales, especially when they use real-time data on patient mobility, nursing observations, and vital sign trends [20–22]. AI-based HAPI prediction models are also said to be better than traditional ones like the Braden Scale because they look at more clinical factors and historical data, and they give more accurate and personalized risk predictions [23–27]. Wearables and remote monitoring systems are also becoming more popular uses of AI. AI-based methods have become better at finding patterns of physiological decline that are missed between clinical observations as continuous physiological monitoring becomes more widely available [13–30]. During and after the COVID-19 pandemic, these systems became very popular as remote monitoring and digital triage became more popular. In this way, AI helps bring safety monitoring to the community level, where it could help find problems early and fix them quickly. But even though things are looking good, reviews often warn that AI is moving too quickly into healthcare for proper clinical evaluation. Several reports are based on retrospective datasets or single-center cohorts or patient groups with very specific inclusion criteria [5–7], and only a limited number of reports have prospectively validated their results or evaluated the effect of the prediction on clinical workflows or patient outcomes. This gap shows how important it is to include safety science principles in the design and use of AI systems. These principles stress real-world system performance, contextual integration, and ongoing surveillance.

Generative AI products, like GPT and complex generative models, can generate myriad healthcare deliverables such as synthetic data, image processing, and clinical decision support (CDS) and can enhance clinical and administrative workflows while raising important ethical, security, and governance considerations [31].

### 7.1.3 Why AI and Patient Safety Are Related

There are powerful structural factors that make AI and patient safety the closest of allies. The challenges to which AI applies itself—delayed recognition of deterioration, variability of monitoring, and the need to integrate complex, multifactorial risk profiling—are those that patient safety science has been struggling with for decades. Threats such as patient deterioration, ADEs, falls, pressure ulcers, and missed early warning signs usually evolve over time and are often overlooked in hectic clinical settings.

This synergy probably also explains why AI is so well-positioned for safety applications. AI systems are able to identify subtle "deltas"—minute but significant shifts in physiological trends, behavioral patterns, or drug combinations that may lead to harm. Discussions and theoretical articles stress that the major qualities of AI, namely pattern recognition, scalability, and continuous data processing, readily correspond to long-standing weaknesses in patient safety systems [1–3, 32].

However, these same features bring with them novel safety concerns. There is evidence that automation bias can result in clinicians placing too much trust in the recommendations provided by AI, even when findings from clinical assessment are sending mixed messages [33, 34]. Disparities in performance among demographic groups also raise issues about fairness and equity, as there could be some subpopulations having late detection of deterioration or suffering disparate harm [35]. Safety failures induced by model drift, that is, degradation in predictive performance as clinical practices, technologies, or population of patients evolve, may be hard to detect unless there is systematic and continuous surveillance [32]. In addition, the brittleness of models—which is a susceptibility for AI systems to act unpredictably in unseen or unexpected circumstances—may further exacerbate challenges in ensuring safe implementation [32–35]. Privacy and security are also key aspects of patient safety. Modern AI systems are more reliant on massive, sensitive datasets, and breaches, data corruption, or integrity failures can interrupt clinical workflows and compromise predictive systems. Reflecting these concerns, many clinical AI systems are classified as high-risk under regulatory frameworks such as the EU AI Act, highlighting the importance of governance, transparency, and oversight along the entire AI life cycle [36–42].

One more common denominator is the human factor. AI is not a substitute for clinical reasoning but a partner to it. Patient safety is contingent on the manner in which clinicians understand and respond to AI-generated predictions, how alerts are integrated within clinical workflows, how uncertainty is conveyed, and how healthcare groups collectively respond to alerts. Safety experts stress that successful risk management depends on robust governance structures, ongoing monitoring of performances, and a learning-oriented culture that understands AI is but one part of a broader sociotechnical system [1–3, 39, 42].

These factors, taken together, account for the increasing hybridization of AI with patient safety. AI provides powerful new instruments for identifying risk and reducing harm early, but only if they are realized with due consideration of systemic effects on safety in clinical practice to the extent real-world settings can permit them. The incorporation of generative AI in healthcare systems adds a new layer to these considerations that further affects clinical decision-making, data trustworthiness, and system transparency, thereby highlighting even more the interconnection of AI uptake and patient safety outcomes [43].

## 7.2 CLINICAL IMPLICATIONS OF AI IN PATIENT SAFETY

AI has become popular in safety-critical clinical areas, in which risk detection on time can dramatically change the care flow. The strongest evidence base is for sepsis and acute deterioration, medication-related harm, in-hospital falls, pressure injuries, and wearable-based continuous monitoring. Although the clinical scenarios differ, these systems have a similar approach: they use very large quantities of EHR or physiological data to find patterns that are precursors of clinical deterioration. In all of these, it is fair to say that studies generally show that AI can identify signals of deterioration missed by traditional tools; however, translating these into real-world tools remains challenging. The following sub-sections provide a brief summary of the current evidence in each of these fields. Table 7.1 shows clinical applications of Artificial Intelligence for patient safety.

### 7.2.1 Predicting Sepsis and Rapid Decline

Sepsis remains one of the most lethal diseases in medicine, necessitating early detection and proper management. AI has shown a lot of promise for fixing problems with traditional scoring systems like SIRS or qSOFA, which are often not

**TABLE 7.1**
**Clinical Applications of Artificial Intelligence for Patient Safety: Use Cases, Safety Mechanisms, and Evidence Base**

| Clinical Safety Domain | Primary AI Use Cases | Safety Mechanism/ Benefit | Representative Evidence Types |
|---|---|---|---|
| Sepsis & Acute Deterioration | Early-warning prediction from EHR time-series data, Deep-learning models for sepsis onset, Automated deterioration alerts, Wearable-enhanced prediction | Earlier recognition of instability, Faster escalation and treatment initiation, Reduced missed deterioration events | Multi center cohort studies, Deep-learning retrospective analyses, Prospective pilot evaluations, Vendor tool audits |
| Adverse Drug Events (ADEs) | Machine-learning risk scores for specific ADE types, NLP extraction of ADE mentions from clinical notes, Algorithmic detection of drug–drug interactions | Prevention of medication-related harm, Enhanced pharmacist decision support, Expanded pharmacovigilance reach | ADE-specific ML studies, NLP scoping reviews, Structured-unstructured hybrid detection models |
| In-Hospital Falls | Dynamic fall risk prediction using EHR variables, Real-time risk score updates, Targeted prevention workflows | More accurate patient segmentation, More efficient preventive resource allocation, Reduced fall incidence and injuries | Prospective fall-prevention evaluations, EHR-embedded ML prediction studies |
| Pressure Injuries (HAPI) | ML-based HAPI risk models, Automated early-warning for skin-integrity deterioration, Real-time nurse-facing risk dashboards | Improved targeting of repositioning, support surfaces, and preventive measures, Reduced false positives from traditional Braden Scale | HAPI ML validation studies, Implementation case studies |
| Wearable & Remote Monitoring | Continuous monitoring of cardiopulmonary signals, ML models predicting unplanned ICU transfer or HF decompensation, Activity/ sleep-based instability detection | Recognition of deterioration between routine observations, Earlier intervention opportunities, Reduced missed warning signs | Wearable-based deterioration studies, Remote monitoring pilots, Heart-failure monitoring research |

sensitive enough to find sepsis early. AI modeling, particularly ML and DL, is propelling the future of precision medicine for hyperacute stroke through the utilization of high-dimensional EHRs, encompassing vital signs, laboratory results, clinical notes, and more, alongside both retrospective and prospective real-time assessments of continuous risk [7–10]. DL models, like recurrent neural networks (RNNs) and gradient-boosting machines, have been shown to be better at predicting sepsis using time-series data. DL models have been shown to be able to find changes in vital signs hours before they are clinically recognized. This lets doctors act sooner, which increases the chances of survival [7]. There are still problems that need to be solved when using these models in other clinical settings because their performance may depend on the local patient population and clinical practice [9, 10]. Also, AI needs to be fully integrated into clinical workflows with real-time monitoring and ongoing calibration to keep its accuracy in changing healthcare settings in order to be able to predict sepsis [11]. Multisite validation studies underscore the essential requirement for local customization of AI tools and governance frameworks to facilitate continuous feedback and recalibration [12]. Another area of research is using AI-based wearable devices to predict when things will get worse. These wearables (like chest patches and wristbands) gather high-frequency physiological data that can help find early signs of sepsis or deterioration that might not be noticed during normal clinical observations [13, 14]. In hospitals and other settings where patients are switching from one type of care to another, where there aren't always many opportunities to take prompt action, this type of monitoring may be beneficial. Even though it seems promising, reviews reveal that integrating AI for sepsis detection into clinical practice can be inconsistent. AI models may not work as well in some places as they do in others because of differences in coding practices, patient populations, alert thresholds, and clinical engagement [7–9]. Therefore, the effectiveness of AI tools will depend on how well they fit into local workflows and how clinicians react to the model predictions, even though they could be very helpful for identifying issues early.

### 7.2.2 Medication Safety and Adverse Drug Events (ADEs)

Medication-related harm is still a big problem for patient safety, and the usual ways to watch for ADEs have been long, boring chart reviews, voluntary reporting, or simple rule-based triggers. They are useful to about the same degree in terms of both scale and effectiveness. AI offers a more scalable and comprehensive method for capturing structured EHR data, laboratory results, longitudinal medication sequences, and even unstructured clinical notes [15–19]. This makes it easier to find latent hazards of interest that are more widespread and active. System reviews show that ML models that were made to predict certain ADEs, such as nephrotoxicity, over-anticoagulation, or drug-drug interactions, usually work better than older methods. They work best when they include time patterns from lab results and interactions between multiple diseases [17, 19]. AI applications can also find complex relationships that are hard to hide during normal clinical work-ups by finding small patterns, like sequences in medication orders or combinations of risk factors spread over multiple encounters. NLP is another way to find ADEs in free-text notes that might not be in structured data fields. This is in addition to ML. We acknowledge reviews indicating that NLP systems can recognize symptom descriptions such as rash, confusion, or bleeding, which are occasionally exclusively present in clinician notes or nursing observations [15, 16]. Hybrid methods that use both structured and unstructured data work better than methods that only use one type of data. They are also better at finding things. However, documenting styles may still differ among institutions [15]. AI-powered pharmacovigilance is another way to make patients safer by letting doctors act sooner. Several studies show that predicted risk scores for ADEs can be used to start pharmacist reviews or focused monitoring, which makes it easier to find problems earlier in the drug's life cycle [17–19]. There are many tools like this, but most of them haven't been thoroughly tested in real-world clinical settings. Like sepsis prediction models, AI's ability to find ADEs depends a lot on how engaged clinicians are, how they get alerts, and whether they are willing to act on them. Even with these problems, new research shows that AI could greatly improve the detection of medication harm, which would make it easier to intervene early and improve patient safety overall. Use cases for safe medication AI are getting bigger. Investigation AI is also used to look through data from different places to find dangerous drug interactions and bad effects on patients. Researchers have used databases like DrugBank, the FDA's adverse event reporting system, and the Observational Medical Outcomes Partnership (OMOP) database to figure out how drugs interact with each other and how they affect people [44–50]. One example of an application that used AI to find drugs that the FDA had taken off the market [51]. Additionally, AI has proven beneficial in predicting drug dosages for medications such as insulin, digoxin, and warfarin [52–55], as well as in scanning hospital EHRs to identify medication errors, including incorrectly issued prescriptions [56]. In a study, AI was employed to monitor the administration of anticoagulant medications in stroke patients [57]. AI has also been used to find drugs that a patient might be taking but that aren't on their medication list or health record [58–60] or to find signs of opioid abuse by looking at clinical notes [61, 62].

### 7.2.3 Risk Prediction for Falls in Hospital Setting

Falls are also one of the most serious threats of adverse outcomes in hospital patients, especially the elderly and those with mobility limitations [13]. AI-based prediction models for fall risk have demonstrated good potential in advancing fall prevention by incorporating more patient information, including vital signs, levels of activity, medications, and fall history [2, 20, 21]. Unlike static and limited traditional fall risk tools (e.g., Morse Fall Scale), AI models are updated in real-time risk predictions with dynamic information to provide more real-time-based interventions and advanced actionable recommendations. Li et al. reviewed ML-based models of fall risk and concluded that AI tools, based on sensor data and EHR variables, were more effective compared to conventional models for fall prediction [20]. Another study showed that introducing AI-based risk predictions into clinical practice allowed a more effective distribution of fall-prevention resources with a diminished rate of incidents in those areas with the highest risk [22]. The major benefit of AI lies in its potential to deliver dynamic observation of real-time risk assessments and give continuous feedback as opposed to static scoring systems [21]. Despite these benefits, there are still challenges associated with fall prediction based on AI, especially in terms of the generalization of models to other clinical sites. For fall risk models to work well in different patient and hospital settings, they need to be validated at more than one site. Additionally, these models need to be implemented in clinical workflows without overburdening the clinicians or contributing to alert fatigue due to false positives [20]. Conventional fall risk instruments—for example, the Morse Fall Scale—process are associated with low predictive accuracy and traditional method do not take into account dynamic changes in patient's status that potentially would lead to increased risk of falls. AI models are designed to overcome this problem by integrating a wider range of clinical parameters, including vital signs, mobility measures, cognitive tests, and nursing notes [20–22]. A systematic review of ML-based fall risk prediction models reveals that the majority of the included studies reporting on predictive accuracy demonstrate enhanced predictive performance when compared to the legacy tools, especially when the models utilize longitudinal data and nonlinear interactions [21]. AI algorithms are able to predict such events hours before they happen, allowing for interventions that are more targeted. For example, algorithms that monitor mobility patterns or sensor-derived activity data are able to detect abrupt alterations in gait or agitation that is frequently associated with attempts to move without assistance [20, 22]. Translation studies show that delivery of AI-powered predictions within the fall-prevention pathways may encourage staff to provide more observation or to apply bed-exit alarms or to offer assistance with mobility to a patient at an increased risk of falling. The first results suggest that combining AI-derived risk scores with strict interventions may lower the number of falls. However, as with other uses of AI, the effect in practice depends on how well it fits into workflows, how engaged clinicians are, and how few alerts there are that don't need to be acted on, which could lead to alert fatigue.

### 7.2.4 HAPI Prediction (Prediction of Pressure Injury)

HAPI is an important nursing-sensitive indicator and a key area of interest for predictive analytics [1, 2]. Instruments like the Braden Scale rely on static evaluations and don't take into account the complicated interactions between comorbidities, mobility, nutritional status, and illness severity. The HAPI prediction models based on AI get around these problems because they use EHR data, which means they can take into account a wider range of patient-specific factors and keep an eye on them over time [23–27]. It has been shown in [23, 26] that machine-learning models are always better at telling the difference between things and making predictions than Braden-based assessments. These models use information from a variety of sources, such as demographics, functional status, hemodynamics, laboratory panels, medication profiles, and nursing assessments, to give each person a unique risk estimate. Comparative studies have shown that AI models can find both short-term and long-term factors that affect tissue perfusion and skin integrity [24, 25]. Recent studies that focused on implementation suggest that predictive HAPI tools work best when they are part of a full prevention program. For instance, one study found that high-risk predictions helped prioritize limited resources for repositioning schedules, percussion-relief surfaces, and focused skin assessment, which led to better prevention outcomes [27]. These results show that AI-powered HAPI tools can greatly improve patient safety, but they need to be fully integrated into nursing workflows to be effective. The field is moving forward as more and more people pay attention to how to use imaging, sensor data, and continuous risk monitoring together in models that can predict HAPI. Even though the current evidence suggests that machine-learning-based models are more sensitive and comprehensive than traditional tools, these models are more likely to be useful if clinical governance and monitoring are put in place during their use.

### 7.2.5 Wearables and Remote Monitoring

Patient monitoring is being revolutionized by AI and wearable technology, especially in the areas of continuous surveillance and early detection of clinical deterioration. Due to integrated sensors within the wearable devices that can record on-body physiological and behavioral parameters, such as heart rate, oxygen saturation, temperature, and motion, real-time early warning signs can be captured. This ongoing collection of data allows for slower recognition of deterioration, less iatrogenic harm, and later clinical intervention [13–30].

Up-to-date evidence suggests that AI algorithms on wearable data can precisely predict acute deteriorations, like sepsis and respiratory failure, by recognizing variations in activity patterns and vital signs. Importantly, Zanos et al. demonstrated that AI models developed using wearable sensor data predicted ICU transfers hours to days before the development of overt clinical symptoms [13]. In addition, AI-based classifiers have been successfully used to predict decompensation of heart failure patients to initiate preventive treatments and therefore improve clinical outcomes [28]. These features are crucial in remote monitoring situations, as patients can be monitored continuously after hospital discharge using wearable technology, thereby bringing hospital-level surveillance to the home [29]. Contrary to low-frequency intermittent bedside vital-sign measurements, wearable sensors provide high-frequency data and longitudinal data with multiple physiological signals, which may reveal subtle physiological changes before clinical deterioration [13–30]. AI algorithms trained on these rich time-series datasets can learn intricate temporal patterns that would be difficult for clinicians to manually track. Recent studies with accelerometry, photoplethysmography (PPG), and continuous heart rate monitoring have reported that AI-based systems can identify early signals of deterioration—including fluid overload or respiratory compromise—within prognostic time horizons that are relevant from a clinical perspective [13, 29]. Further prospective assessments have indicated that prediction systems enabled by wearables outperform classic bedside monitors, especially in ambulatory subjects, as they are capable of providing dependable monitoring even while subjects go about their daily routines [28]. Wearables have also been utilized to forecast postoperative complications, acute heart failure decompensation, and unexpected ICU transfers, promoting earlier triage decisions and mitigating the possibility of unmonitored decline [29, 30].

Miniaturization of wearable-based systems, however, still poses a number of challenges. Motion artifacts, poor device attachment, signal noise, and variability in patient adherence can all potentially influence the quality of the data. Continuous—real-time model training must therefore consider patient activities as well as device operation. In addition, given the large diversity of wearable device types, sensor layouts, and patient groups, models trained in one environment might not be easily transferred to another clinical situation. Multisite validation is thus crucial to ascertain generalizability and performance in varying populations and care settings [29, 30]. Continuous monitoring may also increase alert volume and contribute to alert fatigue and the effectiveness of the escalation pathways, thus again highlighting the need for appropriate workflow integration and governance. In addition to wearable and remote monitoring technologies, generative AI is forming the basis of further data-enabled healthcare solutions, such as automated clinical documentation and personalized patient engagement solutions. Such systems have previously been shown to make use of acquired behavioral and linguistic patterns extracted from large corpora of clinical narratives to support patient–clinician communication and care delivery [63].

Meanwhile, energy-conscious communication protocols based on or inspired by smart city infrastructures are at the core of enabling a dependable data transfer over wearable-based remote patient monitoring systems, a vital need for keeping the patient safe in continuous monitoring applications [64].

## 7.3 SAFETY THREATS CAUSED OR EXACERBATED BY AI TECHNOLOGY

Using AI in clinical work processes brings a number of risks, some of which may be the same as safety issues that are already there or lead to new types of harm. These kinds of risks come from more than just the possibility of algorithmic errors; they also come from how AI models interact with human decision-making, clinical processes, and institutional governance models. AI has the potential to pick up on signs of decline earlier than traditional tools, but these benefits may be lost if the models act in ways that are not expected, are misinterpreted, or are used without enough protection. The next few sections give a brief overview of the four main types of risk that were found in the research, conceptual work, and policy documents that were looked at.

### 7.3.1 Model Error, Brittleness, and Generalization Failure

AI models that are being developed are very sensitive to the data and assumptions that went into making them. When these assumptions are not met in real life, models can become weak or break down. As the literature suggests, systematic reviews of sepsis and deterioration prediction reveal that model performance often declines when utilized in a setting different from its development site [7–9]. External validations conducted in various hospitals, patient demographics, and documentation styles have revealed significant variability in discrimination and calibration. This indicates that even high-performing models may yield erroneous predictions when assessed in unfamiliar contexts [8, 11]. The inconsistency of EHR data is one reason why it is brittle. Models may be affected by differences in charting styles, lab testing rates, patterns of missing data, and clinical workflows. Studies of commercial deterioration tools have shown that models based on historical data may not work well for institutions with different patient populations or ways of measuring things. They may also give a lot of false positives or false negatives [7, 12]. This variability can lead to significant safety issues, especially since AI-driven predictions are used to make quick clinical decisions. Another important thing to think about is calibration drift. As clinical practices evolve (e.g., treatment protocols, documentation standards, and patient demographics), the predictive relationships employed by AI models may diminish. Research on drift detection shows that a model's performance may slowly get worse over the course of months or years without any clear signal. This can lead to systematic misclassification and the under- or overestimation of risk for some groups of patients [32]. Models based on wearables are also vulnerable to the problem of generalization. Continuous physiologic monitoring yields extensive data; however, training models on data from a singular device or sensor has resulted in suboptimal performance when generalized to alternative devices or patient populations [13, 14]. There are many reasons for variability, such as motion artifacts, differences in patient adherence, and differences in sensor algorithms. If these models aren't checked and adjusted every so often, they may become less and less reliable over time. This proof shows that AI models really do depend on the context. If model errors and brittleness are not fixed through ongoing validation, monitoring, and governance, they could lead to new safety problems or make existing ones worse in clinical systems.

### 7.3.2 Automation Bias, Over-Reliance, and the Human Element

AI models produce accurate predictions, but the interface with humans adds an additional layer of risk. One known problem is automation bias—the overreliance on AI textual output. Experiments and observational investigations indicate that clinicians may defer to AI results in the face of conflicting clinical evidence [33]. This conduct may cause omission errors—that is, failing to take action when one is warranted because the model is erroneously indicating low risk—or commission errors—that is, taking wrongful action because one is misled by a prediction.

Studies on human–computer interaction demonstrate that interfaces, notifications, and clarifications play a crucial role in how clinicians act [34]. Excessively salient risk scores, vague statements, or uncalibrated alert thresholds might mistakenly lull users into a sense of certainty and nudge clinicians to trust the model. However, subtle alerts and/or excessive noise may lead to neglect or devaluation of the suggestions of the AI, that is, to under-reliance.

Cognitive load, time pressure, and incomplete information also contribute to increased vulnerability to automation bias [33, 34]. In time-sensitive settings, including emergency departments or medical-surgical units, clinicians might rely on AI as a "cognitive shortcut," particularly when busy. This dependence can decrease situational awareness and result in clinicians being less likely to identify errors or contradictions in the model's outputs.

Also, the team dynamics can be changed by AI. Potentially, if some members of the care team trust AI predictions and others are skeptical, discord could impede communication and the escalation of care. Research in human factors stresses that a safe AI integration is one where model uncertainty is explained in absolute terms, escalation protocols delineated, and the interface is used to support—not supplant—clinical reasoning [13–15].

Automation bias is a sociotechnical hazard and risk factor. It arises not solely from the AI system but also from human cognition, system design, and organizational pressures in a complex interrelation. To mitigate this, a particular process has to be put in place at the start, followed by training and assessment on a continuing basis to make certain that the role of the AI in decision-making is to assist, not replace, clinical judgment.

### 7.3.3 Bias, Fairness, and Unequitable Safety Outcomes

Bias and discrimination are significant safety concerns when medical AI systems are brought into practice. Historical biases in healthcare data, differences in how data are collected, and underrepresentation of certain groups can make these predictive models less accurate—or even harmful—when applied to particular segments of the population. Empirical studies have revealed that clinical prediction models frequently have poorer sensitivity in patients who suffer from rare diseases, at the two ends of the age spectrum, and in racial and ethnic minority groups [35]. Since many AI technologies are developed to facilitate early identification of risk or harm, such disparities can manifest as unequal safety outcomes.

Bias can be introduced in a variety of ways throughout the life cycle of the AI. Training data sets may also reflect historical disparities in access to care, and the models may then learn and propagate such under-treatment or late-recognition patterns. Alterations to documentation practices, like a decline in symptom or pain reporting in certain populations, may lead AI algorithms to fail to detect important safety signals. In addition, proxies used as predictors may contain socioeconomic patterns (e.g., prior healthcare utilization) that lead to unfair treatment of groups.

Consequently, fairness evaluations underline the need to analyze not only overall model performance but also the accuracy, calibration, and error rates of subgroup models [35]. Aggregate good AUC does not imply there are no demographic-specific differences in the clinical utility of a risk model. Such disparities may undermine the trust of clinicians and patients, reduce the impact of safety interventions, and cause further widening of disparities in health outcomes.

Ensuring fairness in medical AI involves conscious design and governance decisions. Approaches include auditing decision pathways, obtaining more representative and diverse training data, performing subgroup calibration and bias testing, and using fairness-aware learning algorithms. Fairness as a principle for core patient safety is increasingly enshrined in AI governance, acknowledging that predictive tools for patients may exacerbate preexisting disparities if they are not vigilantly overseen and managed in their full life cycle.

Concerns with predictive models are also raised in novel applications, including large language models for use in psychological and therapeutic interventions, where questions of bias, fairness, and disparate safety outcomes among diverse patient populations have also emerged [65].

### 7.3.4 Privacy Issues, Data Protection, and Security Challenges

Patient safety depends heavily on privacy, data protection, and cybersecurity because AI systems rely on a lot of sensitive patient data. You can train models without gathering all of the data in one location by using federated learning and other privacy-preserving ML techniques. However, the healthcare sector has not yet made extensive use of these kinds of approaches and solutions. It is common knowledge that AI models are susceptible to re-identification, model extraction, and inference attacks, particularly when they are trained on small or highly detailed datasets. Regulations such as the EU Artificial Intelligence Act classify a number of clinical

AI applications as "high-risk." Strict guidelines for data protection, documentation, post-market monitoring, and transparency are mandated by these bodies [36–38]. According to the Act, safety and privacy are complementary aspects of one another. For instance, not only is patient privacy violated when data security or models are compromised, but predictions also become less reliable. Patient data is increasingly being recognized as a valuable resource that must be safeguarded. In order to reduce these risks, a set of data-centric security procedures, such as audit trails, threat-monitoring systems, and access controls, must be implemented [39–42]. Patient care is directly impacted by security incidents such as ransomware attacks, data corruption, and cloud-based AI service disruptions. The decision-support tools linked to EHRs, particularly those that are used to identify clinical deterioration early or to monitor patients over time, may be impacted by these disruptions. In summary, the most crucial concerns regarding AI-based safety risks are privacy and security. Data integrity will be crucial as AI becomes more prevalent in clinical workflows in order to maintain confidentiality, improve system stability, and deliver safe and dependable care.

SDG in healthcare applying generative AI models can help mitigate ethical/privacy issues by generating plausible artificial datasets that retain certain statistical characteristics of real patient records without leaking private details. These techniques contribute to fulfilling the regulations (e.g., GDPR and HIPAA) by allowing model training and research with less risk to privacy [66].

## 7.4 GOVERNANCE AND REGULATION FOR AI SAFETY

Safe use of AI in healthcare requires more than technical accuracy; it demands the establishment of strong governance that manages AI development, application, monitoring, and long-term performance. As AI technology is integrated into clinical workflows, healthcare organizations need to navigate tools that change over time, that rely on complex social and technical systems, and that exert influence over decision-making in critical situations. Therefore, governance frameworks (internal and external to the organization) are indeed critical to maintaining safety, ensuring accountability, and trust. The regulatory environment is changing swiftly. There is a realization that among the differences between AI and other technologies is the necessity of ongoing monitoring due to unique risks, leading government agencies, professional organizations, and international bodies to begin promulgating guidance and regulations for the safe use of AI. In this section, we consider how organizational governance structures may promote AI safety, review major regulatory initiatives, including the EU AI Act and U.S. FDA guidance, and explore mechanisms by which AI governance may be incorporated into extant patient safety frameworks.

### 7.4.1 Organizational AI Governance Structures

Clinical use and effective governance are prerequisites for the secure integration of AI within healthcare networks. The Institute for Healthcare Improvement (IHI), AMA, and other implementing toolkits emphasize that AI governance should extend across an entire system life cycle from development and selection through monitoring, updating, and decommissioning [39–42]. The objective is to be certain the AI tools are clinically relevant, fair, protected, and in line with organizational priorities.

#### 7.4.1.1 Fairness

Researchers examine fairness within three critical areas in healthcare AI:

It first analyzes bias sources that can be introduced at multiple phases of the ML pipeline. Then it discusses toward the potential impact of such biases on portions of the population of patients receiving different standards of care, loss of trust, and legal/ethical questions.

Processes to monitor and ensure fairness in AI models should be part of AI governance. This includes evaluating the performance of the model in different demographic subpopulations, including race, ethnicity, age, sex, socioeconomic status, and language, to eliminate potential concealed disparities. A multidisciplinary oversight committee should be responsible for these procedures, and models should be retired or retrained when disparities arise. Also, the development of AI models should guarantee procedural justice and distributive justice, for instance, against racial bias, inequalities in society, and so on. Finally, we introduce fairness metrics and trade-offs, providing a means to confront bias while managing the integral tensions between fairness and performance in healthcare. By addressing these issues, this part seeks to highlight the importance of addressing bias in order for AI technologies to drive fair and equitable healthcare for all [35].

#### 7.4.1.2 Trustworthiness

AI governance systems will need to incorporate training for clinicians and patients to help them understand how AI-based tools work in order to build trust. Such training may include case simulations, explanations of model logic, and knowledge of AI limitations to mitigate the risk of over-trusting AI. Furthermore, the use of patient data should be appropriate and authorized or preapproved, and full informed consent should be obtained from the patient before the application of AI in patient care at the least [39, 41].

Transparency fosters open lines of communication between patients and healthcare providers. When patients are empowered with information, they are more at ease voicing their concerns, raising queries, and sharing feedback, which contributes to a more engaged and communicative patient-provider relationship. Open access healthcare organizations exemplify shared decision-making where patients and healthcare professionals work together in order to decide the best course of action [10]. To build psychological safety between physician and patient is crucial to having effective shared decision-making. Shared decision-making is a process in which clinicians and patients work together to decide on the best treatment option for the patient. This method fosters consensus building and is more likely to result in decisions that are well aligned with patient preferences and values [11–13].

#### 7.4.1.3 Transparency

Governance mechanisms should make the decision process for AI models transparent. Both clinicians and patients should have access to the reasons why AI-based decisions are made to maintain autonomy in decisions, whether at the clinician or patient level. Data governance should be open and transparent about how the AI models run and how the decision is made. Issuing model cards or AI fact sheets can help differentiate when clinicians should rely on AI models, reducing misuse and automation bias [39–42]. Transparency in AI ensures that patients and clinicians are better informed and able to jointly make decisions that are thoughtful, value-congruent, and aligned with their healthcare needs.

Take, for example, the use of decision aids to facilitate shared decision-making: it's hard to do this effectively when there isn't a strong shared mental model between the clinicians and patients. Interprofessional healthcare providers with a shared mental model can view the patient as more than just the object of care; they view the patient as a partner, as a decision-maker, as someone who is in collaboration with them, and as their teammates in interprofessional healthcare teams. This entity of "mindset" allows healthcare workers to practice patient-centered care, as they can understand and respect the patient's perspective and decisions. Shared mental models are important for collaboration within healthcare teams, and such collaboration facilitates shared clinical decisions.

Informed consent is a key part of patient-centered care because it respects patients' rights and autonomy by making sure they are involved in decisions about their care. Patients need to fully understand the risks, benefits, and other options that come with their treatment choices. It is the job of healthcare providers to give patients clear information so that they can give informed consent. It is very important to know the difference between informed consent, informed choice, and shared decision-making. Informed consent means that doctors explain and suggest the best care option(s) based on medical exams and clinical evidence, and the patient understands and agrees to them. Informed choice and shared decision-making also use medical exams and clinical evidence. Doctors explain and recommend the pros and cons of different care options. However, shared decision-making also means that the patient and doctor work together to make sure that the treatment plans fit with the patient's values and preferences by taking into account their hopes, wishes, thoughts, beliefs, and social background.

#### 7.4.1.4 Accountability

Responsibility we take the basic definitions of accountability and use them in a healthcare AI setting. We go into more detail about the three main parts of accountability: the actors, the person in charge, and the principal. The healthcare AI system includes everyone who is involved in the process of developing and using AI. This process starts with gathering data, then moves on to development, and finally to deployment. The different institutions and authorities that govern these actors make up the authority that controls the whole ecosystem. The patients are the ones who delegate, so they are the main ones in the framework. Our framework makes it clearer what the governing bodies do to make sure that the accountability mechanisms work. These usually happen when compliance mechanisms and rules give actors the rules and guidelines they need to follow. Also, the actors' actions are justified by the steps they take. AI governance needs to be part of the approval, introduction, and deployment phases of AI tools in healthcare when it comes to accountability. Before AI models are put into use, oversight must make sure that

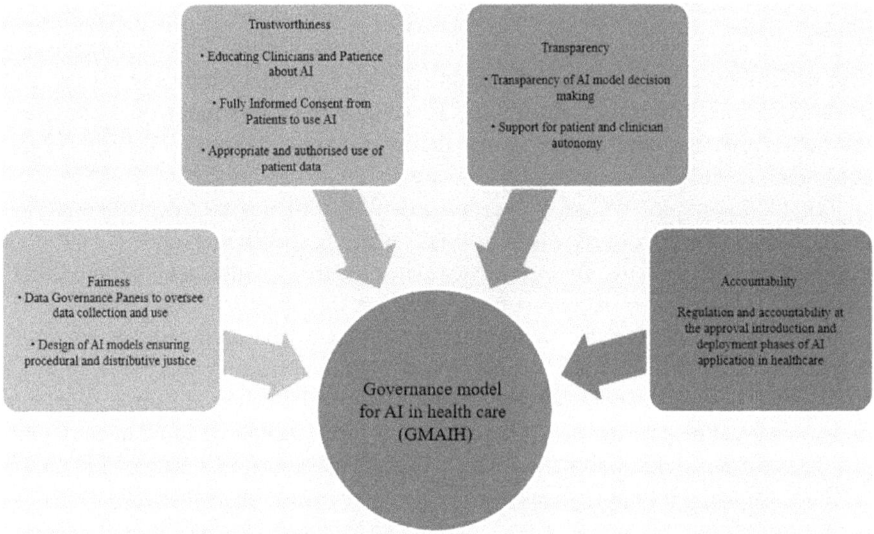


**FIGURE 7.1** Outline of the governance model for artificial intelligence (AI) in healthcare.

they are thoroughly tested for performance and safety. There need to be rules in place to make sure that AI systems are watched over all the time, from the time they are built until the time they are used. This will make sure that they are used in a responsible and ethical way. This includes keeping an eye on AI models while they are being used, with systems in place to keep an eye on how they work in the real world and fix any problems or mistakes that come up [39–42]. In our framework, we see the whole healthcare AI system as a single, complicated group of actors who act as agents to give patients health benefits and as the main actor. The reason for this is that the patients don't know the difference between the different people involved in this system. Also, each step in the pipeline is a step up for the next one. So, even though the actors work on their own, the system affects the patient as a whole. Due to these changes, the healthcare industry is becoming a smart industry along with the growth of AI. This makes it clear that we need to think of the system as a group of actors who depend on each other to get things done. Figure 7.1 shows governance model for artificial intelligence (AI) in healthcare.

### 7.4.2 External Regulatory Legislations

Besides internal governance, the external regulatory mechanism is important to ensure AI security in healthcare. While regulation is expected to be different in certain regions, key frameworks exist that regulate the development, validation, and use of AI in healthcare.

#### 7.4.2.1 The EU AI Act

It has, arguably, the most exhaustive risk-based regulatory approach to AI in which medical AI systems are indeed classified as "high-risk" if utilized for diagnosis, treatment, or CDS 39, 40. Worst yet, they claim the high-risk systems must comply with rigid requirements concerning safety, transparency, data management, cybersecurity, and post-market monitoring. Human oversight should be maintained and included in the monitoring programs post-deployment. Furthermore, the Act promotes the establishment of "regulatory sandboxes" to facilitate innovation and, at the same time, ensure compliance with safety standards. Several analysts suggest that the EU AI Act may serve as a reference for the regulation of healthcare AI worldwide [38].

#### 7.4.2.2 FDA Oversight of AI/ML-based SaMD

In the US, certain AI systems are regulated by the FDA as Software as a Medical Device (SaMD). AI/ML-based systems change over time, and this is in contrast to traditional software, leading to regulatory dilemmas. In response to this, the FDA has suggested the use of Predetermined Change Control Plans (PCCPs) to describe anticipated model changes, validation procedures, and impact mitigation strategies related to model changes in advance of implementation by developers [38].

While still evolving, the PCCP-based framework embodies the growing recognition that AI safety needs to regulate not only the initial model but also its continuous development.

#### 7.4.2.3 Comparative Perspectives across Regulatory Systems

Comparative studies reveal that the EU focuses on risk classification and on transparency and fairness, while the US places more emphasis on technical validation and post-market performance within the SaMD regulation [36–38]. Both systems affirm the significance of human oversight, life cycle management, and cybersecurity. Analysts said they expect an international regulatory convergence over time, with multinational health systems demanding consistent standards, as AI tools globalize.

### 7.4.3 Integrating AI Governance with Established Safety Programs

AI governance cannot exist in isolation. Healthcare systems must integrate AI governance with existing risk management, quality improvement (QI), and incident-reporting systems to develop a unified safety approach. Integration of the two means that the potential for AI mishaps will now be examined with the same seriousness the National Coordinating Council for Medication Error Reporting and Prevention has long accorded to medication errors, device malfunctions, or breakdowns in communication.

#### 7.4.3.1 Connecting AI Oversight to Risk Management Systems

Proactive hazard identification, monitoring of precursors, and systematic evaluation of negative events have been emphasized in risk management models [1–3]. AI governance is expected to fit comfortably within these schemes, delivering information about model functioning, subgroup differences, clinician–model interactions, and novel failure modes. When AI plays a role in causing harm or failing to prevent it, analyses of incidents must consider human factors as well as conduct technical analyses of the model's behavior [2].

#### 7.4.3.2 Integrating AI in Quality Improvement (QI) Initiatives

QI teams have a natural role in monitoring AI systems. QI methodologies could facilitate further tweaking of alert thresholds, monitoring of effects on clinical workflows, detection of model drift, or even evaluation of new escalation procedures in plan-do-study-act mode. Numerous implementation guidelines recommend that AI tools be approached like any other clinical intervention—with iterative refinement, frontline feedback, and reevaluation at certain intervals [39–42].

#### 7.4.3.3 Linking to Incident Reporting Systems

With the increasing prevalence of AI systems, such reporting systems should be expanded with categories describing AI-related alerts, inappropriate predictions, or workflow interruptions. Such reports contribute to the detection of patterns such as excessive alerting or under-alerting, even fairness-related matters and communication issues between healthcare providers. Incident-reporting mechanisms need to be modified to account for AI-specific failures, for example, misclassifications or problems with model updates.

#### 7.4.3.4 Human-Factors Alignment

To successfully integrate AI governance into safety systems, attention must be paid to human-factors-based issues, including cognitive load, usability of decision support, communication paths, and procedures for escalation [1, 4]. AI should enhance, not detract from team, situational awareness. Thoughtful interface design, alerting behaviors, and explanations matter. Governance bodies need to collaborate with human factors teams to evaluate the impact of prediction outputs on clinician behavior, workload, and communication patterns.

#### 7.4.3.5 Developing a Learning System for AI Safety

A strong ecosystem of trust considers AI a component within the broader learning health system. This includes:

- Continuous data monitoring of performance and equity
- Feedback loops that are timely to both developers and frontline users
- Procedures to retire or replace underperforming models
- Open communication about risk and updates

These are well-established patient-safety mindsets in thinking about resilience, system learning, and organizational mindfulness [1–3, 39–42].

#### 7.4.3.6 AI-Driven Insights for Health Policy

In health policy, AI introduces exciting new possibilities for evidence-informed decision-making, enhanced understanding through data analytics, and advancement of health equity. AI enables policymakers to develop effective policies and model potential outcomes by allowing them to gather and analyze precise data. This is an asset, especially in tackling such emerging health issues such as pandemic preparedness and distribution of vaccines [67, 68]. It is also pivotal in the detection of disparities in healthcare as AI analyzes trends in health data, allowing policymakers to confront systemic inequalities and widen access to care for marginalized communities [69–72]. AI is revolutionizing healthcare policymaking by delivering better insights from data for stronger policy formulation [73]. Automation in health data analytics, AI reduces human errors and offers real-time analysis, enabling policymakers to rapidly revise strategies in the face of public health threats. For instance, logistic activities and resource distribution for public health problems, such as vaccine distribution [74], can be optimized by AI models. Nevertheless, data privacy and ethical implications remain to be the significant issues. Compliance with regulations such as the General Data Protection Regulation (GDPR) reads as required, further underlining the importance of comprehensive AI governance frameworks [69]. AI also has an impact on fair health policies by noticing inequalities in access to healthcare. Using ML techniques, one can identify the gaps in service delivery, which may be addressed by focused health interventions [70]. For instance, with AI's analysis of big data, it identifies social determinants of health, leading to the formulation of better-informed policies that deal with systemic inequities [75]. Further, AI-informed analyses facilitate proactive policies to address and mitigate existing disparities in healthcare, allowing for the concentration of resources toward areas of highest demand [76].

In addition to these, AI is indispensable for monitoring the success of health policies. AI enables policymakers to evaluate the effects of prospective policy interventions through predictive modeling, improving the policymaking process and reducing uncertainty [77, 78]. This is especially true when considering the long-term effects of policies on chronic disease management [79] and on public health efforts [80, 81]. Real-time policy monitoring Based on real-world health outcomes, AI can facilitate continuous policy adjustments [69]. Yet the debates surrounding AI in healthcare policy continually revolve around ethical issues of accountability, transparency, and the risk of biased decision-making. There should be strong regulations to promote accountability and ensure responsible use of AI in policymaking processes [67].

However, substantial challenges around data privacy, fairness, and regulatory compliance must be overcome for AI to have full transformative effects on health policy [67, 69, 82]. Establishing the right regulatory framework and fostering international harmonization on AI regulation are pivotal in attenuating risks and unleashing AI's potential in healthcare.

## 7.5 MONITORING, EVALUATION, AND LEARNING SYSTEMS

Clinical care AI systems also need to be constantly monitored to ensure stable and reliable performance, safe operation, and consistency with institutional objectives. Traditional decision-support tools are generally assessed only once, prior to widespread use, but AI-based tools are different. Their performance varies by setting, is susceptible to drift, and relies on human interpretation. Therefore, monitoring and evaluation should be integrated throughout an AI tool's life cycle and contribute to a learning system in which data, governance, feedback from the clinic, and safety science intersect to sustain safety and efficacy over time.

The components of AI monitoring systems are described in the following subsections: evaluation and validation approaches, continuous monitoring and drift detection, and AI-specific incident reporting.

## 7.5.1 Methods for Evaluation and Validation of AI

Systematic reviews have repeatedly pointed out a key limitation in the literature on medical AI: insufficient rigorous clinical validation, especially via prospective and multisite studies [1, 5–7]. Although numerous AI models—many arising from highly controlled benchmark or hard-coded baseline spaces (HCBS)—demonstrate strong performance on retrospective datasets, only a fraction have been prospectively evaluated in real clinical sites. This lack of evidence leaves us with limited knowledge about how these models work when they are embedded in real workflows, interacting with heterogeneous clinical teams and under different documentation cultures.

The lack of rigorous validation is particularly worrisome given the expanding use of generative AI tools in medicine. Holistic reviews of generative AI use cases indicate that structured and stringent validation frameworks are required to achieve trustworthy performance, generalizability, and patient safety in various clinical practices [83].

### 7.5.1.1 Study Designs to Evaluate AI

There is increasing methodological literature that highlights traditional randomized controlled trials (RCTs) as valuable but not necessarily feasible among AI-based early-warning systems. Alternative study designs have been suggested that accommodate scientific rigor and practical feasibility in complex healthcare environments:

- Pragmatic trials: These trials test AI tools in real clinical settings with physicians in the field retaining methodological rigor, providing a better understanding of the real-world performance.
- Stepped-wedge trials: In these trials, units are crossed over to the intervention at different intervals, allowing comparisons to be made, while also enabling all units to ultimately be exposed to the intervention.
- Interrupted time-series designs: This design can be used to analyze trends prior to implementation and after implementation, in order to determine if observed changes may be associated with an AI tool.

These alternative designs allow for a more practical and relevant approach to evaluate AI tools in a dynamic healthcare environment where conventional randomization can interfere with workflows or result in disparities of care.

### 7.5.1.2 The Contribution of Multisite Validation

Multisite validation schemes highlight the need to validate AI tools in other populations and settings [6, 7]. A model trained in one institution may not perform the same in another due to differences in patient population, measurement protocols, or staffing levels. Testing a model at multiple sites offers the advantage of understanding the extent to which calibration, sensitivity, specificity, and subgroup performance vary. It is also critical as a measure of how well the model generalizes, a key condition for its safe use.

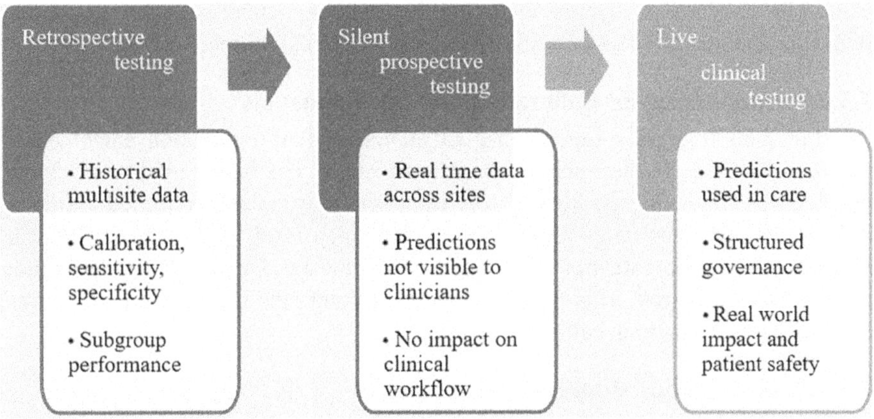


**FIGURE 7.2** Multisite phased validation framework for clinical AI systems.

Some validation frameworks suggest a three-step process for testing AI tools.

Retrospective testing: Evaluation of model performance with historical data.

Silent prospective testing: Predictions are produced, but not viewed by clinicians, assessed in a manner that does not influence clinical practice.

Live clinical testing: Predictions used in care decisions under structured governance to evaluate real-world impact.

This two-tiered approach allows to identify early potential issues and, at the same time, to ensure patients safety during the entire evaluation process. Figure 7.2 depicts Multisite phased validation framework for clinical AI systems.

#### 7.5.1.3 Workflow and Usability Evaluation

Clinical validation alone is not sufficient from a usability perspective. Research in human–computer interaction shows that several additional factors influence the real-world safety and effectiveness of clinical systems. These in-clude the design of the user interface, the frequency and manage-ment of system alerts, the clarity and format of explanations pro-vided by the system, and how well the technology is integrated into existing clinical workflows. Together, these elements play a crucial role in determining whether a system can be used effectively and safely in real clinical environments.

Such evaluations underscore that AI systems are not fixed instruments; rather, they are embedded in a sociotechnical system that includes clinicians, workflows, and organizational culture.

### 7.5.2 Monitoring Performance and Detecting Drift

The performance of an AI system can also deteriorate even after it has been validated and successfully deployed. Drift—changes to the data or clinical setting that degrade model accuracy – are now recognized as a danger to AI safety. Drift may be caused by a variety of sources, including the following: changes in patient populations, documentation practices, new therapies, or clinical protocols [7–9, 32].

#### 7.5.2.1 Monitoring for Calibration and Discrimination

The literature frequently reports that AI models drift in calibration much sooner than expected [12]. In these situations, the estimates of risk output by the model may become systematically too high or too low, even as it maintains a good ability to discriminate between cases and noncases. This may result in unnecessary alarm, non-detection, or slow attrition of confidence by clinicians. Hence, regular calibration monitoring is required. This may be achieved through the use of calibration plots, E–O ratios, and subgroup calibration plots.

#### 7.5.2.2 Continuous Monitoring Frameworks

Continuous surveillance systems based on principles of safety sciences and QI are vital for drift detection. These systems often report trends on key metrics, such as prediction error over time, outcome rates among high-risk and low-risk groups, subgroup performance across demographic variables, alert rates, clinician response patterns, and data-quality metrics (e.g., missing data, measurement frequency).

There is evidence to support that continuous monitoring should be regarded as a fundamental governance function, rather than an optional step, given that many AI tools are deployed at scale and affect many decisions daily [32].

#### 7.5.2.3 Fairness and Subgroup Monitoring

Fairness monitoring is an important part of ensuring AI safety. Studies have revealed that AI models may result in disparate predictive accuracy for individuals of different races, ethnicities, ages, or income levels—even if the overall performance of the model is satisfactory [35]. As such, continuous monitoring must involve:

- Subgroup–level AUROC (Area Under the Receiver Operating Characteristic Curve) and Calibration indicators
- Evaluation for false positive or false negative skew of particular subpopulations
- Drift detection that considers demographic shifts
- Testing predictions to see if they exacerbate or mitigate inequity

Equity is becoming recognized as a foundational component of AI safety, and governance bodies should consider failures of fairness to be significant safety events warranting immediate attention and remediation.

#### 7.5.2.4 Feedback Loops and Model Updates

Surveillance in real time naturally invokes decisions about when and how to revise models. Predetermined Change Control Plans (PCCPs) are examples of regulatory frameworks that provide a methodology for implementing updates in a controlled manner. PCCPs define the types of changes that can be made and the extent of validation that must take place prior to implementation [36–38].

Companies, however, should define their own internal update policies based on these regulatory principles. This allows any change to the model to be fully auditable, comprehensively validated, and approved by multidisciplinary governance committees to ensure safety and efficacy [39–42].

### 7.5.3 Incident Reporting and AI-Specific Taxonomies

"Conventional patient-safety incident-reporting systems were not designed for AI." As predictive analytics tools are increasingly integrated into clinical care, incident reporting also needs to adapt to identify errors and near-misses emanating from AI-based interactions. In the absence of such mechanisms, communities may fail to see important trends in failure or to recognize covert hazards. Synthesizing data and generative AI model outputs can also contribute to AI incident reporting by allowing for the secure simulation and categorization of unusual occurrences without breaching real patient data, which in turn can help with the development of taxonomies and data sets for evaluating AI safety [66].

#### 7.5.3.1 AI-Related Incident Categories

Safety experts recommend incident-reporting taxonomies also have AI-specific elements, such as:

- Wrong or misleading outputs
- Non-escalation after an AI alert
- Over-escalation as a result of false positives
- Ambiguous or unintelligible explanations of models
- System outage or data corruption impacting predictions
- Differences in predictions for different patient groups
- Failures in Human–AI communication [74]

These subcategories elucidate some of the mechanisms by which AI tools may be involved in harm, building on categorization frameworks for medication errors, device malfunctions, and communication failures [1–3].

#### 7.5.3.2 Using NLP on Incident Reports

Standard NLP approaches have previously been used to analyze traditional patient-safety reports [14], and the same approaches can be extended to support AI-specific taxonomies. Studies demonstrate that narratives encoded by NLP on incident reports can reveal trends, identify event type clusters, and detect novel, potential risks more so than human analysis [15, 16]. In relation to AI-specific events, NLP may even be able to detect specific problems such as widespread clinician confusion about risk scoring, not acting on alerts, or systematic differences in predictions by demographic group.

#### 7.5.3.3 Incorporating AI Incidents Within Systemic Safety

The governance structures insist that AI-related incidents are not to be considered in isolation. They need instead to be embedded within established mechanisms of risk management and QI [39–42]. For example:

- A human-factors team can investigate interface errors
- Quality teams may investigate outcome variation
- Data science teams can explore calibration failures or drifts
- Frontline staff can describe local workflow and communication issues

This assimilation is part of a larger movement toward embedding AI within the clinical infrastructure as a whole and not as a separate space for experimentation.

This integration reflects a trend of consolidating AI into the core clinical rather than providing it as an experimental add-on.

#### 7.5.3.4 Learning from AI-Related Events

A mature learning system uses AI-related incidents to drive further improvement of tools and workflows. This could include changes to alert thresholds, revisions to interfaces, enhancements to clinician training, or updates to models via PCCP-consistent processes [36–42]. Importantly, learning well requires transparency with psychological safety to report without blame.

## 7.6 HUMAN FACTORS, EXPLAINABILITY, AND TRUST

Successful translation of AI into the clinic relies on not just on model performance but also on how clinicians comprehend, interact with, and ultimately trust the system. Predictive accuracy enables an AI tool to produce meaningful signals, while human factors and explainability determine whether those signals result in modifying the clinical practice in a safe and appropriate manner. Well-functioning predictive models are capable of causing harm, for example, by changing workflows such that clinicians are inundated with alerts or by masking uncertainty in communication [1–4]. Additionally, poor training, limited knowledge about AI, or a deficient safety culture may contribute to increase automation bias and result in the misinterpretation of model outputs [33, 34].

This section reviews three critical elements of safe human-AI collaboration: workflow and usability design, explainability approaches that support clinician reasoning, and the training, literacy, and cultural enablers required for trusted adoption.

As AI tools are increasingly embedded within clinical workflows, their success will hinge not only on technical development and robust governance mechanisms but also on their ability to adjust and respond to real-world dynamics. The intricacies of human–AI interaction, explainability, and trust highlight the need for continuous progress in both AI design and clinician engagement ahead, significant gaps in the evidentiary foundation remain to be filled, and promising technological breakthroughs that can further advance safety, fairness, and model reliability can still be realized. This section describes and considers these future directions and highlights the way research needs to focus on how to scale AI safely and effectively in healthcare settings.

### 7.6.1 Workflow Integration and Usability Design

The integration into clinical workflows is perhaps the most important factor in determining if an AI solution improves patient safety or brings a new source of risk. Insights from AI adoption studies suggest that models that perform well in retrospective studies can break when deployed in the real world if they are out of sync with clinical workflows and the professional duties and communications modalities of their users [1, 3]. AI systems that produce risk scores without well-defined paths for escalation, or alerts delivered at suboptimal points in the clinical workflow, are often ignored, misunderstood, or misused.

These challenges underscore the criticality of usability and workflow-aware design in clinical AI systems. For instance, an active AI-based dental treatment planning system embedded within the panoramic X-ray workflow demonstrates how strong consideration of workflow in the design at all phases is paramount for enabling clinicians, not inhibiting them, and engaging patients too [84].

#### 7.6.1.1 Alert Fatigue and Signal Overload Are on the Increase

Alert fatigue is a known impediment to safe digital decision support. Studies on alerts embedded in EHRs suggest that alert volume may dilute the perceived salience of clinically relevant signals, resulting in both omissions and commissions of errors [2, 4]. This issue is exacerbated with AI tools, with risk scores being dynamic rather than fixed, rule-based alerts. If thresholds are too low, clinicians will be faced with a flood of alerts for now-actionable issues and of no concern to them. Over time, this "noise" can erode confidence in the system and reduce responsiveness.

Human-computer interaction studies highlight that timing, modality, intrusiveness, and brevity influence alert design [33]. Alerts should be generated at a time when clinicians can intervene—not busy periods—and when it is clear what level of escalation or assessment is needed. AI products that produce vague risk scores without associating them with clinically meaningful next steps may be misunderstood or ignored.

#### 7.6.1.2 Interface Design and Communication of Uncertainty

Usability studies demonstrate that clinicians' interpretations and actions on predictions can be heavily influenced by the decisions of small interface designs [34]. Color-coded risk bars, probabilities, and textual summaries influence risk perception. Interfaces that create false confidence could encourage automation bias, and interfaces that are poorly designed or too busy could exacerbate cognitive load. A good interface should have sufficiently clear: risk level, trend direction, uncertainty, and suggested response.

Implementation studies indicate that interface design is likely to be a process of iterative design and testing with direct users. The most successful implementations are those in which clinicians have a role in co-designing the presentation of predictions, the actions they prompt, and their integration with handovers, rounding routines, and escalation protocols [1, 3].

#### 7.6.1.3 Team Coordination and Sociotechnical Alignment

AI predictions affect not just decisions made by individuals but also by teams. Such scenarios are commonplace in hospital-admitted patient units and multidisciplinary rounds, and it is essential in such situations to clearly define who is responsible for responding to AI alerts. Studies indicate that ambiguity in roles can cause bystanding and delayed intervention, particularly when predictions are uncertain or without adequate context [2, 4].

For successful integration with clinical workflow, responsibilities need to be clearly specified, lines of escalation delineated, and a shared understanding established of how the AI tools align with existing safety mechanisms. This sociotechnical alignment enables teams to more effectively respond to AI-generated insights and supports collaboration in patient care.

### 7.6.2 Explainable AI Techniques Applicable to Safety

Explainability has become a core element for trusted AI in healthcare. Although some AI models are excellent, clinicians require enough visibility into why the model made a specific prediction to decide whether to accept that prediction in their clinical decision-making. Explainability promotes safety by supporting human supervision, diminishing inappropriate trust of the system, and aiding in the identification of errors or biases in the model output [85–87].

#### 7.6.2.1 Global vs. Local Explainability

Explainability can be achieved by employing two different strategies:

- Global explainability: what does the whole model look like? Which variables it is using, which ones are most important, and how it treats the data. These give a global understanding of the behavior of the model, but not always why a particular prediction was produced [85].
- Local explainability: This examines individual predictions, applying techniques such as SHAP, LIME, and counterfactual narratives to determine which features contributed to a particular risk score or alert. They are critically important for safety-critical decisions, as they permit a clinician to verify if a prediction is appropriate for a given patient.

#### 7.6.2.2 Clinician-Focused Explanation Design

Explanations must be able to facilitate clinical reasoning, according to usability studies. Clinicians have been shown to prefer explanations that conform with known cognitive models—such as a summary of important clinical features of the patient, an estimate of patient trajectory, and a degree of uncertainty [86]. Expert systems (e.g., raw SHAP values or complex decision boundaries) can end up confusing rather than illuminating.

Relevant aspects for explainability are:

- Actionable relevance: "Factors explained should be ones a clinician can act on, e.g. increasing respiratory rate, deteriorating kidney function".

- Parsimony with fidelity: Visuals and textual components should achieve the simplification of complex information without distorting model logic.
- Contextual positioning: Explanations are provided at the point of decision within the clinical workflow.
- Expression of uncertainty: AI systems should also report confidence levels or uncertainties if relevant, so that clinicians can assess the trustworthiness of predictions and act accordingly.

#### 7.6.2.3 Explainability as a Safety Feature

Explainability also contributes to that ongoing safety surveillance. When predictions are interpretable, clinicians are more likely to identify potential model drifts or errors and report these to governance bodies. In this sense, explainability acts as a preventative warning system for the model itself, which promotes a form of continuous improvement through feedback loops.

### 7.6.3 Training, Literacy, Safety Culture

Even if the AI system is optimally designed, thoughtful training and a positive safety culture are essential to safe utilization. In the absence of sufficient AI literacy, clinicians could potentially misunderstand predictions, place too much trust in the model, or not be aware of contradictions between predictions and clinical judgment [39–42].

#### 7.6.3.1 Developing AI Literacy

AI literacy is about knowing what the model does, how it works, when it does well, and when it fails. Training curricula are increasingly including

- Basic notions of ML and predictive risk-modeling
- Managing model uncertainty and limitations
- Understanding risk scores and alerts
- Recognizing signs of drift or bias
- How and when to escalate based on predictions

Governance frameworks also underlie that training should be continuous and professional-group specific to address disparities in digital literacy and clinical responsibilities [39].

#### 7.6.3.2 Embedding AI into Safety Culture

Strong safety culture also affects how clinicians respond to the AI-generated predictions and report concerns. Safety cultures encourage open communication, psychological safety, and everyone doing their part to keep systems safe [1, 3]. What it means for AI is that clinicians should be able to comfortably challenge predictions, report errors, and engage in conversations about model performance.

AI products should be used as tools, not as experts. Governance bodies advocate simple messaging designed to reinforce clinician judgment, denote that AI is not a substitute for clinical reasoning, and promote shared decision-making [39–42].

When AI is presented as a tool for learning as opposed to telling, it is likely that use will be safer and more reflective.

Implementation Science and Sustained Learning Implementation Science studies suggest that ongoing positive outcomes are contingent upon reinforcement of continuous learning cycles.

Post-deployment, teams must:

- Keep a regular check on clinician responses to alerts
- Monitor outcomes data and performance in subgroups
- Ask for input on usability and explanations
- Modify thresholds, workflows, and training materials, if necessary.
- Disseminate best practices within and across services.

These behaviors foster a learning system in which AI is an ongoing element of safety improvement rather than a one-time intervention.

These practices encourage a learning system where AI is perpetually woven into safety enhancements as opposed to being considered a fixed solution.

## 7.7 CONCLUSION

AI is reshaping the patient safety field to facilitate earlier risk detection, more tailored decision support, and continuous monitoring in ways that extend beyond traditional tools. In areas such as sepsis, ADEs, falls, pressure injuries, and surveillance for deterioration based on wearables, AI has demonstrated the capability to detect signals that are otherwise extremely challenging to identify in real-world clinical settings [3]. Together, these developments indicate that AI could play a critical role in augmenting current safety frameworks—especially in environments where slow recognition of clinical changes remains a key contributor to preventable injury.

Yet the promise of AI also brings a familiar and novel set of risks with it. Problems like brittleness, failure to generalize, automation bias, unequal performance across subgroups, and vulnerabilities in data protection all underline the importance of careful, ongoing scrutiny. These challenges make clear that AI should not be considered a solely technological solution, but rather a sociotechnical one, dependent on how algorithms work combined with human judgment, clinical workflows, and organizational culture. Bringing AI into healthcare delivery will require not just technical innovation but also substantial investment in training, governance, and system-level monitoring to ensure it is deployed safely.

With the adoption of AI-driven tools on the rise within healthcare systems, the challenge will be to create environments in which they can be used safely, transparently, and equitably. This necessitates the development of robust governance structures, evaluation methods, ongoing vigilance of performance, and a commitment to learn from these real-world experiences. It also necessitates nurturing the human dimensions of trust, training, communication, and shared decision-making that facilitate clinicians' thoughtful—not unthinking—use of AI. It is equally important to focus on the financial and labor force consequences of AI so that these applications enhance care rather than strain resources.

In the end, the future of AI for patient safety will be determined not only by advances in ML methodologies but also by the ability of healthcare organizations to adopt these tools and integrate them into complex care systems. As AI systems mature, their socio-technical context will need to be considered (including continuous feedback, collaboration, and governance) to contribute to a safer, more reliable healthcare environment. Designed with care, governed well, and subject to ongoing scrutiny, AI can increase clinicians' capacity to detect risk, to react to deterioration, and to provide safer, more reliable care—which has the potential to improve patient outcomes and safety at scale and, in doing so, to advance the quality and safety of care internationally.

## REFERENCES

1. Bates DW, et al. The potential of artificial intelligence to improve patient safety: a scoping review. NPJ Digit Med. 2021;4(1):54.
2. Ratwani RM, Bates DW, Classen DC. Patient safety and artificial intelligence in clinical care. JAMA Health Forum. 2024;5(2):e235514.
3. Tighe P, Mossburg S, Gale B. Artificial intelligence and patient safety: promise and challenges. AHRQ PSNet Perspective. 2024.
4. Reason J. Human error: models and management. BMJ. 2000;320(7237):768–770.
5. Yeung AWK, Torkamani A, Butte AJ, Glicksberg BS, Schuller B, Rodriguez B, Ting DSW, Bates D, Schaden E, Peng H, Willschke H, Van der Laak J, Car J, Rahimi K, Celi LAC, Banach M, Kletecka-Pulker M, Kimberger O, Eils R, Islam SMS, Wong ST, Wong TY, Gao W, Brunak S, Atanasov AG. The promise of digital healthcare technologies. Front Public Health. 2023;11:1196596. doi:10.3389/fpubh.2023.1196596.
6. Klang E, García-Elorrio E, Zimlichman E. Revolutionizing patient safety with artificial intelligence: the potential of natural language processing and large language models. Int J Qual Health Care. 2023;35(3):mzad049.
7. Yan MY, et al. Sepsis prediction, early detection, and identification using clinical text for machine learning: a systematic review. J Am Med Inform Assoc. 2022;29(3):559–575.
8. Mohammed A, et al. Machine learning-based early prediction of sepsis using electronic health record data: a systematic review. J Clin Med. 2023;12(17):5658.
9. Kumar R, et al. Sepsis in liver failure patients: diagnostic challenges and recent advancements. World J Crit Care Med. 2025;14(2):101587.
10. Papareddy P, et al. Transforming sepsis management: AI-driven innovations in early detection and tailored therapies. Crit Care. 2025;29:366.
11. Subramanian M, et al. Data-driven machine learning approaches for predicting in-hospital sepsis mortality. Comput Biol Med. 2024;173:108023.
12. Mohammed AA, et al. Vital signs-only machine learning model for acute inpatient deterioration prediction. NPJ Digit Med. 2025;8 (online ahead of print).
13. Zanos TP, et al. Development and validation of a clinical wearable deep learning-based continuous in-hospital deterioration prediction model. Nat Commun. 2025;16:1–14. doi:10.1038/s41467-025-65219-8.
14. Ting LP-Y, Chen HP, Liu AS, Yeh CY, Chen PL, Chuang KT. Early detection of patient deterioration from real-time wearable monitoring system. arXiv [preprint]. 2025; arXiv:2505.01305.
15. Golder S, et al. Leveraging natural language processing and machine learning methods for adverse drug event detection in electronic health/medical records: a scoping review. Drug Saf. 2025;48(4):321–337.
16. Bakker M, et al. Adverse drug event detection using natural language processing: a scoping review. PLoS One. 2022;17(1):e0279842.

17. Wang J, et al. Predicting adverse drug events using machine learning based on electronic health records: a systematic review. Front Pharmacol. 2024;15:1497397.
18. Hwang Y, et al. Artificial intelligence-powered pharmacovigilance: a review of machine and deep learning in clinical text-based adverse drug event detection. J Biomed Inform. 2024;152:104522.
19. Mifsud M, et al. Machine learning techniques for predicting drug-related side effects: a scoping review. Pharmaceutics. 2023;15(6):795.
20. Li Y, et al. Applying artificial intelligence to predict falls for inpatients. Front Med (Lausanne). 2023;10:1285192.
21. Lin FC, et al. AI-driven fall prediction across generations: integrating deep learning and machine learning for young, middle-aged, and older adults. Gerontology 2025; 72(1):3–18.
22. Chang L, et al. Digital healthcare approaches for fall detection and prediction in older adults in hospital and long-term care settings: a systematic review. Medicina. 2025; 61(11):1926.
23. Lee J, et al. Supervised machine learning-based prediction for in-hospital pressure injuries using electronic health records. Int J Med Inform. 2021;151:104471.
24. Fleming R, et al. Machine learning approaches for hospital-acquired pressure injuries: a comparative study. Front Med Technol. 2022;4:926667.
25. Guo Y, et al. Electronic medical record-driven machine learning predictive model for hospital-acquired pressure injuries. J Clin Med. 2024;13(4):1175.
26. Choi J, et al. Predicting pressure injury risk in hospitalised patients using machine learning compared with standard care. BMJ Open. 2024;14:e082540.
27. Howard A, et al. Implementable prediction of pressure injuries in hospitalized adults using EHR data. JMIR Med Inform. 2024;12(1):e51842.
28. Kroll RR, et al. Accuracy of a wrist-worn wearable device for monitoring heart rates in hospital inpatients: a prospective observational study. J Med Internet Res. 2016; 18(9):e253.
29. Olson MC, et al. Predicting fall risk through automatic wearable monitoring: a systematic review. Int J Progn Health Manag. 2021;12(4):1–14.
30. Khan MM, et al. AI-driven wearable sensors for postoperative monitoring in surgical patients: a systematic review. Comput Biol Med. 2025;196:110783.
31. Taheri A, Farhadi A, Zamanifar A. Application of GenAI in Clinical Administration Support. In: Zamanifar A, Faezipour M, editors. Application of Generative AI in Healthcare Systems. Cham: Springer; 2025. p. 91–117. doi:10.1007/978-3-031-82963-5_4
32. Wiens J, et al. Do no harm: a roadmap for responsible machine learning for health care. Nat Med. 2019;25(9):1337–1340.
33. Fernandes C, et al. Exploring the risks of automation bias in healthcare artificial intelligence systems: a Bowtie analysis. AI Ethics. 2024;4(1).
34. Hoffman B. Automation complacency: risks of abdicating medical decision making to AI. AI Ethics. 2025;5(2):5783–5793.
35. Cross JL, et al. Bias in medical AI: implications for clinical decision-making. PLoS Digital Health. 2024;3(11):e0000651.
36. European Parliament. The EU Artificial Intelligence Act: implications for healthcare. Health Policy. 2024;149(1):105152.
37. Florido-Benítez L. Hyper-segmentation and hyper-personalization in the tourism industry. Int J Tourism Cities. 2024; vol 11, 105–152.
38. Szadeczky T, et al. Risk, regulation, and governance: evaluating artificial intelligence across diverse application scenarios. Secur J. 2025;38(1):35.
39. Albaadani MM, et al. Ten quality improvement initiatives to standardize healthcare processes. Contemp Top Patient Saf. 2024;3:xx.

40. Burrell DN. Dynamic evaluation approaches to telehealth technologies and artificial intelligence (AI) telemedicine applications in healthcare and biotechnology organizations. Merits. 2023;3(4):700–721.
41. Morley J, et al. Governing data and artificial intelligence for health care: developing an international understanding. JMIR Form Res. 2022;6(1):e31623.
42. Stanford HAI. Facilitating responsible governance of healthcare AI tools. White paper. 2024;1–4.
43. Rashidieranjbar F, Farhadi A, Zamanifar A. Revolutionizing Healthcare with Generative Artificial Intelligence Technologies. In: Generative Artificial Intelligence (AI) Approaches for Industrial Applications. Cham: Springer Nature Switzerland; 2025. p. 189–221.
44. Song D, et al. Similarity-based machine learning support vector machine predictor of drug-drug interactions with improved accuracies. J Clin Pharm Ther. 2019;44(2):268–75.
45. Bean DM, et al. Knowledge graph prediction of unknown adverse drug reactions and validation in electronic health records. Sci Rep. 2017;7(1):16416.
46. Cai R, et al. Identification of adverse drug-drug interactions through causal association rule discovery from spontaneous adverse event reports. Artif Intell Med. 2017;76:7–15.
47. Dandala B, Joopudi V, Devarakonda M. Adverse drug events detection in clinical notes by jointly modeling entities and relations using neural networks. Drug Saf. 2019; 42(1):135–46.
48. Chapman AB, Peterson KS, Alba PR, DuVall SL, Patterson OV. Detecting adverse drug events with rapidly trained classification models. Drug Saf. 2019;42(1):147–56.
49. Huang L, Wu X, Chen JY. Predicting adverse side effects of drugs. BMC Genomics. 2011;12(Suppl 5):S11.
50. Dey S, Luo H, Fokoue A, Hu J, Zhang P. Predicting adverse drug reactions through interpretable deep learning framework. BMC Bioinformatics. 2018;19(Suppl 21):476.
51. Onay A, Onay M, Abul O. Classification of nervous system withdrawn and approved drugs with ToxPrint features via machine learning strategies. Comput Methods Programs Biomed. 2017;142:9–19.
52. Simon ACR, et al. Safety and usability evaluation of a web-based insulin self-titration system for patients with type 2 diabetes mellitus. Artif Intell Med. 2013;59(1):23–31.
53. Hu Y, Tai C, Tsai C, Huang M. Improvement of adequate digoxin dosage: an application of machine learning approach. J Healthy Eng. 2018;2018:3948245.
54. Hu Y, Wu F, Lo C, Tai C. Predicting warfarin dosage from clinical data: a supervised learning approach. Artif Intell Med. 2012;56(1):27–34.
55. Reddy M, et al. Clinical safety and feasibility of the advanced bolus calculator for type 1 diabetes based on case-based reasoning: a 6-week nonrandomized single-arm pilot study. Diabetes Technol Ther. 2016;18(8):487–493.
56. Schiff GD, et al. Screening for medication errors using an outlier detection system. J Am Med Inform Assoc. 2017;24(2):281–287.
57. Labovitz DL, Shafner L, Reyes Gil M, Virmani D, Hanina A. Using artificial intelligence to reduce the risk of nonadherence in patients on anticoagulation therapy. Stroke. 2017;48(5):1416–1419.
58. Hasan S, Duncan GT, Neill DB, Padman R. Automatic detection of omissions in medication lists. J Am Med Inform Assoc. 2011;18(4):449–458.
59. Long J, Yuan MJ, Poonawala R. An observational study to evaluate the usability and intent to adopt an artificial intelligence-powered medication reconciliation tool. Interact J Med Res. 2016;5(2):e14.
60. Li Q, et al. An end-to-end hybrid algorithm for automated medication discrepancy detection. BMC Med Inform Decis Mak. 2015;15:37.
61. Choudhury A, Asan O. Role of artificial intelligence in patient safety outcomes: systematic literature review. JMIR Med Inform. 2020;8(7):e18599.

62. Carrell DS, et al. Using natural language processing to identify problem usage of prescription opioids. Int J Med Inform. 2015;84(12):1057–1064.
63. Farhadi A, Taheri A. Application of GenAI in Synthetic Data Generation in the Healthcare System. In: Zamanifar A, Faezipour M, editors. Application of Generative AI in Healthcare Systems. Cham: Springer; 2025. p. 67–89. doi:10.1007/978-3-031-82963-5_3
64. Zamanifar A, Nazemi E. EECASC: an energy-efficient communication approach in smart cities. Wirel Netw.2020;26(2):925–940.
65. Naghib A, Gharehchopogh FS, Zamanifar A. The Role of Large Language Models in Delivering Artificial Intelligence-based Psychological Interventions and Therapies. In: Applications of Large Language Models (LLM) in Healthcare Systems. Boca Raton (FL): Chapman and Hall/CRC; 2025. p. 142–178.
66. Farhadi A, Zamanifar A, Faezipour M. Application of Generative AI in Drug Discovery. In: Farhadi A, Zamanifar A, Faezipour M, editors. Application of Generative AI in Healthcare Systems. First online 26 February 2025. p. 155–174.
67. Lakkimsetti M, et al. Optimizing the clinical direction of artificial intelligence with health policy: a narrative review of the literature. Cureus. 2024;16:e58400.
68. Chirico F, Teixeira da Silva JA. Evidence-based policies in public health to address COVID-19 vaccine hesitancy. Future Virol. 2023:261–273.
69. Amini MM, et al. Artificial intelligence ethics and challenges in healthcare applications: a comprehensive review in the context of the European GDPR mandate. Mach Learn Knowl Extr. 2023;5:1023–35.
70. Goralski MA, Tan TK. Artificial Intelligence: Poverty Alleviation, Healthcare, Education, and Reduced Inequalities in a Post-COVID World. In: Mazzi F, Floridi L, editors. The Ethics of Artificial Intelligence for the Sustainable Development Goals. Springer International Publishing; 2023. p. 97–113.
71. Kluge EH. The ethics of artificial intelligence in healthcare: from hands-on care to policy-making. Healthc Manage Forum. 2024;37:406–8.
72. Chen RJ, et al. Algorithmic fairness in artificial intelligence for medicine and healthcare. Nat Biomed Eng. 2023;7:719–42.
73. Kim ES. Can data science achieve the ideal of evidence-based decision-making in environmental regulation? Technol Soc. 2024;78:102615.
74. Cauët E, et al. Policy brief Belgian EBCP mirror group artificial intelligence in cancer care. Arch Public Health. 2024;82:142.
75. Guevara M, et al. Large language models to identify social determinants of health in electronic health records. NPJ Digit Med. 2024;7:6.
76. Rueda J, et al. "Just" accuracy? Procedural fairness demands explainability in AI-based medical resource allocations. AI Soc. 2022;39:1–12.
77. Ramezani M, et al. The application of artificial intelligence in health policy: a scoping review. BMC Health Serv Res. 2023;23:1416.
78. Shumway DO, Hartman HJ. Medical malpractice liability in large language model artificial intelligence: legal review and policy recommendations. J Osteopath Med. 2024;124:287–90.
79. Badidi E. Edge AI for early detection of chronic diseases and the spread of infectious diseases: opportunities, challenges, and future directions. Future Internet. 2023;15:370.
80. Shah NH, et al. A nationwide network of health AI assurance laboratories. JAMA. 2024;331:245–9.
81. Addy A, et al. Analysis of Ghana's public health act 2012 and AI's role in augmenting vaccine supply and distribution challenges in Ghana. J Law Policy Globalization. 2024;139:14–20.
82. Pasham SD. The function of artificial intelligence in healthcare: a systematic literature review. Int J Acta Informatica. 2023;2(1):32–42.

83. Zamanifar A, Faezipour M. Application of Generative AI in Healthcare Systems. Cham: Springer; 2025.
84. Rashidi Ranjbar F, Zamanifar A. Autonomous dental treatment planning on panoramic X-ray using deep learning-based object detection algorithm. Multimedia Tools Appl. 2024;83(14):42999–43033.
85. Sadeghi Z, et al. A review of explainable artificial intelligence in healthcare. Comput Electr Eng. 2024;118:109370.
86. Basiouni A, et al. Unlocking the future: systematic review of the progress and challenges in explainable artificial intelligence (XAI). SSRN. 2023;5049330.
87. Holzinger A, et al. Causability and explainability of artificial intelligence in medicine. Wiley Interdiscip Rev Data Min Knowl Discov. 2019;9(4):e1312.

# 8 Future Directions and Challenges in AI Safety for Healthcare

*Farshid Babapour Mofrad and Midya Yousefzamani*

## 8.1 INTRODUCTION

Artificial intelligence (AI) has emerged as one of the most innovative phenomena now taking place in medicine, with dramatic implications for how healthcare is rendered, provided, and experienced. In recent years, computer technology has passed through a gradual evolutionary phase whereby, from a situation in which simple machines were employed merely to carry out human commands, we have come to the recognition of the possibility of intelligent machines competent in intelligent autonomous evaluation and decision-making [1, 2]. The new computer programming and advances in brain mapping have generated intelligent (or semi-intelligent) software systems (chatbots, diagnostic tools, and robotic surgery) that simulate human thinking through processes that include the integration of perception, inference, and reasoning [3]. These developments have provided new opportunities for prevention, diagnosis, and treatment in the actual responsibilities of both physical and mental health. AI models are able to analyze complex biological data, reach earlier diagnoses, and individualize therapeutic choices for patients vis-à-vis [4, 5]. In this manner, AI helps physicians to reach more rapid and precise diagnoses, to decrease medical errors, and to improve the operational efficiency [6]. A notable innovation is the advent of generative AI, now able to produce human-like text, pictures, and molecular designs.

DALL·E, are being applied with more and more success to drug development, clinical documentation, and point of education of patients [7–11]. Their facility for extracting and generalizing the same patterns from enormous databases accelerates innovation but involves a continual realization of the new risks that are connected with the interpretability, accountability, and safety of the same. Understanding this goal, global initiatives such as those spearheaded by the European Union and European Commission have heavily invested in R&D of AI to increase capacity to deliver healthcare, deal with a lack of personnel, and equalize care [12]. However, even with these advances, the speed of integration of AI by clinicians into work practices has been slower than originally believed [13]. Many systems are still difficult to use, non-transparent, and difficult to interpret. In an area such as healthcare, where decisions relevant to human life are made, clinicians and patients require more than just "performance" from such agencies but require transparency of issues such as understandability, safety, and non-hazarding. As identified in various studies,

 DOI: 10.1201/9781003743422-8

medical AI systems cannot be seen categorically as safe or trustworthy when it can be seen that practitioners are unable to explain or authenticate algorithmic reasons why something has occurred [14]. Without interpretability, it is impossible for clinicians to ensure the safety of patients or meaningfully trust AI-mediated systems. The relationship between AI safety and trust is at the center of responsible innovation in healthcare. Trust is what determines if AI systems are accepted or adopted by clinicians, regulators, or the general public. Trust is also a psychological and ethical process that allows humans to deal with uncertainty and to act on their knowledge despite the risks involved [15]. This trust ostensible must be established on the basis of demonstrable safety. An AI system that offers no proven ways of guaranteeing patient protection or ethical conduct will, in any event, be distrusted on the grounds of its perfect correctness or refined structure; men are such that they will never believe in anything, of whatever nature, in which there is no protection against risks, be it ever so small. Thus, safety is not a mere technical product but the ethical and productive basis for belief. An AI system, to be trustworthy, must show itself, to merit trust, to be capable of doing its duty with ability and trustworthiness. It must perform its function dependably, but on the other hand, it must also possess knowledge of handling ethical conduct with regard to human welfare [16, 17]. This implies descriptive knowledge and the knowledge of the ethical basis, which admits of liberal and effective conduct, which will imply such a large amount of transparency that the clinician will obtain the information and education to be able to interpret, if necessity, and justify AI decisions. Hence, the "Black-box" quality of many modern machine-learning models undermines this desirable state of things, for there creeps in a consideration opposed to the one introduced into the design for transparency and knowledge of the reliability of the system, together with the risk of equality and accountability of results [18]. Therefore, the interpretability of such imports becomes a prime condition of safety, for such systems as cannot explain the words of their predictions will be likely to commit the errors of unreliability, discrimination, misevaluations, or inopportune intercessions, and that without the possibility obtained by the physician of interceding. To address these concerns, AI Trust Frameworks were suggested by researchers and policymakers in order to balance innovation with both ethical and clinical standards [19–21]. These frameworks cover issues of fairness, accountability, and privacy while explicitly stating that safety validation has to stretch further than technical accuracy and be rendered to the ethical and social considerations surrounding their use. The intent is that innovation is carried out firstly with responsibility but also through collaboration of engineers, clinicians, ethicists, and regulators. Despite significant advances in AI applications, especially in diagnostic imaging, drug discovery, and digital health, serious issues remain. Many models work well in research but fail to generalize across populations [4, 5]. The issues pertaining to data quality, interoperability, and cybersecurity continue to deflate reliability and trustworthiness, while the regulatory and ethical frameworks have not progressed to keep pace with innovation [14, 18]. Successful and reliable implementation of AI in healthcare will require continuing efforts: robust validation, clear reporting, continuous monitoring, and compliance with ethical principles in a patient-centered way. Ultimately, safety leads to trust, which in turn leads to an acceptance of AI as a complement to human decision-making rather than a replacement in our mutual endeavor for improved health, safety, and well-being. This chapter considers where AI safety in healthcare might go next and what challenges remain unresolved, and it seeks to describe the principles and practice for building a system that is both transformative and trustworthy.

## 8.2 MODEL RELIABILITY AND GENERALIZATION

The assurance of reliability and generalizability of AI systems remains one of the most challenging problems of achieving safety in healthcare. The accuracy and efficacy of AI models are based on traditional metrics such as accuracy, sensitivity, and specificity, which enter into the devotion of clinical validation [5, 21]. Although preclinical and experimental results may appear satisfactory, previous clinical studies have not shown comparable performance for these systems. This is because of differences in population demographics, prevalence of disease, and clinical pathways in different centers, a fact that demonstrates the necessary immunity and generalizability of the AI systems when applied in their training mode to the real clinical setting [3, 5, 22]. Hence, external validation of the AI systems has arisen as one of the most important requirements for ensuring reliability of the model. Davahli et al. (2021) emphasize that the variations in demographics and pathology of disease cannot possibly all be elucidated in initial clinical trials, and thus it is necessary to validate the model externally with the demographic data that has been supplied from the place for which the model is intended for deployment [22]. If external validation is not pursued, the AI systems may well have the capacity to supply inconsistent outputs or unsafe outputs on examination of application in different ethnic populations, which discredits clinical confidence in the data and the patient's safety.

A reliable AI model must also display stability, producing repeatable outputs given almost identical inputs, and robustness, defined as preserving accuracy after the introduction of noise or uncertainty in data [23, 24]. The lack of stability and robustness can erode the confidence of clinicians and patients alike, which limits the availability for which the system can safely be used in decision-making of a safety-critical nature. At the same time, algorithmic bias remains a serious barrier to achieving fairness and generality, since AI models that are trained by imbalanced or non-representative datasets can retain, and perhaps accentuate, current inequities in healthcare delivery [25–27]. Three main strategies have been proposed to avoid the bias, namely preprocessing (the handling of data bias), in-processing (the adjusting of learning algorithms to reduce bias), and post-processing (the rectifying of biased outputs) [28, 29]. Bias regularized learning and topological data analysis are examples of current efforts that attempt to design AI models that are both fair and robust [29]. In the final analysis, however, reliability in AI for healthcare consists not only of technical performance but also of continuous monitoring, recalibration, and ethical vigilance throughout the model's lifetime [21].

### 8.2.1 Model Drift: Data, Concept, and Temporal Drift

Notwithstanding their protracted development and extensive validation, the performance of AI models in medicine often deteriorates over time as a result of a phenomenon called model drift. Model drift is the gradual diminution of a model's predictive efficacy that occurs over time as a result of changes in data distributions, disease patterns, or clinical practice. In terms of patient populations, disease prevalence, and diagnostic criteria that are undergoing change, all being interpreted by the model, drift poses a particular challenge for safety and efficacy in healthcare [21, 22]. Drift of input into models is known as data drift and occurs when the statistical distribution of the input data changes over time, producing a mismatch between the training and deployment environments. An example of this may be an imaging AI model trained on data from one hospital, as opposed to data from a population having different demographic or equipment characteristics [5]. Similarly, varying data acquisition protocols could produce major drift as a result of change in the electronic health record or vice versa. Concept drift, on the other hand, occurs when the relationship obtained between input features as presented to the algorithm and the target outcome changes. This may occur with changes to definitions of disease states; for example, new WHO definitions for hypertension teach us that threshold values for hypertension or diabetes will change, together changing the meaning of the target that the model is predicting [22]. Temporal drift reflects long-term shifts caused by evolving epidemiological or environmental conditions. For example, the emergence of new pathogens, changes in treatment guidelines, or population aging can all result in temporal performance degradation in AI systems. Ongoing monitoring, periodic recalibration, and retraining with updated data sets are therefore necessary components of AI life cycle management in order to mitigate those risks. Ethical vigilance, along with those technical interventions, is also required to ensure transparency and accountability of the evolving models. Continuous adaption is therefore not only a technical necessity but also a fundamental principle of safety for sustainable AI deployment for healthcare [18, 21].

As is shown in Table 8.1, it is due to specific types of data or practice variation, which need particular mitigations, that there are different forms of model drift. Distinguishing them is crucial in the design of adaptive and safe AI systems, which can ensure uniform clinical performance over time.

**TABLE 8.1**
**Types of Model Drift and Their Implications in Healthcare AI**

| Type of Drift | Definition | Causes | Mitigation Strategies |
|---|---|---|---|
| Data Drift | Change in data distribution between training and deployment environments | New data sources, imaging devices, population differences | Continuous monitoring, input data normalization |
| Concept Drift | Change in the relationship between input and output variables | Updated diagnostic criteria or treatment standards | Periodic retraining, recalibration with updated labels |
| Temporal Drift | Gradual shifts in data patterns over time | Epidemiological or demographic changes | Time-based model retraining, performance auditing |

### 8.2.2 Life Cycle Management: Monitoring, Recalibration, and Continuous Retraining

The reliability of AI systems in healthcare does not conclude with deployment but rather relies on continuous life cycle management that enables reliable and ethical performances throughout its clinical usage phase. Unlike traditional medical devices, AI models show a dynamic evolution that requires constant monitoring to ensure their concordance with the realities of clinical practice and needs of patients [21]. Monitoring is the first pillar of such a life cycle management. Constant post-deployment monitoring will identify early warning signs such as model drift, unexpected errors, or data quality problems. The most effective monitoring systems incorporate performance indicators, fairness metrics, and uncertainty estimation tools that alert clinicians and developers about differences from the expected level of behavior [22]. Such systems are especially important in high-risk applications such as radiology or predictive diagnostics, where undetected drift may directly impact outcomes for patients. Recalibration of the model is a periodic adjustment of the model to restore performance without necessarily retraining the model from the beginning. This may involve changing or updating probability distribution thresholds and geometric boundaries or introducing very small curated data sets representing new disease presentations. Recalibration of the cycle ensures that predictions remain reliable as population factors or the environmental [20] change. Continuous retraining represents the highest level of life cycle maintenance, which incorporates systematic relearning from adjusted data or data sources. Relearning sustains that AI models remain applicable to novel diseases, adjusted attending medicines, or devices. However, this effort must be aligned with appropriate or rigorous version logging, remaining documentation, and appropriate release or validation measures against subsequent quality degradation or amplification of biases [18]. Finally, life cycle management is not just a technical issue. It also embodies ethical awareness and regulatory accountability. Lysaght et al. (2019) state that the safe introduction of AI requires making clear records of updates in the models, explainability of changes in algorithms, and the participation of interdisciplinary teams in governance. Thus, safety requires a living ecosystem where the technical maintenance and ethics of the system grow together [19]. In Figure 8.1, as previously described, the safe and sustainable AI deployment process involves a cyclic process of monitoring, recalibrating, retraining, and ethical oversight, thereby aimed at designing for various aspects of reliability and governance.

## 8.3 DATA QUALITY, INTEROPERABILITY, AND BIAS

The groundwork for safe AI in healthcare is provided by good quality, representative, interoperable data. The quality of AI predictions depends on the algorithm design but also on the extent, completeness, and differences of the data on which training and validation have been performed [5, 22]. However, the health data trade is often stored separately in several institutions and stored in incompatible formats and is constrained by incompleteness or inconsistency of the record [12, 20]. These interoperability barriers constrain the safety with which the generalizing AI systems

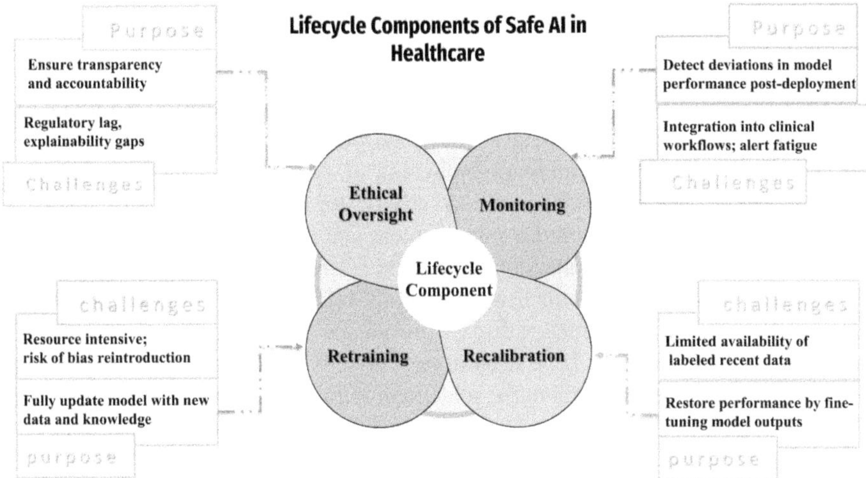


**FIGURE 8.1** Conceptual framework illustrating the four key components of AI life cycle management for healthcare safety: monitoring, recalibration, retraining, and ethical oversight. Each component serves a distinct purpose in maintaining model reliability and clinical trust, while facing unique implementation challenges such as data quality, transparency, and regulatory adaptation.

may be used in differing populations and clinical contexts. As a result, future AI safety initiatives must emphasize the creation of standardized, federated data ecosystems that support secure, ongoing learning and sharing of AI without sacrificing privacy to broker developments of trust [3, 21]. This kind of framework would facilitate not only external validation but also ongoing recalibration of models with the introduction of new information, an important device for preventing model drift and ensuring longitudinal reliability. Addressing algorithmic bias is also essential to health equity and patient safety [27]. Bias can result from sampling, measurement, and historical inequities that can spread through AI and reinforce disparities in the outcome front [25, 26]. Future areas of emphasis around AI safety will have to include bias-aware learning strategies, transparency in reporting, and governance strategies to effectuate fairness across demographic and clinical cohorts [19, 28]. Ultimately, building trustworthy, safe AI for healthcare will be closely related to data quality, interoperability, and equity principles coalescing around continuous technical and ethical vigilance.

### 8.3.1 Data Quality and Representativeness

Data of high quality, representative, and interoperable is the basis of AI safety in healthcare. The reliability of AI models is based not only on their algorithmic sophistication but also on the correctness, completeness, and diversity of their "training data" [5, 22]. Clinical databases are often subject to inconsistencies, missing values, and diverse recording standards, which reduce the reliability and reproducibility of AI predictions [21, 30]. These failings, together with heterogeneous, nonuniform structures for data, increase the risk of unsafe recommendations and "data drift," where model performance degrades as the nature of the data varies [22]. The primary ethical challenge in future AI safety remains the representativeness of the data. Models that are trained on homogeneous datasets consistently perform poorly on different demographics of patients and clinical environments [25, 26]. Noting this issue, Soenksen et al. (2022) [30] and Crossnohere et al. (2022) [31] indicate that the AI implementation frameworks that are currently in use remain immature and that an early (and further) requirement for improvement and fairness is the extension of the representativeness of data collection from "other" groups who are presently underrepresented. The issues examined are especially relevant in global health systems, with their intrinsic complexities of disease prevalence, factors of socioeconomics and methods of delivery of care [27]. In summary, effective and inclusive federated data collection methods will be vital in the solution of improving representativeness, while still being mindful of promoting and preserving issues of privacy [3, 12]. Another aspect that needs to be addressed concerning trustworthiness in AI is that the safety and privacy of data are important dimensions. There is enormous need for data anonymization, access regulation, and statistical protection for safe handling of sensitive patient data. Ethical standards are also needed in case this data may be compromised [32, 33]. Another aspect needed is transparency and interpretability, for not only does the patient need to understand the reasoning of the models, but also the clinician [34]. However, emerging AI Trust Frameworks include these principles as cited by Lysaght et al. (2019) [19] and Dwivedi et al. (2021) [20] so as to ensure data integrity and fairness in an environment of accountability. In the future, the focus of AH needs to shift closer towards the use of functional, quality-assured, ethically driven data pipelines that guarantee that social responsibility is aligned to technical validation. This is of immense value in relation to the safety and equity of AI technology in AH [35, 36].

### 8.3.2 Data Interoperability and Access Barriers

The interoperability of data in healthcare—that is, the capacity for the seamless exchange of and access to information across systems, institutions, and geographies—is a necessary precondition for the safety and trustworthiness of AI. Despite advances in electronic health record (EHR) systems and data standards, most healthcare data remain siloed, fragmented, and inconsistent across clinical settings [12, 20]. This fragmentation inhibits the ability of AI systems to generalize, validate, and adapt to real-world conditions. Barriers to interoperability also impede reproducibility and limit partnerships between institutions, thereby restricting the build-up of the diverse, high-quality datasets necessary for safe, fair AI delivery [30, 31]. Interoperability challenges arise as a result of differences in data schemas, storage modalities, and coding systems between hospitals and research centers [5]. The lack of standardized ontologies and semantic alignment of data frequently leads to either duplicated data or gaps in data; this can make datasets difficult to match or merge without creating bias in the sample or losing data integrity [22]. Furthermore, organizational requisite for privacy and institutional policies surrounding the access of data that arise as an important product of the protection of patient confidentiality can lead to a slower rate of AI innovation [33]. Thus, the acquisition of proper measures for a balance between data access opportunities and data protection is an important headset, and consideration for the next generations of AI safety frameworks. Future developments in AI safety should place federated learning and privacy-preserving collaborative architectures at the forefront to overcome matters of interoperability while maintaining proper regard for privacy. Federated models allow for decentralized implementation of model training across different institutions, allowing algorithms to learn from large data stores while keeping sensitive data resident [3, 12]. In addition, if universal interoperability standards are developed, such as Fast Healthcare Interoperability Resources (FHIR) and HL7 protocols, this will facilitate the trading of structured data and ensure that the metadata representing data in the healthcare system are uniform [20]. Besides technical harmonization, governance structures must also be built so that transparency, accountability, and fair participation of all stakeholders in the initiative prevail. Interoperable ecosystems should not become exclusionary with regard to existing inequalities in terms of access or representation [19, 35]. Ultimately, the question of interoperability is not just a problem of data management but a question of safety. Unless data flow freely, AI systems cannot be validated, monitored, or recalibrated properly, making interoperability a necessary building block for achieving safe and adaptive AI in healthcare.

### 8.3.3 Algorithmic Bias and Health Equity

Algorithmic bias is likely one of the most longstanding and ethically charged challenges related to AI safety in healthcare. While AI systems may be remarkably accurate in their diagnostic and predictive capabilities, they may also be able to perpetuate and even amplify inequities in health outcomes if the data on which they are trained is biased and/or unrepresentative of the real-world phenomenon [25, 26]. These biases may derive from various sources of bias, such as sampling bias, measurement bias, and historical bias, all of which affect how well the models learn to generalize to real clinical populations [27, 28]. Sampling bias derives from the underrepresentation of some demographic and/or socioeconomic groups among the training data; measurement bias derives from the nature of the gathering of the data and the variability entailed in these techniques; and historical bias is a reflection of the built-in inequities of previous medical practices or policies. The science of AI has shown that biases in algorithms could give rise inappropriately to recommendations for therapy, to wrong diagnoses of diseases, and to inequities in access to care that various populations would receive [27]. For instance, predictive algorithms for disease states have been found to underrepresent the needs of ethnic populations when trained mainly on high-resource system data [26]. The implications of this bias are a danger to patient safety and an erosion of trust in and acceptance of AI in clinical practice. Thus, addressing this problem requires a multifold approach to the technical, ethical, and governance strategies [19]. Various methods have been suggested as solutions to the issue of bias and inequality in AI systems, including three recommended strategies, those being preprocessing, in-processing, and post-processing [13, 28]. Preprocessing methods are concerned with solving biased data samples through sampling, reweighting, or data augmentation; in-processing methods add constraints relating to bias and fairness into the learning algorithm, while post-processing methods change the predictions made after the model has been trained to promote fair outcomes. Newer methods, such as adversarial learning and topological data analysis, have also been developed, which enhance the ability to measure and rectify structural biases in complex data. Such techniques alone, however, have to be supplemented by continuous monitoring of bias over the entire life cycle of AI systems to avoid the re-emergence of inequality again post-development [27, 29]. It is crucial to stress from a governance standpoint that justice in health AI cannot be achieved with merely technical optimization. It requires institutional accountability, transparency as to data provenance, and stakeholder engagement (especially of those groups historically marginalized in health research) [19, 35]. Ethical oversight bodies and AI Trust Frameworks are increasingly recommending "bias audits" and equity impact assessments prior to the clinical rollout of algorithms [31]. These ensure that model validation does more than consider the accuracy metrics but also incorporates metrics of fairness, interpretability, and patient safety. Future directions, therefore, should consider the need for governance structures that are bias-aware, as well as inclusive data ecosystems, so that AI achieves health equity and does not, at worst, unintentionally reinforce inequities [30]. In conclusion, the realization of fairness and equity within an AI-driven mechanism for healthcare will necessitate a collective movement towards uniformity of data quality assurance, interoperable structure, and bias-adapted governance for the models. The areas coincide. Bad data quality produces greater degrees of bias, insufficient interoperable infrastructure reduces inclusiveness, and a deficiency of regulatory means and methods reduces accountability. As healthcare systems continue to go digital and data-driven, future AI safety frameworks need to converge on continuous ethical validation systems, whereby fairness and transparency are monitored in real time rather than considered static outputs [20]. This transition—from reactive bias-correcting initiatives to proactive bias-prevention initiatives—is essential to developing trustworthy AI that contributes to, rather than threatens, health-equity benefits. If fairness is metaphorically "baked" into every stage of the AI life cycle—from collection of data to implementation of systems—the next generation of intelligent systems will be capable of acting as true instruments of inclusive, safe, and sustainable healthcare innovation [35].

## 8.4 PRIVACY, SECURITY, AND SAFETY RISKS

The pace at which AI is becoming integrated into healthcare systems has outstripped the rate at which corresponding regulatory oversight and ethical safeguards are being developed. While AI technologies hold out the promise of greater diagnostic accuracy, efficiency, and access, their safe and equitable use turns on the presence of sound governance structures designed to manage new risks [19, 20]. Traditional regulatory structures like the Health Insurance Portability and Accountability Act (HIPAA), the General Data Protection Regulation (GDPR), and the Food and Drug Administration (FDA) device approval processes are not capable of addressing the adaptive, data-driven, and often opaque properties of AI algorithms [36]. The result is a situation in which the AI used currently in healthcare is largely subject to a regulatory framework that is both fragmented and reactive—one that is struggling to achieve the right balance between innovation, patient safety, and accountability. Equally important, ethical oversight has become crucial as AI systems begin to operate to influence medical decision-making, patient privacy, and public trust [35]. Issues such as algorithm bias, opacity, and ambiguous accountability architectures create difficulty for established ethical principles of autonomy, beneficence, and justice. Thus, the future of AI safety will depend not only on technical validation but also on the establishment of adaptive, transparent, and ethically valid regulatory ecosystems, which can sustain both innovation and safety [33]. The following subsections detail the current landscape of AI regulation and ethics within the field of healthcare: gaps that exist, frameworks that are emerging, and possible future options to reconcile AI innovation with the validity of clinical practice and social trust.

### 8.4.1 The Need for Regulation in AI-Driven Healthcare

Due to the growing embeddedness of AI in healthcare delivery, the quest for regulation is one of the key elements of both patient safety and reliability of the system. Unlike traditional medical devices and pharmaceutical products, the AI models are continually learning and changing [19]. This creates risks that would not be present in regulatory frameworks because these frameworks were not designed to address risks that are dynamic in nature. Current legislation, such as the HIPAA in the United States and the GDPR in Europe, mainly protects issues like data privacy and consent, not considering algorithmic transparency on an ongoing basis, validation, or post-deployment monitoring [33, 37]. These limitations have increasingly severe implications for safety and accountability as AI applications move from research to clinical decision-making. The regulatory assessment must therefore consider not only its technical functioning but also everything that makes up its life cycle: that is, the collection and processing of data through to implementation and retraining [38]. It is necessary to evaluate thoroughly the privacy and security measures of AI systems to be able to ensure confidentiality, integrity of data, and resilience to cyber threats. This includes a thorough review of consent mechanisms, data anonymization processes, encryption protocols and access controls in order to establish that sensitive patient data continue to be secure and are used [39]. Compliance with global data protection standards should be supplemented by constant monitoring and protocols of incidents to ensure that breaches or anomalies of performance are very rapidly detected and transparently resolved. Open communication of practices of privacy and security are also necessary in order to guarantee trust of the patient and clinician [38, 39]. According to the degree of potential impact of AI systems on patient outcomes, they may be classified into A and B categories from the standpoint of safety. Type A systems (e.g., diagnostic or treatment decision-support systems) are high-risk, and they require rigorous regulatory validation and post-marketing surveillance. These systems might include diagnostic or therapeutic decision support systems; these are high-risk devices and require regulatory clearance and post-market surveillance. Type B systems (for example, those related to administrative automation or transcription systems) are of low clinical risk but require monitoring for appropriate data use [40]. This new regulatory paradigm must therefore be flexible and include a risk strategy which will demand the necessary modifications to grant of safety according to clinical setting and algorithmic safety. This regulatory model, which will include technical, ethicists, and procedural safeguards, is the necessary structure that must facilitate the forward thrust of innovation and society's protection and safety in the context of AI in health [21, 36].

### 8.4.2 Ethical Dimensions and Accountability

The ethical dimension of AI in healthcare constitutes one of the key pillars of a safe and trustworthy implementation. The increasing independence and complexity of AI systems increase the urgency for established ethical principles and accountability measures. This demand is reflected in AI Trust Frameworks, as a developing response to the moral, social, and technical challenges created by intelligent technologies [41]. These frameworks were originally aimed at establishing general ethical borders for AI but have now developed into instructions for specific practices to reduce bias, ensure data privacy, and guarantee fairness and inclusiveness in algorithmic decision-making [20]. Regulatory advances such as the GDPR (EU, 2016) continue to be a critical development in core changes, which seek to encode ethical principles into the legal basis that governs data-based technologies. Likewise, cross-disciplinary partnerships, like the Partnership on AI and the Global Partnership on AI (GPAI), have furthered the cause of international standardization of trust and accountability norms, which facilitate communication among technologists, policymakers, and civil society [42]. These efforts allude to the fact that ethical governance is not static but must change with developments in technology and social aspirations if they are to be relevant and efficacious. The ethical frameworks that govern medicine serve two roles: they uphold the rights of patients while also protecting the ethical integrity of the profession. Ethical systems create protocols regarding data use, permission, and de-identification, which create a higher principle of privacy and confidentiality for medical AI [38, 39]. By being transparent about the use of personal information of patients, they ameliorate concerns regarding misappropriation of information and violation of patient privacy. Fairness principle is as important as any other moral law: it places the burden of continually demonstrating the algorithms' ability to detect bias so as to spare underrepresented populations unfair exposure [43]. The detection of bias and perpetuation of fairness are not technical aims; they have ethical significance in themselves in generating trustworthiness and justice for patients [44, 45]. Transparency and accountability are prerequisites for the ethical application of AI in healthcare, as they ensure that decision-making can be interpreted, reproduced, and altered in the interest of patient safety. The concept of explainability allows for understanding by clinicians of the logical paths to product suggestions made by AI algorithms, engendering confidence in the suggestions made by the system and aiding in error detection [46]. The advent of Explainable AI (XAI) tools, which employ rule-based logic, saliency maps, and can be model-agnostic, is an important means of closing the cognitive gap between prediction by computational means and human being reasoning [4]. Transparent presentation of aspects of model development, data provenance, and outcome data enhances the auditability and regulatory oversight of AI, changing the character of AI development in clinical implications of practice from a "black box" to a more accountable partner [26]. Responsibility covers not simply technical accuracy but also ethical and professional responsibility throughout the complete AI trajectory. A central problem to be solved in establishing trust is who is accountable when automated systems malfunction or cause damage [18]. It is by systems such as CONSORT-AI and SPIRIT-AI that responsibility has received operational listing, obliging traceable documenting, monitoring for bias, and verification after deployment of ML models [3, 47]. Adaptive governance also seeks to advance continuous auditing and recalibrating models to ensure that AI systems grow safely with clinical practice [38, 42]. The change from static compliance to dynamic oversight demonstrates a growing recognition that AI ethics must change when algorithms learn, the data change, and societal expectations evolve. To build ethical AI, it needs to be inclusive and based on human-centered design. A diverse population should be included in data collection and validation to reduce systemic bias and improve generalizability across demographic groups [27]. Transparent processes for consent to data use, effective patient communication tools, and clear mechanisms for feedback from users reinforce transparency and consent [44]. The guidelines for ethical design also emphasize building systems of AI that are supplementary rather than substitutive to human expertise, a way of development that ensures technology is used as an aid to empowerment rather than as a substitution [48]. It is the combination of transparency, accountability, and inclusivity that renders this tripartite essential for trustworthy AI in healthcare. The combination of these practices reduces ethical principles from nebulous ideas into measurable quotients without compromising the trust between clinician and patient and technology. As AI becomes more abundant in future decision-making, this balance is to determine not only whether future health systems are safe and fair but, in fact, the legitimacy in the eyes of their users and those whom they are to serve (See Figure 8.2 for the integrated governance structure linking regulatory, ethical, and oversight dimensions of AI safety).

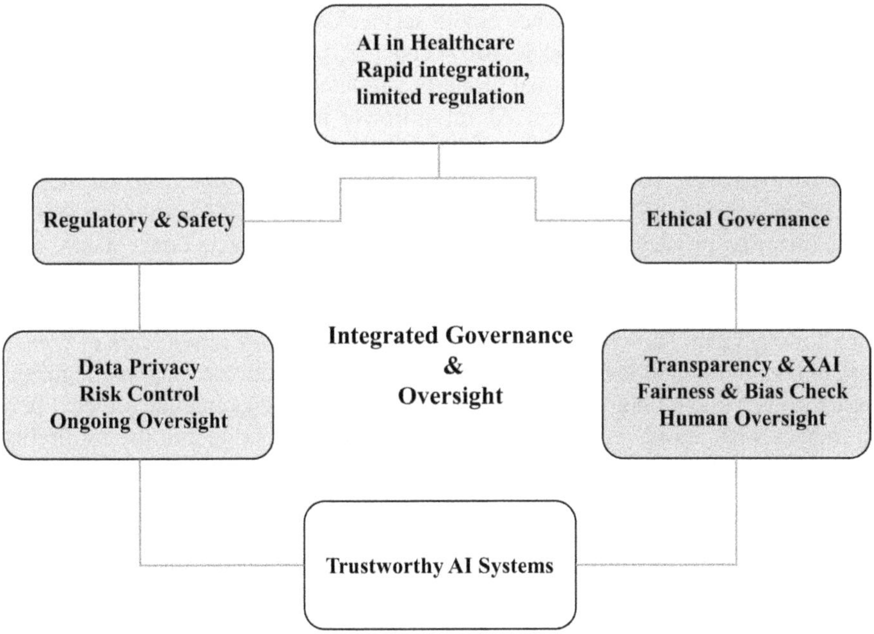


**FIGURE 8.2** Integrated framework of regulatory and ethical governance for trustworthy AI in healthcare.

## 8.5 CLINICAL INTEGRATION AND HUMAN FACTORS

The essence of safety, as it relates to healthcare, is minimizing risk and uncertainties that could lead to harm [49, 50]. The introduction of AI into healthcare systems is changing the definitions of safety. Increased use of machine learning (ML) and AI is evident in the enhancement of diagnostic accuracy and management of patients while minimizing the risk of both predictable and unpredictable harm. As a result, risk minimization has become the cornerstone of clinical AI applications. This focus is essential for ensuring safety, which in turn forms the basis of trust and ultimately supports the acceptance of AI in practice. ML systems are commonly classified as type A (diagnostic) and type B (administrative or transcription) applications, each carrying different implications for safety and risk management. [49]. From a risk perspective, type A applications require far more rigorous validation and stricter ethical oversight because they directly influence clinical decision-making, whereas type B applications carry substantially lower risk. However, in situations of low-risk exposure, the remote possibility of future risk implementation emphasizes the necessity of both capital and algorithmic transparency and also accountability in approaches to ensure clinician confidence. The world of clinical research clearly indicates that AI has the capability of meeting the issues of modern safety. The study of Swaminathan et al. [51] attests to finding that the ML program to monitor chronic obstructive pulmonary disease (COPD) attained improved triaging accuracy compared to that gained by physicians, leading to reduced under-triaging and enhanced patient safety. Also, electronic triaging (e-triaging) systems have been shown to perform above regular severe stress indices in emergency health services with a higher level of detection of high-risk cases that required definitive care [52, 53]. This gives further credence to AI giving clinical safety when properly validated and improving efficiency in workflow. The incorporation of AI into clinical practice provides innumerable advantages. Nevertheless, certain barriers to wider applications remain. Many clinicians, even with proven succor, are wary of relinquishing their decision-making for fallen Abraham to "AI systems" due to problems associated with transparency, data integrity, privacy, and medicolegal culpability [5]. Ethical concerns are also spawned by the prodigious data dependence and potential misuses of sensitive patient data. Inter-organization data sharing of a great mass is indeed a sine qua non for algorithm harvesting. However, this simultaneously raises fears of breach of confidentiality and loss of patient autonomy [14]. In addition, ongoing algorithmic bias is a continuing threat to equitable healthcare, inducing unequivocal performance when measured across demographic lines and a threat to the credibility of AI-based decision-making systems [25, 26]. Another serious impediment is to ensure that AI systems developed under controlled research environments will generalize to clinical environments. Inordinate variability in patient demographics, prevalence of disease, and complexity of personnel workflow will regularly lead to model performance degradation when undertaken in an environment outside of that for which the model was developed [4, 5]. For instance, very high performance in the predictive capability of certain diagnostic algorithms in retrospective datasets may not model the same high degree of performance when evaluated in multiple differing clinical environments due to a lack of consistency in data integrity and context variability. The complication of clinician over-reliance on automation, often referred to as automation bias, complicates the issue. Repetitive exposure to the recommendations of the AI systems may potentially lessen human vigilance, which results in clinicians placing too much trust in what the output of the system is [17]. Embedding mechanisms to make AI explainable and confidence scores within AI interfaces may assist in calibrating clinician trust such that AI-derived insights are viewed skeptically rather than trusted [19]. Furthermore, the phenomena of model drift and unpredictability of automated system behavior mean that there will be a need for ongoing monitoring and regulation. Due to continuous learning of AI systems, their decision thresholds may change, resulting in, on occasion, unintended events that may have patient safety implications [14]. Ongoing (recalibration), post-deployment auditing, and the need for ongoing human-in-the-loop supervision will be necessary to maintain reliability and clinical alignment. Ultimately, the alignment of AI with the clinical arena is not merely a technological shift but a transformation in human–machine cooperative paradigms [4]. The design must be transparent, ensuring the safety of the patient with responsibility in terms of governance on exploration by humans. There must be collaboration with a sustainable relationship and partnership between technology and clinicians. If AI is used intelligently, it has the potential to improve outcomes through enhanced accuracy of diagnostics and operational efficiency, working as an intelligent assistant to clinicians, augmenting rather than replacing human judgment in healthcare [22]. The key human and organizational factors that affect the safe uptake of AI into clinical operations are summarized in Table 8.2, along with their key risks and approaches to foster sustainable trust-based adoption.

**TABLE 8.2**
**Key Human Factors and Challenges in Safe AI Integration**

| Aspect | Description | Key Risks | Mitigation Strategies |
|---|---|---|---|
| **Model Drift and Unpredictability** | Changes in model behavior due to evolving data or autonomous learning. | Unsafe recommendations; decreased reliability. | Life cycle monitoring; recalibration; documentation of updates. |
| **Workflow Integration** | Alignment of AI systems with existing clinical processes and decision pathways. | Disruption of workflow; user resistance. | Early clinician involvement in design; iterative usability testing. |
| **Clinician Trust and Acceptance** | Building confidence in AI recommendations through transparency and interpretability. | Distrust due to "black box" models or unclear reasoning. | Use of explainable AI (XAI); clear communication of model logic and uncertainty. |

*(Continued)*

**TABLE 8.2 *(Continued)***
**Key Human Factors and Challenges in Safe AI Integration**

| Aspect | Description | Key Risks | Mitigation Strategies |
|---|---|---|---|
| **Training and Digital Literacy** | Equipping clinicians with AI literacy and operational competence. | Misuse or misunderstanding of AI tools. | Continuous professional training; inclusion in medical education curricula. |
| **Automation Bias/ Over-reliance** | Over-trust in AI recommendations leading to reduced vigilance. | Skill degradation; missed anomalies. | Confidence scoring; human-in-the-loop monitoring; cross-check protocols. |
| **Ethical and Legal Accountability** | Assigning responsibility for AI outcomes and ensuring ethical compliance. | Ambiguity in liability; ethical lapses. | Regulatory alignment (e.g., GDPR and HIPAA); audit trails; transparent reporting. |
| **Data Privacy and Security** | Protection of sensitive patient information in AI-enabled environments. | Breaches, unauthorized access, or misuse. | Encryption, role-based access control, anonymization, and regular security audits. |

## 8.6 POLICY, REGULATION, AND ECONOMIC CHALLENGES

The safe and fair introduction of new technology in healthcare depends on social and political arrangements of regulation and legislation, as well as the economic contingencies that render it viable, and technical soundness [20]. Rapidly-developing systems of AI face a regulatory infrastructure that does not have the capacity to match the dynamic and self-developing learning algorithms and complex data ecologies [14]. Therefore, the dual demand on policymakers and healthcare institutions is to obtain the innovation while protecting patient welfare and accountability [19]. If AI is to become a reliable, representative, and ethically governed force in contemporary healthcare delivery, these problems of law and economic justice must be faced [18].

### 8.6.1 Regulatory and Ethical Governance of AI in Healthcare

The burgeoning use of AI in healthcare is yet insufficiently scrutinized, despite its increasing clinical potential. It is therefore imperative that standard evaluation frameworks for the testing of the efficacies and safety of all medical devices based on AI are set up in order to ensure uniformity and the preservation of patient health [54]. US and European regulatory bodies such as the FDA and EMA have set up working groups charged with the evaluation and validation of digital and AI tools used in clinical health [54]. The approval by the FDA of Arterys' deep learning imaging platform in 2017 is the world's first acknowledgment of a system based on AI, thus ushering in a new era in the regulation of digital health [54]. However, legislative revision is still necessary to ensure that data can be exchanged between countries in a safe and efficient manner without jeopardizing privacy and compliance [55]. Among the most important elements of the AI safety policy are legislation, liability, and continuing development [56]. It is through commitment to existing data protection frameworks and legal regimes that any trustworthy AI governance can develop [56]. The EU's GDPR is a global legal scheme that provides strict rules for anonymization techniques and strictures on inter-organizational data sharing that prioritize privacy over unfettered innovation [42, 56]. Although the existence of the GDPR provides a strong ethical foundation, it has unintentionally tied up international data aggregation and collaboration because of fears of penalties arising from non-compliance [42]. Conversely, the U.S. regulatory paradigm, shaped largely through the HIPAA, emphasizes innovation and flexibility in lieu of rigid constraint [57]. The latter protects personal health information (PHI) but permits broader use of de-identified data, creating a framework that is adaptable but unequal in breadth [57]. On the other hand, the Chinese regulatory paradigm treats AI as a generator of economic and strategic power, permitting large-scale collection of health data with modest initial privacy oversight, although recent reforms have begun to institute personal data protections [20]. In addition to legislative regimes, the notion of Software as a Medical Device (SaMD) is increasingly important and may be defined as software that solves medical problems through computations [37, 42]. The FDA's Digital Health Software Precertification (Pre-Cert) Program allows the regulatory focus to shift from product level to developer accountability, which increases transparency and ongoing regulatory oversight [41]. Such efforts indicate a trajectory toward adaptive regimes of regulation in which safety validation ceases to be confined to premarket approval but rather extends to post-market surveillance and feedback loops based upon data [58]. For ethical governance, it is also necessary to establish accountability and liability. Who is responsible for what—developers, clinicians, or healthcare facilities?—is a huge unanswered question in AI [42]. The regulators could create an accountability framework by implementing laws requiring life cycle monitoring, bias auditing and reporting, and transparency. Especially important are post-marketing surveillance systems to ensure effectiveness in the real world and the safety of medical devices using AI [58, 59]. Finally, adaptive regulation must strike a balance between innovation and patient safety. A global effort for a legal and ethical framework to link GDPR, HIPAA, and the new AI acts will be necessary to create safe, equitable, and sustainable AI use in the healthcare system [54].

### 8.6.2 Economic and Implementation Barriers to Safe AI Adoption

The integration of AI into healthcare systems has formidable economic and implementation barriers. The greatest of these barriers pertains to the availability and accessibility of quality AI-ready datasets for analysis. Most medical data are held privately by hospitals and are often lacking, unstructured, or out of date [4, 60]. Public dataset resources are limited in terms of diversity and frequency of updates, which leads to difficulties with the generalization and reproducibility of models. Data collection, annotation, and maintenance require huge amounts of capital and human resources, excluding those institutions and technology companies that cannot afford these amounts. In addition to these economic barriers, the aggregation of data across healthcare organizations runs into further economic and technical barriers of differing formats, standards, and interoperability [61]. In order to develop unified infrastructures, including cloud-based areas of repository and the use of standardized data formats, for example, FHIR, there will be high implementation costs incurred, and there will need to be cooperation between institutions [62]. Although simulated environments and the generation of synthetic data have been put forward as a way to solve this problem, this solution remains expensive and is less well matured in healthcare technology than in other areas of AI [63]. One other economic barrier relates to the preeminence of the big technology companies and their control of the area of innovation for healthcare-related AI. These companies have access to huge amounts of behavioral and biomedical data related to patients through the use of sensors and wearables, thus giving these companies a competitive advantage in the field in relation to the academic and public institutions [64]. Although partnerships between technology companies and healthcare systems may accelerate advancement, there is a danger of concerns for data ownership, patients' privacy, and unequal access to innovation. Security vulnerabilities increase the economic and ethical risks. Adversarial attacks, in which deliberately modified inputs cause misclassification, impose an economic burden due to regulatory compliance requirements and the need for post-market surveillance [14, 18]. The cost of upgrading security features is well observed, such as imposing blockchain-based information redirects additional costly infrastructure, but it is necessary to maintain patient safety and trust in the institution. Furthermore, technological limitations such as the so-called "memory wall," meaning the widening gap between processor speeds and data transfer rates, must be taken into account when considering the hardware costs of implementing AI in healthcare [65]. Continued investment in computational infrastructure, model retraining, and system updating is also essential if the costs and constraints of current technologies are to be overcome. In conclusion, it should be perceived that the economic sustainability of AI in health will depend on the balance of the requirements for innovation with equity with all healthcare systems for security (economic, personal, and societal implications) [6]. Overcoming financial, infrastructural, and ethical differentiation will achieve successful implementation of AI within the health framework, which will protect the rights of individuals to be benefited by AI rather than limit this advantage to economically rewarding environments [42]. Table 8.3 outlines the main policy, regulatory, and economic issues influencing the safe integration of AI into healthcare systems. The table contains existing frameworks such as GDPR, HIPAA, and FDA Pre-Cert. Major barriers to convergence include interoperability, liability, and cost. Strategies for sustainable, compliant, equitable governance of AI are recommended.

**TABLE 8.3**
**Key Policy, Regulatory, and Economic Challenges in Safe AI Adoption in Healthcare**

| Domain | Key Focus | Current Example/ Framework | Challenges Identified | Proposed Solutions/ Strategies |
|---|---|---|---|---|
| **Regulatory Governance** | Establishing oversight for AI medical tools | FDA, EMA, WHO Digital Health Guidelines | Lack of unified global standards; fragmented regulatory scope | Develop international harmonization (e.g., alignment of the FDA, EMA, and EU AI Act.) and adaptive regulatory frameworks |
| **Legal Frameworks** | Data protection and patient rights | GDPR (EU), HIPAA (US), China's Data Protection Law | Divergent privacy laws; restricted data sharing; ethical liability gaps | Create interoperable data governance and global ethical frameworks; strengthen accountability laws |
| **Software Classification** | Defining AI as medical-grade software | Software as a Medical Device (SaMD); the FDA Pre-Cert Program | Lack of post-market surveillance and ongoing validation | Continuous life-cycle monitoring; developer certification and auditing |
| **Liability and Accountability** | Assigning responsibility for AI-driven errors | Institutional and developer-level accountability models | Ambiguity over liability (developer vs. clinician vs. institution) | Introduce clear liability policies and mandatory reporting of AI-related incidents |
| **Economic Barriers** | Cost and access disparities | Public vs. private data ownership; big tech dominance | High costs of data curation, annotation, infrastructure | Encourage public–private partnerships and open-access datasets |
| **Technological Constraints** | Hardware and system interoperability | Cloud-based data platforms, FHIR standards | Fragmented data formats; limited interoperability; "memory wall" issue | Standardized infrastructure; investment in computation capacity and data harmonization |
| **Security and Sustainability** | Cybersecurity and long-term viability | Blockchain, encryption, adversarial testing | Security breaches; high maintenance costs; inequitable access | Secure data sharing protocols; equitable resource distribution; continual reinvestment |

## 8.7 FUTURE OUTLOOK AND MULTIDISCIPLINARY COLLABORATION

In conclusion, as AI continues to transform contemporary society and healthcare, the future implementation of it consistently and securely will depend upon interdisciplinary cooperation and a nonstop trust of the public. The complex interplay of technology, ethics, and human factors shows that no single discipline may be relied upon to enforce responsible innovation. Engineers, clinicians, ethicists, policymakers, and patients must work together to create frameworks for the advancing of equity, accountability, and transparency in AI-driven healthcare [26, 27]. The development of trust remains the key goal of this future. There must be trust from patients that AI systems are ethically utilized and properly safeguard privacy, and trust from the health professions that they supplement and do not supersede human intelligence. To this end, there needs to be investigation of algorithmic bias and interpretability. Interdisciplinary collaboration can allow groups of scientists to work together through all of the steps of model development from data capture to algorithm validation to address the issue of bias [25]. Transparency in design and interpretability in outputs will allow clinicians to make recommendations from AI-driven recommendations and promote both accountability and acceptance [66]. Environmental factors play a significant role in shaping access to care, and inclusive training should guide clinicians in responding effectively to these conditions. Rather than becoming the focus of predicted AI-related "disruptions, physicians should be equipped with essential background knowledge on AI, how it is primarily dependent on big data, and its resultant capacity for precision." All physicians should be educated on health-related AI, including standards of care and the foundation of AI. Ethical practice in medicine must be a core content area of this education, though other important supervisory structures would also need to be developed for all health-AI-related innovations and should become part of medical education [4, 6, 19]. In the end, the ongoing and true application of AI in medicine will depend on the ongoing collaboration of various disciplines. Engineers, clinicians, ethicists, policymakers, and patients all bring important perspectives that need to be unified to create safety, equity, and trust. This interdisciplinary intersection can be conceptualized as a model of the Responsible AI in Healthcare, which includes overlapping technological, clinical, and ethical dimensions that comprise a comprehensive framework for sustainable innovation.

As shown in Figure 8.3, the future of medicine does not rest in the isolated improvement of different disciplines but in the integration of them. It is in the overlapping realms of technology, clinical skill, and ethical governance that the basis of reliable AI systems lies. Only in this way can we ensure that the future of healthcare innovation remains human-centered and ethically grounded. Conclusively, the AI future of medicine needs to take place in the ethical landscape as well as the inclusive global environment. Justice and dignity, confidentiality of data, and ethical assessment in all the phases of AI registration and deployment should be in evidence. If this could be allied with academic strength in a well-diversified and multidisciplinary development, then AI can become potently applied in the concentration of achieving world health. The object is not to replace the physician but to enhance their practice efficiency by means of AI-uncovered technology to aid precision-medical, compassioned, and more available means of diagnosis and therapy. This bridging and tying together between novel technology and ethical standards will herald the next era in which the AI component of medical interventions will be ethically impregnable, safe and secure, completely acceptable, and a well-functioning humanistic ally-involved product [12, 42, 67].

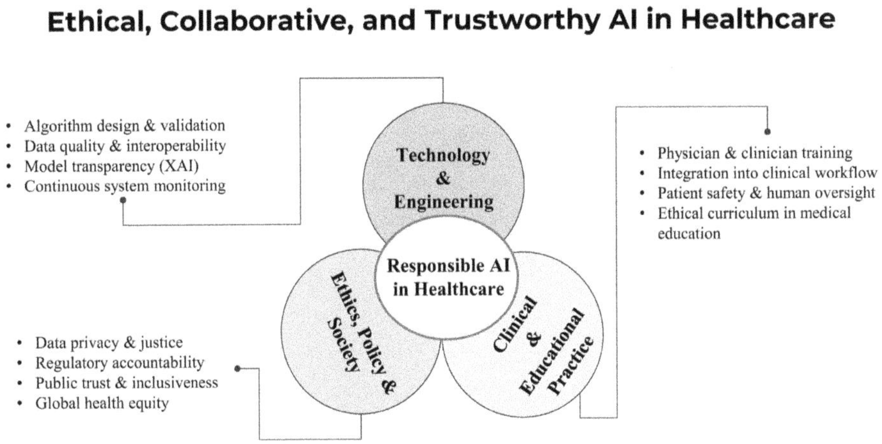


**FIGURE 8.3** Interdisciplinary convergence for the future of trustworthy AI in healthcare, illustrating the overlap between engineering, clinical, and ethical-policy domains.

## REFERENCES

1. Luhmann N. Familiarity, confidence, trust: problems and alternatives. Trust: making and breaking cooperative relations. 2000;6(1):94–107.
2. Petersson L, Larsson I, Nygren JM, et al. Challenges to implementing artificial intelligence in healthcare: a qualitative interview study with healthcare leaders in Sweden. BMC health services research. 2022;22(1):850.
3. Rivera SC, Liu X, Chan A-W, et al. Guidelines for clinical trial protocols for interventions involving artificial intelligence: the SPIRIT-AI extension. The Lancet digital health. 2020;2(10):e549–e560.
4. Topol EJ. High-performance medicine: the convergence of human and artificial intelligence. Nature medicine. 2019;25(1):44–56.
5. Bajwa J, Munir U, Nori A, Williams B. Artificial intelligence in healthcare: transforming the practice of medicine. Future healthcare journal. 2021;8(2):e188–e194.
6. Mehta N, Pandit A, Shukla S. Transforming healthcare with big data analytics and artificial intelligence: a systematic mapping study. Journal of biomedical informatics. 2019;100:103311.
7. Eke CI, Norman AA, Shuib L. Multi-feature fusion framework for sarcasm identification on twitter data: a machine learning based approach. PLoS One. 2021;16(6):e0252918.
8. Eke CI, Norman AA, Shuib L. Context-based feature technique for sarcasm identification in benchmark datasets using deep learning and BERT model. IEEE access. 2021;9:48501–48518.
9. Eke CI, Norman AA, Shuib L, Nweke HF. Sarcasm identification in textual data: systematic review, research challenges and open directions. Artificial intelligence review. 2020;53(6):4215–4258.
10. Mannuru NR, Shahriar S, Teel ZA, et al. Artificial intelligence in developing countries: the impact of generative artificial intelligence (AI) technologies for development. Information development. 2025;41(3):1036–1054.
11. Hayawi K, Shahriar S, Alashwal H, Serhani MA. Generative AI and large language models: a new frontier in reverse vaccinology. Informatics in medicine unlocked. 2024;48:101533.

12 Tangi L, Combetto M, Martin BJ, et al. Artificial Intelligence for interoperability in the European public sector. European Commission. 2023.
13. Sharma M, Savage C, Nair M, et al. Artificial intelligence applications in health care practice: scoping review. Journal of medical Internet research. 2022;24(10):e40238.
14. Albahri AS, Duhaim AM, Fadhel MA, et al. A systematic review of trustworthy and explainable artificial intelligence in healthcare: assessment of quality, bias risk, and data fusion. Information fusion. 2023;96:156–191.
15. Gille F, Jobin A, Ienca M. What we talk about when we talk about trust: theory of trust for AI in healthcare. Intelligence-based medicine. 2020;1:100001.
16. O'neill O. Linking trust to trustworthiness. International journal of philosophical studies. 2018;26(2):293–300.
17. Ryan M. In AI we trust: ethics, artificial intelligence, and reliability. Science and engineering ethics. 2020;26(5):2749–2767.
18. Eke CI, Shuib L. The role of explainability and transparency in fostering trust in AI healthcare systems: a systematic literature review, open issues and potential solutions. Neural computing and applications. 2025;37(4):1999–2034.
19. Lysaght T, Lim HY, Xafis V, Ngiam KY. AI-assisted decision-making in healthcare: the application of an ethics framework for big data in health and research. Asian bioethics review. 2019;11(3):299–314.
20. Dwivedi YK, Hughes L, Ismagilova E, et al. Artificial intelligence (AI): multidisciplinary perspectives on emerging challenges, opportunities, and agenda for research, practice and policy. International journal of information management. 2021;57:101994.
21. Balagurunathan Y, Mitchell R, El Naqa I. Requirements and reliability of AI in the medical context. Physica medica. 2021;83:72–78.
22. Kelly CJ, Karthikesalingam A, Suleyman M, et al. Key challenges for delivering clinical impact with artificial intelligence. BMC medicine. 2019;17(1):195.
23. Carvalho DV, Pereira EM, Cardoso JS. Machine learning interpretability: a survey on methods and metrics. Electronics. 2019;8(8):832.
24. Hüllermeier E, Waegeman W. Aleatoric and epistemic uncertainty in machine learning: an introduction to concepts and methods. Machine learning. 2021;110(3):457–506.
25. Celi LA, Cellini J, Charpignon M-L, et al. Sources of bias in artificial intelligence that perpetuate healthcare disparities—a global review. PLoS digital health. 2022; 1(3):e0000022.
26. Rajkomar A, Hardt M, Howell MD, et al. Ensuring fairness in machine learning to advance health equity. Annals of internal medicine. 2018;169(12):866–872.
27. Yang J, Soltan AA, Eyre DW, Clifton DA. Algorithmic fairness and bias mitigation for clinical machine learning with deep reinforcement learning. Nature machine intelligence. 2023;5(8):884–894.
28. Mehrabi N, Morstatter F, Saxena N, et al. A survey on bias and fairness in machine learning. ACM computing surveys (CSUR). 2021;54(6):1–35.
29. Zhang BH, Lemoine B, Mitchell M, editors. Mitigating unwanted biases with adversarial learning. Proceedings of the 2018 AAAI/ACM Conference on AI, Ethics, and Society; 2018.
30. Soenksen LR, Ma Y, Zeng C, et al. Integrated multimodal artificial intelligence framework for healthcare applications. NPJ digital medicine. 2022;5(1):149.
31. Crossnohere NL, Elsaid M, Paskett J, et al. Guidelines for artificial intelligence in medicine: literature review and content analysis of frameworks. Journal of medical Internet research. 2022;24(8):e36823.
32. Narayanan A, Shmatikov V, editors. Robust de-anonymization of large sparse datasets. 2008 IEEE Symposium on Security and Privacy (sp 2008); 2008: IEEE.
33. Mylrea M, Robinson N. Artificial Intelligence (AI) trust framework and maturity model: applying an entropy lens to improve security, privacy, and ethical AI. Entropy. 2023;25(10):1429.

34. Lukyanenko R, Maass W, Storey VC. Trust in artificial intelligence: from a foundational trust framework to emerging research opportunities. Electronic markets. 2022; 32(4):1993–2020.
35. Kiseleva A, Kotzinos D, De Hert P. Transparency of AI in healthcare as a multilayered system of accountabilities: between legal requirements and technical limitations. Frontiers in artificial intelligence. 2022;5:879603.
36. Sujan M, Smith-Frazer C, Malamateniou C, et al. Validation framework for the use of AI in healthcare: overview of the new British standard BS30440. BMJ health & care informatics. 2023;30(1):e100749.
37. Amann J, Blasimme A, Vayena E, et al. Explainability for artificial intelligence in healthcare: a multidisciplinary perspective. BMC medical informatics and decision making. 2020;20(1):310.
38. Naik N, Hameed B, Shetty DK, et al. Legal and ethical consideration in artificial intelligence in healthcare: who takes responsibility? Frontiers in surgery. 2022;9:862322.
39. Farhud DD, Zokaei S. Ethical issues of artificial intelligence in medicine and healthcare. Iranian journal of public health. 2021;50(11):i.
40. Sullivan Y, de Bourmont M, Dunaway M. Appraisals of harms and injustice trigger an eerie feeling that decreases trust in artificial intelligence systems. Annals of operations research. 2022;308(1):525–548.
41. Floridi L, Cowls J, Beltrametti M, et al. AI4People—an ethical framework for a good AI society: opportunities, risks, principles, and recommendations. Minds and machines. 2018;28(4):689–707.
42. Norman AA, Eke CI, Phiri M, et al. Digital health and deep learning: opportunities, challenges, and the imperative of data protection in wearable devices. 2024, https://doi.org/10.2139/ssrn.4703449.
43. Peters D, Vold K, Robinson D, Calvo RA. Responsible AI—two frameworks for ethical design practice. IEEE transactions on technology and society. 2020;1(1):34–47.
44. Nasir S, Khan RA, Bai S. Ethical framework for harnessing the power of AI in healthcare and beyond. IEEE access. 2024;12:31014–31035.
45. Eke CI, Norman AA, Mulenga M. Machine learning approach for detecting and combating bring your own device (BYOD) security threats and attacks: a systematic mapping review. Artificial intelligence review. 2023;56(8):8815–8858.
46. Samek W, Montavon G, Vedaldi A, et al. Explainable AI: interpreting, explaining and visualizing deep learning. Vol. 11700. Springer Nature; 2019.
47. Liu X, Rivera SC, Moher D, et al. Reporting guidelines for clinical trial reports for interventions involving artificial intelligence: the CONSORT-AI extension. The Lancet digital health. 2020;2(10):e537–e548.
48. DignumV, editor Responsible artificial intelligence—from principles to practice: a keynote at TheWebConf 2022. ACM SIGIR Forum; 2023: ACM New York, NY, USA.
49. Varshney KR, editor Engineering safety in machine learning. 2016 Information Theory and Applications Workshop (ITA); 2016: IEEE.
50. Varshney KR, Alemzadeh H. On the safety of machine learning: cyber-physical systems, decision sciences, and data products. Big data. 2017;5(3):246–255.
51. Swaminathan S, Qirko K, Smith T, et al. A machine learning approach to triaging patients with chronic obstructive pulmonary disease. PLoS One. 2017;12(11):e0188532.
52. Kim D, You S, So S, et al. A data-driven artificial intelligence model for remote triage in the prehospital environment. PLoS One. 2018;13(10):e0206006.
53. Levin S, Toerper M, Hamrock E, et al. Machine-learning-based electronic triage more accurately differentiates patients with respect to clinical outcomes compared with the emergency severity index. Annals of emergency medicine. 2018;71(5):565–574. e2.
54. Diebolt V, Azancot I, Boissel F-H, et al. "Artificial intelligence": which services, which applications, which results and which development today in clinical research? Which impact on the quality of care? Which recommendations? Therapies. 2019;74(1):155–164.

55. Jiang F, Jiang Y, Zhi H, et al. Artificial intelligence in healthcare: past, present and future. Stroke and vascular neurology. 2017;2(4): 230–243.
56. Forcier MB, Gallois H, Mullan S, Joly Y. Integrating artificial intelligence into health care through data access: can the GDPR act as a beacon for policymakers? Journal of law and the biosciences. 2019;6(1):317–335.
57. Price WN, Cohen IG. Privacy in the age of medical big data. Nature medicine. 2019; 25(1):37–43.
58. Callahan A, Fries JA, Ré C, et al. Medical device surveillance with electronic health records. NPJ digital medicine. 2019;2(1):94.
59. Salazar JW, Redberg RF. Leading the call for reform of medical device safety surveillance. JAMA Internal medicine. 2020;180(2):179–180.
60. He J, Baxter SL, Xu J, et al. The practical implementation of artificial intelligence technologies in medicine. Nature medicine. 2019;25(1):30–36.
61. Patel NM, Michelini VV, Snell JM, et al. Enhancing next-generation sequencing-guided cancer care through cognitive computing. The oncologist. 2018;23(2):179–185.
62. Miotto R, Li L, Kidd BA, Dudley JT. Deep patient: an unsupervised representation to predict the future of patients from the electronic health records. Scientific reports. 2016;6(1):26094.
63. Camacho DM, Collins KM, Powers RK, et al. Next-generation machine learning for biological networks. Cell. 2018;173(7):1581–1592.
64. Wang F, Preininger A. AI in health: state of the art, challenges, and future directions. Yearbook of medical informatics. 2019;28(01):016–026.
65. Rong G, Mendez A, Assi EB, et al. Artificial intelligence in healthcare: review and prediction case studies. Engineering. 2020;6(3):291–301.
66. Char DS, Shah NH, Magnus D. Implementing machine learning in health care—addressing ethical challenges. The New England journal of medicine. 2018;378(11):981.
67. Díaz-Rodríguez N, Del Ser J, Coeckelbergh M, et al. Connecting the dots in trustworthy artificial intelligence: from AI principles, ethics, and key requirements to responsible AI systems and regulation. Information fusion. 2023;99:101896.

# Index

*Note:* **Bold** page numbers refer to tables and *Italic* page numbers refer to figures.

## D



## E



## F



## G

## O



## P



## Q



## R



## S

## T



## U



## V



## W



## X

For Product Safety Concerns and Information please contact our EU representative GPSR@taylorandfrancis.com
Taylor & Francis Verlag GmbH, Kaufingerstraße 24, 80331 München, Germany

www.ingramcontent.com/pod-product-compliance
Ingram Content Group UK Ltd.
Pitfield, Milton Keynes, MK11 3LW, UK
UKHW020201200926
475702UK00004B/553
* 9 7 8 1 0 4 1 2 4 9 6 1 0 *